IT L... UH

An ISEB Foundat...

rvices

9AB

is,

herts.ac.uk

The British Computer Society

BCS is the leading professional body for the IT industry. With members in over 100 countries, BCS is the professional and learned society in the field of computers and information systems.

BCS is responsible for setting standards for the IT profession. It is also leading the change in public perception and appreciation of the economic and social importance of professionally managed IT projects and programmes. In this capacity, the society advises, informs and persuades industry and government on successful IT implementation.

IT is affecting every part of our lives and that is why BCS is determined to promote IT as the profession of the 21st century.

Joining BCS

BCS qualifications, products and services are designed with your career plans in mind. We not only provide essential recognition through professional qualifications but also offer many other useful benefits to our members at every level.

BCS membership demonstrates your commitment to professional development. It helps to set you apart from other IT practitioners and provides industry recognition of your skills and experience. Employers and customers increasingly require proof of professional qualifications and competence. Professional membership confirms your competence and integrity and sets an independent standard that people can trust. Professional Membership (MBCS) is the pathway to Chartered IT Professional (CITP) Status.

www.bcs.org/membership

Further Information

Further information about BCS can be obtained from: BCS, First Floor, Block D, North Star House, North Star Avenue, Swindon SN2 1FA, UK.

Telephone: 0845 300 4417 (UK only) or + 44 (0)1793 417 424 (overseas)

Email: customerservice@hq.bcs.org.uk

Web: www.bcs.org

IT Law

An ISEB Foundation

Jon Fell (Editor)

John Antell

Jonathan Exell

Vivian Picton

Adrian Roberts-Walsh

Louise Townsend

 BCS

The British Computer Society
Publishing and Information Products
First Floor, Block D
North Star House
North Star Avenue
Swindon
SN2 1FA
UK

www.bcs.org

ISBN 978-1-902505-80-0

British Cataloguing in Publication Data.
A CIP catalogue record for this book is available at the British Library.

All trademarks, registered names etc. acknowledged in this publication are to be the property of their respective owners.

Disclaimer:
The views expressed in this book are those of the authors and do not necessarily reflect the views of the British Computer Society except where explicitly stated as such.
Although every care has been taken by the authors and the British Computer Society in the preparation of the publication, no warranty is given by the authors or the British Computer Society as publisher as to the accuracy or completeness of the information contained within it and neither the authors nor the British Computer Society shall be responsible or liable for any loss or damage whatsoever arising by virtue of such information or any instructions or advice contained within this publication or by any of the aforementioned.

 Captured, authored, published, delivered and managed in XML
CAPDM Limited, Edinburgh, Scotland   www.capdm.com

Contents

List of figures and tables

Contributors

John Antell is a barrister who specializes in contractual disputes, particularly those involving IT and engineering. He also practises in employment law, particularly cases within the IT and engineering sectors where the use of freelance workers, subcontracting and outsourcing is widespread.

A chartered member of the BCS, he worked in IT for 15 years before being called to the Bar in 1992. He is a member of the Technology and Construction Bar Association and of the Employment Law Bar Association.

Jonathan Exell is a qualified British and European Patent Attorney at Williams Powels, a private practice firm of patent and trademark attorneys. His practice area focuses on the computer sciences and business method areas and he spends a considerable amount of his time dealing with cases where the subject matter falls close to that excluded from patentability by law. Jonathan regularly lectures on patent law and particularly on aspects relating to computer-implemented inventions. One of Jonathan's main aims is to improve intellectual property awareness in UK small and medium-sized enterprises (SMEs).

Jon Fell is a partner in the Outsourcing, Technology and Commercial Group of the international law firm Pinsent Masons. Since 1995 he has advised on all aspects of internet-related law and ecommerce issues. Jon is one of the founders of OUT-LAW.COM and his clients range from start-ups to multinationals and include suppliers and users of technology. He has written and lectured extensively on all aspects of IT law, ecommerce, internet regulation, legislation and EU directives. Jon is a member of the supervisory board of the Computer Learning Research Centre Royal Holloway University of London.

Jon is a trustee of the CodesandCiphers Heritage Trust, which is in the process of establishing the National Museum of Computing.

Vivian Picton is a lecturer at the University of Glamorgan where he teaches on a wide range of courses including the law degree (legal research and use of information technology in the legal environment) and computing degree (computer/information technology law and security).

He has acted as consultant to many small legal offices in their pursuit to harness and develop systems to create a more economical working environment and to benefit from the gains.

Adrian Roberts-Walsh has over 20 years experience of teaching, lecturing and training, management and examining in business, computing and information and communication technologies (ICT) in both the UK and overseas, across a variety of sectors including: educational, financial, commercial aviation and military. He currently teaches information management and management at both undergraduate and postgraduate levels.

Louise Townsend is a senior associate in the Outsourcing, Technology and Commercial Group of Pinsent Masons. She advises and provides training on data protection, freedom of information and IT Law including carrying out data protection audits, advising on information security, records management, website compliance and marketing. She holds the ISEB qualifications in data protection, freedom of information and IT Law, and is an accredited ISEB trainer in each of these areas. She speaks regularly at conferences and seminars and writes extensively on these subjects.

Preface

The purpose of this book is to provide an overview of some of the key legal topics facing anyone involved in the IT sector. It is designed to accompany the ISEB IT Law Essentials course and, as far as possible, we have adopted the numbering used in the syllabus to make it easier to look up topics as the course progresses. However, in a number of chapters, we have gone on to consider other related topics and these are dealt with at the end of the relevant chapter. The law covered by this book is that of England and Wales.

The topics covered by this book are constantly evolving. Throughout the book there are details of where to find additional information and wherever possible online information resources have been cited.

The ISEB IT Law Essentials course was first conceived back in 2004. A working party comprising practitioners and academics was brought together to develop a course for IT professionals. Our first task was to decide which of the many areas of law would be most useful to those involved in the IT sector. In the end we decided upon six areas:

(1) **Contract**: Contract law underpins all commercial arrangements. As such, it is essential to have an understanding of how contracts work and the key factors to consider in relation to any agreement.

(2) **Privacy**: The obligations imposed by the Data Protection Act 1998 permeate virtually all aspects of the use, exploitation and management of IT systems. Equally nearly every commercial agreement contains a clause imposing a duty of confidentiality. Privacy is also increasingly affected by EU and human rights legislation.

(3) **Evidence**: Increasingly business records are being maintained electronically and the way in which those electronic documents and records are maintained and retained has grown in importance. It is essential that such records are managed in a way in which they can be relied upon in the event of a dispute.

(4) **Intellectual property**: Intellectual property rights determine who owns the underlying rights in all IT systems, applications, data or business systems. An understanding of these rights and how to manage them is fundamental to the management of such systems, applications and businesses.

(5) **Employment**: IT managers are increasingly involved in human resources matters in relation to their own teams, outsourcing projects and in relation to the development and management of IT and communications

policies. It is important for all managers to have a working knowledge of the key principles of employment law.

(6) **Information security and accessibility:** Both of these topics are essential to the development and management of any IT system.

Each member of the working party was responsible for developing the syllabus and examination questions for one of these areas. It was my privilege and pleasure to chair the working party and help guide it towards its goals. I would like to thank all of the members of the working party (John Antell, Jonathan Exell, Stephen Mason, Vivian Picton and Adrian Roberts-Walsh) for their hard work over the past three years. My thanks also go to Tracy Kurzeja and Matthew Flynn from the British Computer Society for all of their hard work and support in bringing the course and this book to fruition.

If you are about to embark on the ISEB course, I hope that you will find it both interesting and useful. In any event I wish you luck with your studies.

Jon Fell
Partner
Pinsent Masons
October 2007

1 Contract Law

JON FELL

For centuries people have been trading and entering into agreements. Contract law has developed to enable people to rely on promises made to them and is the foundation of all forms of commerce. In our personal lives, we make contracts every day. For example, by using public transport or by buying a newspaper we are entering into contracts. In the business world, contracts tend to be more complicated and their terms are often set out in documents.

A contract is an agreement that is legally enforceable and will arise if the essential elements of a contract are present and any specific statutory requirements are met. This is in contrast to a mere promise, which the parties do not expect to be enforced by the courts. Contract law has an important function to play in regulating relationships. If one party to a contract agrees to provide services, it is important that it knows that it is able to rely on the other party's promise to pay for those services.

On the whole the parties to a contract are free to decide upon the terms that will apply to the contract entered into between them. However, there are certain exceptions to this general principle and there are various legislative and other restrictions on the way in which certain provisions or clauses may be framed. For example:

- clauses in standard terms and conditions that seek to limit the liability of a party have to be 'reasonable';[1]
- there are numerous legislative provisions that seek to protect consumers (such as the Consumer Protection (Distance Selling) Regulations 2000[2]);
- certain provisions may be unenforceable due to statute or common law restrictions (such as limiting liability for death or personal injury or seeking to impose a penalty on a party for failing to comply with its obligations under a contract[3] or a contract term in a software licence that prohibits absolutely the reverse engineering of the licensed software);[4] and
- certain terms may be implied into an agreement by statute.[5]

1.1 CONTRACT LAW ESSENTIALS

1.1.1 Elements of a contract

Before the aspects of contract law that apply to the IT world in particular can be considered, it is important to understand the essential elements of a contract and to dispel some of the commonly held myths. For example, under English law there is no legal requirement for a contract to be in writing.[6]

A binding agreement will be formed only if the essential elements of a contract are present. This means that there must have been:

- an unconditional offer;
- which has been accepted unconditionally;
- with consideration passing between the parties;
- who intend to enter into a binding agreement.

Offer and invitation to treat

An offer is a statement made by a person wishing to enter into a contract, by which he shows a willingness to enter into a binding contract. The person making an offer is known as the 'offeror' and the person to whom the offer is addressed is known as the 'offeree'.

In order to be effective an offer must be communicated to the intended offeree. Such communication may be to a specific individual or organization, to a class of offerees or even to the world at large.[7]

The concept of an offer needs to be contrasted with what is known as an 'invitation to treat'. An invitation to treat arises when a person invites others to make offers to him. This is best explained by means of an example. When a person goes into a supermarket, the goods on the shelves constitute an invitation to treat.[8] The supermarket owner is inviting its customers to take the goods to the checkout and to make an offer to the supermarket owner to buy them. It is important to note that a binding contract is only made at the point at which the supermarket agrees to sell the goods to the customer. In this way, the supermarket owner is not making an offer to sell goods at a particular price nor to someone who is prohibited by law from purchasing those goods.[9] Further, the courts have decided that goods displayed in a shop window also amount to an invitation to treat.[10]

It is important to contrast an invitation to treat with a 'unilateral offer', which is an offer made by a person that is capable of acceptance by anybody complying with the requirements set out in the offer (for example, a person handing over a lost item in return for a reward). In order for there to be a unilateral offer, it must be clear that the person making the offer intended it to be capable of acceptance and to be bound by the consequences of that acceptance. In the *Carbolic Smoke Ball case*[11] the owners of a medical preparation known as 'The Carbolic Smoke Ball' issued an advertisement in which they offered to pay £100 to any person who contracted influenza after having used one of their smoke balls three times daily for two weeks. In order to establish the bona fides of the offer, the sum of £1,000 was deposited in the Alliance Bank in Regent Street, London. It was held that the advertisement constituted an offer to the world, which was capable of acceptance. The deposit of the sum of £1,000 in a bank account emphasized the intention of the offeror to make an offer that was capable of acceptance and to be legally bound. However, it is important to note that the general rule is that an advertisement in a newspaper will be a unilateral invitation to treat and not an offer.[12]

The above distinction is particularly important in the online world. Most, if not all, commercial websites will be treated in the same way as a shop window. The goods or services marketed on them will amount to an invitation to treat. The importance from an ecommerce point of view can best be illustrated by means of an example. In 1999 Argos ran into difficulties in relation to Sony television sets it was selling from its website. The televisions were being sold for £299.99. However, the price was rounded up on the site, but for some reason the decimal point was put in the wrong place giving a price of £3.00 as opposed to £300.00. Not surprisingly, Argos was inundated with orders for the television sets. Argos argued that its website amounted to an invitation to treat and as such it was up to Argos to decide whether to accept the offers made by potential customers. Argos declined to accept the offers. The wording of the acknowledgements sent out by the Argos website in response to the orders was crucial. The acknowledgement did not amount to an acceptance of the offers contained within the orders. While the matter did not go to court, it seems unlikely that Argos had entered into any legally binding agreements to sell television sets at £3.00.[13]

The offeror may revoke his offer provided that he does so before his offer is accepted and he communicates the revocation to the offeree. Where a person has started to fulfil the acceptance requirements under a unilateral offer, the offeror cannot revoke the offer in relation to that person. An offeror may provide that the offer will expire after a fixed period and in any event an offer will no longer be capable of acceptance after a reasonable period has expired. An offer will come to an end once it has been accepted.

Acceptance and counter offers

In the same way as there cannot be a contract without an offer, a contract will not be formed until that offer has been accepted. An acceptance must be unconditional. In other words it must not seek to vary the terms of the offer. If it does so, then it will amount to a counter offer, and not an acceptance, with the consequence that the original offer will no longer be capable of acceptance unless reissued by the offeror.

In addition to the requirement for the acceptance to be unconditional, the acceptance must be communicated to the offeror and there must be an intention on the part of the offeree to enter into a binding agreement. In general, silence will not constitute acceptance of an offer. However, acceptance of a unilateral offer does not need to be communicated and acceptance may take the form of the actions of the offeree.[14] If an offer specifies that acceptance must be provided in a particular form or by a particular method, then in order to be effective the acceptance must be given in that form or by that means.

When considering the giving of acceptance, it is worth bearing in mind that it is quite possible for two machines to enter into binding contracts on behalf of their owners.[15] This is important in relation to the use of computers for stock control and management and also emphasizes the potential difficulties surrounding the use of automated responses in relation to online sales.

Consideration

In order for there to be a binding agreement, there must be a consideration passing from each of the parties. Consideration has been defined by the courts as 'some right, interest, profit or benefit accruing to one party, or some forbearance, detriment, loss or responsibility given, suffered or undertaken by the other'.[16] In a contract for the sale of goods, it is relatively straightforward. One party provides the goods and the other makes a payment for them. However, contract law does not regulate whether the parties have made a good bargain. In other words, the consideration given by each party need not be of equal value. However, it must be sufficient in that it must be real and of some value. It does not matter if the value is negligible, although this may impact on the level of damages that can be claimed in the event of breach of contract.

An important point to note is that consideration must not be past. The consideration to be provided by each party must be something that they will give, do or forgo in the future. For example, if a person makes a donation to a charity on Monday, then that payment cannot be used as consideration for a contract entered into on the Wednesday with the charity for the supply of goods or services. However, if a person undertakes on Monday to make a donation in consideration of the charity performing some service on Wednesday, then a binding contract may be made.

If a person is under an existing obligation to make a payment, that payment cannot be used as consideration for a further contract. This raises interesting issues in relation to the release of debts. If a person to whom money is owed agrees to accept the payment of a lesser sum from the debtor in full satisfaction of the loan then, in the absence of any other consideration, there is no binding agreement and the remainder of the debt can be recovered at a later date. This rule seems harsh on the face of it and does not appear to make commercial sense. However, there are ways around this issue. For example, the part payment of the debt on a date earlier than it would otherwise be due is good consideration.[17] The parties can enter into a deed of release of the debt. A deed is an agreement that is in writing, signed by the parties in the presence of witnesses and is delivered. The document must be clearly identifiable as a deed on the face of it. If the formalities are met, then a binding agreement will have been entered into as there is no need for there to be any consideration.

The equitable doctrine of promissory estoppel is also relevant. Where one party to a contract makes a promise not to enforce its rights under a contract and the other party relies on that promise to its detriment, then it would be inequitable for the first party to subsequently renege on its promise and seek to enforce its rights. The promise not to enforce must have been clear and unambiguous. Further, the doctrine works as a defence only and cannot be used to found an action to enforce a right under a contract or to cure a lack of consideration.

Intention to create legal relations

A binding agreement will only come into existence if both parties to the agreement have the necessary intention to create legal relations. This rule applies so as to exclude social and domestic arrangements from the ambit of contract law. Purely gratuitous promises do not give rise to binding contracts. A promise made by one friend to another in the pub to run in the London marathon is unlikely to be enforceable in a court. However, a promise made by a professional athlete to a shoe manufacturer to run in the London marathon in return for sponsorship most likely will be enforceable.

The rule in relation to intention to create legal relations is based on two rebuttable presumptions. In relation to domestic and social arrangements, it is presumed that there is no intention to create legal relations unless the contrary is shown. For example, where payment has been made.

In business and commercial transactions, it is presumed that there is an intention to create legal relations unless the contrary is shown. For example, a specific statement seeking to exclude legal enforcement such as making the document 'subject to contract'.

Certainty

A contract may be void if its terms are uncertain. In order for there to be a binding agreement, there must be certainty as to the identity of the parties, the subject matter of the contract and the terms of the contract. Where there is uncertainty as to the terms on which the parties have contracted, then terms may be implied by statute[18] and the courts will on occasion imply terms into contracts so as to give them efficacy.

Capacity

The parties to a contract must have the capacity to enter into a legally binding contract. Most companies will have capacity to enter into most contracts. However, the ability of a company to contract will depend upon its constitutional documents. The key provision used to be the main objects clause in a company's memorandum of association, but with the widespread adoption of general objects clauses, this became less of an issue. However, capacity is still important when dealing with minors,[19] statutory bodies or agencies and partnerships.

Any person over the age of 18 who is able to understand the consequences of his or her actions can enter into a binding contract. In addition any entity with legal personality can enter into binding agreements. This includes companies, corporations and statutory bodies. There may be restrictions imposed either in the constitutional documents or by statute as to the type of contracts that such entities may enter into. In England and Wales, partner-ships do not have a legal personality separate from the individual partners. This means that it is necessary to either enter into contract with all of the partners or with a one or more partners on behalf of the partnership. The way in which contracts may be signed on behalf of a partnership and the identity of those who may sign on behalf of the partnership is usually set out in the relevant partnership deed.

Postal Rule

As a contract is formed upon an offer being accepted, it is important to know when this occurs. Under English law, the Receipt Rule[20] and the Postal Rule[21] deal with when an acceptance is sent and received.

The Receipt Rule provides that the acceptance is only deemed to have been received when it is actually received. This is used where, for example, the parties are either in each other's presence or talking over the telephone or are using a form of communication such as telex where the transmitting party knows that the intended recipient has received the message and will have done so legibly.

The Postal Rule applies where the person accepting the contract does so by means of the post. The time of acceptance and deemed receipt by the other party is when the person posting the acceptance puts it into the postal system, provided that the letter is properly addressed and the offer did not expressly exclude the use of the postal system. The rationale behind this rule is to distribute the risk of miscommunication between the parties. It is open to the offeror to exclude the use of the postal system to accept his offer. However, the offeree must accept the offer by the means specified in it.

It is usual for commercial contracts to include specific clauses in relation to the giving and acceptance of notices under the contract as the same rules will apply to all such notices between the parties.[22] The contractual provisions will override both rules. It is particularly important to include such provisions if the parties intend to communicate electronically as there are as yet no set rules for the time of dispatch and receipt of emails.[23]

1.1.2 Contract formation and incorporation of terms

A contract is formed upon acceptance of an offer. The time at which accept-ance occurs will depend on the means of communication adopted. If a party wishes to rely on certain terms in a contract, then it is essential that those terms are made known to the other party prior to acceptance. By way of example, if a company wishes to trade on its standard terms and conditions it must provide its customer with those terms prior to the conclusion of the contract. Sending the terms out with an invoice is too late as the contract will have been made already.

It is important to bear in mind that there are very few formal requirements for a contract. It is very easy to make a contract for the supply of goods or services over the telephone or by email provided that there are sufficient details concerning the goods or services and the price.

The so-called battle of the forms arises when two parties seek to contract on their own standard terms and conditions. It is increasingly common for businesses to have terms and conditions both in relation to the goods and services that they provide and the goods or services that they purchase.

Typically, the business seeking to provide the services will submit its standard terms and conditions to its prospective customer. The response from the customer may be to accept the price offered to it in relation to the goods or services, but to state that it will purchase on its own terms. This amounts to a counter offer and is not an acceptance of the offer made by the supplier. If the supplier goes ahead and supplies the goods or services, without having rejected the purchaser's standard terms, then the supplier will be bound by the terms and conditions of its customer. The basic rule of thumb is that the last set of terms and conditions will be the one that applies to the contract (see Example 1). However, most commercial terms and conditions include provisions that state that the terms and conditions of the party will take precedence notwithstanding any other terms and conditions put forward by the other side. Often the battle of the forms leads to ambiguity as to the terms on which parties have contracted. The courts will be reluctant to provide that there has been no valid offer that has been accepted, particularly if one party has started to perform its obligations. However, the precise terms of that contract will be determined by the court.

EXAMPLE 1: THE BATTLE OF THE FORMS

(1) **Binding Agreement on Party A's standard terms of agreement**

Party A offers to sell 10 units at £10 per unit on A's standard terms. Party B then accepts Party A's offer to sell 10 units at £10 per unit on A's standard terms. The resulting contract is on Party A's standard terms of agreement.

(2) **Binding Agreement on Party B's standard terms of agreement**

Party A offers to sell 10 units at £10 per unit on A's standard terms. Party B then accepts Party A's offer to sell 10 units at £10 per unit but on Party B's standard terms. Party A then delivers 10 units to Party B and sends it an invoice for £100. Party B's 'acceptance' amounted to a counter offer, which was then accepted by Party A delivering the units. The resulting contract is on Party B's standard terms of agreement.

1.1.3 Representations and warranties

A representation is a statement of fact. It is not an opinion nor is it a statement of an intention. A misrepresentation is a representation that is false for whatever reason. A representation will be actionable only if it has been made by one party to another with a view to inducing that other party to enter into a contract. By its nature a representation is made before a contract is made. If a party to a contract has altered its position in reliance on a misrepresentation, then contract law will provide a remedy. The nature of the remedy will depend upon the reason for the misrepresentation but will typically be the right to rescind the contract and/or receive damages.

As a general rule, silence will not constitute a representation. However, a person's actions, such as a smile, nod or a wink, may convey a representation. There is no general obligation to provide information prior to a contract being entered into, even if such information may affect the decision to enter into the contract. There are exceptions to this general rule. If a person remaining silent owes a fiduciary duty to the person entering into a contract, then he may not remain silent about salient facts. Equally it is not permissible to remain silent if by doing so a representation that has been made is distorted. This may be the case where a person provides only some of the facts about a situation, but leaves a material fact untold without which the information conveyed is misleading. Similarly, if there is a change in circumstances before the contract is made that renders the representation misleading or false, then failure to disclose the new information may amount to a misrepresentation. Some contracts, such as contracts of insurance, require the parties to act in utmost good faith. Failure to disclose pertinent information will amount to a misrepresentation in such circumstances.

An action may be brought for misrepresentation if and to the extent that the misrepresentation in question induced the party bringing the action to enter into the contract. While there is no requirement for the misrepresentation to be the sole reason for entering into the contract, it must have played a material part in the decision to do so. This means that where a person relies on his own judgment or investigations or knows the statement to be incorrect before entering into a contract, no action for misrepresentation will arise. It follows that unless the misrepresentation has been communicated to the contracting party before the contract is entered into, no case for misrepresentation will arise.

Originally the law recognized only two types of misrepresentation: innocent and fraudulent. A fraudulent misrepresentation is a false statement that is 'made (i) knowingly, or (ii) without belief in its truth, or (iii) recklessly, careless as to whether it be true or false'.[24] In essence a fraudulent misrepresentation will be made if the person making the representation does not honestly believe the facts stated to be true. Only fraudulent misrepresentations gave rise to a right to claim damages.

In 1967 the Misrepresentation Act was passed. As a consequence, there are now three types of misrepresentation under English law:

- fraudulent misrepresentation;
- negligent misrepresentation; and
- innocent misrepresentation.

The concept of negligent misrepresentation was introduced by section 2(1) of the Misrepresentation Act 1967, which provides as follows:

Where a person has entered into a contract after a misrepresentation has been made to him by another party thereto and as a result thereof he has suffered loss, then, if the person making the misrepresentation would be liable to damages in respect thereof had the misrepresentation been made fraudulently, that person shall be so liable notwithstanding that the misrepresentation was not made fraudulently, unless he proves that he had a reasonable ground to believe and did believe up to the time the contract was made that the facts represented were true.

This means that it is no longer just an absence of honest belief in the truth of a statement that is necessary to give rise to action for damages. If the person making the statement had no basis for believing the truth of the statement or did not check into the facts before making the statement then he will be liable in damages.

An innocent misrepresentation is exactly as it sounds. It is a statement of fact, which when made was honestly believed to be true by the person making it and which the person making the statement believed to be true up to the time the contract was entered into.

There are two remedies for misrepresentation, namely rescission and damages. Rescission means setting aside the contract and putting the parties back into the position they would have been in if the contract had not been entered into. However, the right to rescind a contract may be lost if the party concerned has affirmed the contract once he is aware of the misrepresentation either by his actions or through the passage of time. The right to rescind will not be available if it is impossible to put the parties back into the position in which they were before the contract was entered into or if a third party has acquired for value some rights that will be adversely affected if rescission occurred.

Damages will be payable for both fraudulent and negligent misrepresentations. While damages cannot be claimed for an innocent misrepresentation, a right of rescission may arise. If the contract is rescinded an order may be made for a payment to be made to the party rescinding the contract if it is needed to put him back in the position in which he would have been but for the contract. Such a payment will cover out of pocket expenses etc. If the contract cannot be rescinded, then damages may be ordered in lieu of rescinding the contract. Section 2(2) of the Misrepresentation Act 1967 provides a specific right to receive damages in relation to negligent misrepresentations in lieu of the right to rescind the contract.

Unlike a representation, a warranty is a term within a contract that if breached may give rise to a right to receive damages but will not give rise to a right of termination. A 'warranty' needs to be contrasted with a 'condition', which is a term in a contract which if breached may give rise to a right to treat a contract as repudiated. This means that the affected party may give notice to the other party to the effect that it considers the contract to have been repudiated by the other party and that it considers itself to be released from further performance under the contract. A right to damages will also arise.

1.1.4 Remedies

If one party to a contract does not fulfil its obligations under the contract, it is said to be in breach. There are various remedies available under contract law to deal with breaches of contract.

Damages

The principle underlying the recovery of damages for breach of contract is to place the innocent party in the same position as he would have been if the contract had been duly performed.

The key to making a claim for damages is to establish that the loss suffered by the innocent party arises naturally from the failure of the other party to comply with its obligations under the contract or, at the time the contract was made, would have been in the minds of both parties as the probable result of such failure to comply with its obligations.[25] The vast majority of commercial contracts include provisions that limit the liability of the parties in certain circumstances. Typically, this may include an overall cap on the parties' liability under the contract. This is subject to a reasonableness test imposed by the provisions of the Unfair Contract Terms Act 1977.[26]

Where a party seeks to claim damages under the terms of an agreement, it is under a duty to mitigate its loss. This means that the claimant must take all available steps to reduce the actual loss that it has suffered. This may include obtaining the services that the other party has failed to provide from another source so that the level of damages is reduced to the difference between the cost of obtaining the services from the first party and the actual cost of obtaining them from a third party.

An indemnity[27] is an express obligation to compensate by making a money payment for some defined loss or damage as opposed to a contractual obligation giving a right to sue for damages for breach. As with damages, loss needs to be shown. The sum recoverable will be the amount required to compensate the party as a result of the occurrence that has been indemnified against. The damages that may flow following indemnity may be wider in that they may be in relation to 'all losses' arising from a particular failure to comply with an obligation.

While a claim for damages under an agreement will compensate a party for the failure by the other party to comply with its obligations, it will not force the other party to fulfil those obligations. There are various other remedies available to an injured party under a contract such as the granting of an injunction preventing the other party to the contract acting in breach of any restriction imposed upon him under the terms of that contract and an order for specific performance.[28]

Liquidated damages and penalties

Under English Law, it is not permissible to include within a contract a clause that imposes a penalty for failure to comply with an obligation. In this respect, a penalty would be seen as a clause that requires a punitive payment to be made in the event of a breach of contract. A penalty is a payment that is extravagant and unconscionable in relation to the greatest loss that may arise in relation to the breach in question.

In order to avoid a term being treated as a penalty, the parties to a contract may decide to include a liquidated damages clause. In essence the parties agree, at the time that the contract is entered into, what the financial consequences are of failure to comply with a particular obligation. In order to be enforceable, the parties have to have reached a genuine pre-estimate of the likely level of damages that would be payable in the event of that breach. In such circumstances, it is permissible to include a provision within the agreement that provides for the party to pay to the other such amount in the event that it fails to comply with certain obligations. The advantage of this is that the amount of the liquidated damages will, if they fall due for payment, be treated as a contractual debt and so be easier to enforce.

The courts will determine whether a payment amounts to liquidated damages or a penalty. The fact that the amount payable under a liquidated damages provision is large does not in itself mean that it is a penalty. It will depend on whether the liquidated damages are proportionate to the loss suffered and whether they represent a genuine pre-estimate of the parties. Equally, the mere fact that a clause is dressed up to look like liquidated damages will not prevent it being a penalty if the sum payable is excessive.

Equitable remedies

Equitable remedies are not available as of right, but are available only at the discretion of the courts. The two forms of equitable relief typically sought are an order for specific performance and an injunction.

An order for specific performance is a court order compelling a party to fulfil its obligations under a contract. However, an order for specific performance will be awarded only where an order for damages would not provide a sufficient remedy and will not be made in respect of contracts for personal services.

An injunction is an order of the court to prevent the breach of a contract term. It is not generally an order to perform an obligation, but rather an order to stop doing something that is in breach of a contract term. Unlike an order for specific performance, it may be used in relation to contracts for personal services.

Termination

In addition to a right to rescind a contract or to treat it as repudiated, a party may have a right to terminate the contract.[29] This will typically be a contractual right, which will arise in certain circumstances.[30]

1.1.5 Assignment, novation and rights of third parties

Under the common law rule of privity, a person who is not a party to a contract may not enforce the terms of a contract nor have the terms of a contract to which he is not a party enforced against him. While it is reasonable on the face of it not to expect a person to be bound to perform obligations agreed between two other parties, it is less reasonable for a person not to be able to enforce a benefit conferred upon him by a contract just because he was not a party to it.

There are a number of exceptions to the rule. Unless there is a restriction within a contract, a party may assign the benefit of a contract to a third party provided that it gives notice of the assignment to the other party to the contract. A benefit under a contract is the right to receive payment, goods or services from the other party. However, it is not possible to assign the burden of the agreement to the other party.

If a party enters into a contract as an agent for a third party, then the third-party principal will be able to enforce the contract. This will be the case even if the identity of the principal has not been disclosed. It is also open to a party to a contract to receive a benefit on behalf of a third party as a 'trustee' for that third party. This will enable the third party to enforce the contract by asking the trustee to sue on his behalf.

The common law position was changed fundamentally by the Contracts (Rights of Third Parties) Act 1999. Section 1(1) of the 1999 Act provides as follows:

> . . . a person who is not a party to a contract (a 'third party') may in his own right enforce a term of the contract if
>
> (a) the contract expressly provides that he may, or
>
> (b) subject to subsection (2), the term purports to confer a benefit on him.

Subsection (2) provides that no benefit will be conferred upon a third party if on a proper construction of the contract it appears that the parties did not intend the term to be enforceable by the third party. It is usual to see provisions in contracts that disapply the operation of the Contracts (Rights of Third Parties) Act 1999.

In order to be able to enforce rights under a contract, a third party must be 'expressly identified in the contract by name, as a member of a class or as answering a particular description . . .'.[31]

In view of the ability to assign the benefit of a contract, it is common for contracts to include provisions that restrict the ability of parties to assign the benefits under it. Typically, such a restriction will either be an absolute prohibition or a requirement to obtain the prior consent of the other party. The rationale is usually that the parties to the contract have agreed to do business with each other on the terms set out in the relevant contract and do not want to have to deal with third parties particularly if they are competitors.

On occasion it becomes necessary to change the party who is obliged to perform under the agreement. This may arise where a company has sold its business and the contracts need to be transferred to the purchaser. In these circumstances, the contract will need to be novated. In essence this will involve an agreement between three parties. The two original parties to the contract and the new party. Under the terms of the novation the continuing party to the original contract will release the exiting party from further obligations under the original contract in return for the new party undertaking to fulfil those obligations.

1.1.6 Electronic contracts

Most contracts are capable of being entered into electronically and can even be entered into without any human intervention – other than putting the necessary processes and programs in place. The normal rules of contract law apply to electronic contracts. However, the way in which electronic contracts are formed may give rise to slightly different risks to those arising in the real world.

Contract formation

The way in which contracts are made electronically reflects the real world. A contract will be formed at the point at which an offer is accepted. When this occurs will depend upon the means of electronic communication used. It will depend also on whether the parties have agreed how contracts will be entered into electronically between them.

It is very important that the terms on which people are contracting are very clear and are understood by both parties. The importance of getting it right online has been demonstrated already.[32]

In order to protect itself a business should have clear terms of business. However, these terms will be of no use to the business unless they are incorporated into the contracts it enters into.

Incorporation of terms

When considering the question of incorporation of terms in an online contract, it is useful to consider two separate situations. First, contracts entered into by email and, second, contracts entered into by means of websites.

An email is just another means of communication. As such all of the rules that apply to contract formation in the real world apply. However, there are some points that need to be borne in mind. While sending an email is akin to sending a letter, the Postal Rule does not apply. In fact there are as yet no hard and fast rules that apply to email to determine the point at which an email is sent and the point at which it is received. While there have been calls for the government to address this issue,[33] it is for the parties to a contract to determine this in the contract and for the offeror to determine how it wants to receive acceptance of its offer.

It is also important to remember that terms will only be incorporated into a contract if they are brought to the attention of and accepted by the other party before the contract is entered into. This means that if the terms are attached to an email, the person seeking to rely upon them needs to ensure that their existence is sufficiently drawn to the attention of the offeree and that the terms are capable of being read – i.e. that they can be opened and have not become corrupted in the course of transmission.

In relation to websites it is important that the terms and conditions on which the online vendor wishes to do business are brought to the attention of the customer. In this respect, it is useful to go back to the software industry's practice of using shrink-wrap licences. The term shrink-wrap comes from the practice of placing the licence for the software on the outside of the package containing the disks on which the programs are stored and then sealing the same with clear cellophane. The idea being that the terms of the licence are to be read through the clear cellophane before the package is opened. The potential licensee therefore had the opportunity to either accept or decline the terms before loading the software on to his system.

The problem is that it is very difficult to read a complex legal document through crinkled cellophane. If any of the terms of the licence are hidden or are illegible then those terms will not be enforceable against the licensee. The software industry got round this by placing the disks or CD-Rom in an envelope with a notice on it saying that the envelope should only be opened once the accompanying licence had been read and accepted by the licensee.[34] The same principle can be adopted with online terms and conditions.

Click-wrap, web-wrap and browse-wrap agreements

In essence these work in exactly the same way as a shrink-wrap licence. Before the contract is made, a potential customer is taken through the terms and conditions, which he can either accept or decline by clicking on the relevant acceptance button. The courts in the USA have held that this type of agreement to be enforceable in the decision in *Hotmail Corporation v Van Money Pie*.[35] Hotmail offers an online email service. This is a free service that is subject to various authorized use conditions. In particular, Hotmail prohibits the use of the Hotmail account for spamming. Hotmail can be accessed only if the account is set up online and Hotmail's terms are accepted by clicking on the accept button. Van Money Pie opened up an account by clicking on the accept button and then used its Hotmail account to send unsolicited commercial email. Hotmail was successful in its claim against Van Money Pie for breaching its terms and conditions and the case shows the court's willingness to accept the validity of click-wrap agreements.

If a business simply has a statement on its website that terms and conditions are available upon request, then this will not be sufficient to incorporate those terms into any agreement that is entered into online as the potential customer will not have had an opportunity to receive the terms before placing an order. Until recently, some people argued that a hypertext link to the terms and conditions that the potential customer may follow was sufficient. This led to the use of 'browse-wrap' agreements. A browse-wrap agreement involves the supplier placing its terms and conditions on its website and then permitting its potential customers access to those terms and conditions via a hypertext link. This approach is seen to have the least interference with the purchasing process.

On 3 July 2001 the US Southern District New York Federal court ruled on a preliminary issue in the case of *Sprecht and others v Netscape and AOL.*[36] The validity of the licence agreement was questioned following challenges to the use of a tracking device, which was incorporated into the SmartDownload software to monitor users' online activities. Netscape removed the tracking device but argued that the licence agreement obliged any users who had complained about it to participate in an arbitration process rather than filing a suit in the courts. The court held that a mere reference to a licence agreement purporting to bind users downloading free software did not create an enforceable contract. The statement inviting users to review the terms of a licence agreement appeared on the Netscape web page when users went to download its SmartDownload software.

Judge Alvin K. Hellerstein ruled that because there was simply an opportunity to read the terms and conditions and the users' attention was not clearly drawn toward reading them, they did not form the basis for a binding contract. Moreover, the user was not required to give express consent to the agreement and so could not be shown to have agreed to its terms. One way of managing this issue is place a tick box next to the hypertext link to the terms and conditions. The customer will be required to check the tick box before proceeding to place an order to indicate that he has accepted the vendor's terms and conditions. This method can be used to demonstrate the customer's agreement to the terms (see Example 2).

EXAMPLE 2: USE OF A TICK BOX TO INCORPORATE STANDARD TERMS AND CONDITIONS

☐ Tick this box if you accept our <u>terms and conditions</u>.

Place Order

However, the safest way to ensure that terms and conditions set out on a website are fully incorporated is to use a 'web-wrap' agreement.

A web-wrap agreement works in exactly the same way as a click-wrap licence. Before the contract is made, a potential customer is taken through the terms and conditions in a dialogue box and has the opportunity to either accept or decline the terms by clicking on the relevant acceptance button (see Figure 1.1).

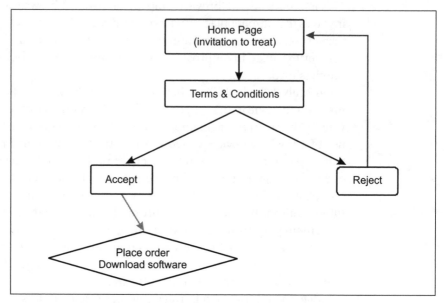

FIGURE 1.1   *Use of web-wrap agreements*

1.1.7 Regulation of electronic contracts

Consumer Protection (Contracts concluded by means of Distance Communication) Regulations 2000

The Consumer Protection (Distance Selling) Regulations 2000[37] ('DSRs') transposed into English law the provisions of the EU Directive on the Protection of Consumers in respect of Distance Contracts.[38]

The DSRs provide additional protection to consumers who are purchasing goods or services at a distance, which means that the purchaser and the vendor are not both physically present when the contract is entered into. The DSRs apply when a consumer enters into a 'distance contract', which is defined in Regulation 3 as being:

> any contract concerning goods or services concluded between a supplier and a consumer under an organized distance sales or service provision scheme run by the supplier who, for the purpose of the contract, makes exclusive use of one or more means of distance communication up to and including the moment at which the contract is concluded.

The DSRs define a 'means of distance communication' as 'any means which, without the simultaneous physical presence of the supplier and the consumer, may be used for the conclusion of a contract between those parties'.

The DSRs apply to distance contracts entered into by a means of communication other than the 'excepted contracts' set out in Regulation 5 as being contracts:

(a) **for the sale or other disposition of an interest in land . . .;**

(b) **for the construction of a building . . .;**

(c) **relating to financial services;**[39]

(d) **concluded by means of an automated vending machine or automated commercial premises;**

(e) **concluded with a telecommunications operator through the use of a public pay-phone;**

(f) **concluded at an auction.**

Prior information

Regulation 7 of the DSRs provide that consumers must be provided with certain information before they enter into a distance contract. The information to be provided is as follows:[40]

- full details of the name and address of the supplier;
- a description of the main characteristics of the goods or services;
- the price of the goods or services including all taxes;
- the delivery costs;
- the arrangements for payment, delivery or performance;
- the existence of a right of cancellation;
- the period for which the offer or price remains valid; and
- where appropriate the minimum duration of the contract.

The information must be provided in a 'clear and comprehensible manner appropriate to the means of distance communication used'.[41] There is no requirement for the information to be given in writing.

Written confirmation and extra information

The DSRs provide that the information to be provided under Regulation 7(1) and certain other information must be provided to the consumer either before the formation of the contract or in good time thereafter during the performance of the contract and at the very latest at the time of delivery of the goods to the consumer. The information must be provided in writing or in another durable medium. This will include the provision of the information by email.

The information to be provided under Regulation 8(2)[42] must include:

- the information to be provided in accordance with regulation 7(1);
- information concerning the right to cancel under Regulation 10, including information about returning any goods and who is responsible for

the cost of returning them and information as to how the right to cancel may be affected by the consumer agreeing to performance of the services;

- geographical address for complaints;
- details of any after-sales service or guarantees; and
- any conditions for exercising a contractual right to terminate the contract if it is of an unspecified duration or exceeds one year.

Following a consultation on proposed changes to the DSRs undertaken by the Department of Trade and Industry (DTI) in early 2004, the DSRs were amended with effect from 6 April 2005.[43]

The key change affected the way in which the cancellation right in relation to a contract for services operates under the DSRs.[44] As originally drafted, a consumer lost the right to cancel a contract if 'the performance of the services has begun with his agreement' provided that the consumer had been told that this was the case in writing or other durable form prior to the conclusion of the contract in question.[45] This caused concern in relation to contracts entered into by telephone as a written notice could not be given prior to the conclusion of the contract that was made over the telephone. The example given in the consultation related to vehicle hire.[46]

In essence, the obligation to provide information in relation to the right of cancellation under Regulation 8 of the DSRs has been clarified. The original regulation 8(3), which required the notice to be in writing, has been repealed. The DSRs have been amended so that the obligation to provide such information has been added to the list of information to be provided in accordance with the provisions of regulation 8(2). It is no longer a prerequisite that information regarding the consumer losing his or her right of cancellation must be given in writing prior to the conclusion of the contract in question. The obligation imposed on a supplier is that at the time that the consumer enters into a contract for the provision of services, the consumer must be advised that if the services are commenced with his consent during the cancellation period then the consumer's rights of cancellation will be lost.

As a consequence of the amendments to Regulation 8, the period during which the right of cancellation runs has also been amended. A new Regulation 12(3)A has been inserted into the DSRs that provides that where information in Regulation 8 has not been provided then the cancellation period will be a period of seven days from the date that the information was given to the consumer or if shorter until the performance of the contract in question has been completed.

Right of cancellation

The right of cancellation granted to consumers is dealt with in Regulations 10–13. Once a distance contract has been entered into and the consumer has been provided with the information required by Regulation 8(2) the consumer then has a period of seven working days after the goods have been delivered within which to return them or within which to cancel the contract for services. The period of seven working days will run from the date on which the consumer receives the information required to be provided under regulation 8(2) or at the latest from the date that is 30 days after the date on which the contract is concluded.[47]

The effect of cancellation is that the contract shall be treated as if it had never been made. This means that there is no cost to the consumer, other than the actual cost of returning the goods in certain circumstances. Any credit agreement entered into by the consumer is cancelled at no cost to the consumer.

Regulation 13 sets out the following exceptions to the right of cancellation in relation to distance contracts:

(a) for the supply of services if the performance of the contract has begun with the consumer's agreement

    (i) before the end of the cancellation period applicable under regulation 12(2); and

    (ii) after the supplier has provided the information referred to in regulation 8(2);[48]

(b) for the supply of goods or services the price of which is dependent on fluctuations in the financial market which cannot be controlled by the supplier;

(c) for the supply of goods made to the consumer's specifications or clearly personalised or which by reason of their nature cannot be returned or are liable to deteriorate or expire rapidly;

(d) for the supply of audio or video recordings or computer software if they are unsealed by the consumer;

(e) for the supply of newspapers, periodicals or magazines; or

(f) for gaming, betting or lottery services.

On 10 March 2005 the European Court of Justice pronounced judgment in the case of *easyCar (UK) Limited v Office of Fair Trading*.[49] easyCar is a car hire company that enters into agreements with its customers over the internet. The price of hiring a car is determined by supply and demand. As fewer cars remain available, the price of hire goes up. In theory, the earlier that a customer hires a vehicle the cheaper the price.

There had been a number of complaints to the Office of Fair Trading (OFT) that easyCar did not comply with its obligations under the DSRs. easyCar applied to the High Court for a declaration that its rental agreements were exempt from the cancellation rights granted under Regulations 10 and 12 on the basis that car hire contracts fell within the exception of 'contracts for the provision of transport services'.[50] The OFT then sought an order to make easyCar comply with the provisions of the DSRs. There was no dispute as to the fact that the car hire contracts in question constituted 'distance contracts' for the purposes of the DSRs nor that there was a provision of services within the meaning of the DSRs. The matter was referred to the European Court of Justice for determination.

The European Court of Justice decided that the term 'transport services' should be treated as a sectorial exemption. Accordingly, the exemption applied to services that were generally available in the transport sector. In the court's view, the exemption within the Directive[51] was intended to cover all services provided within the transport sector and not merely some forms of agreement relating to specific transport services. If that had been the intention, then there would have been explicit provisions dealing with the contracts in question. While the Distance Selling Directive had been adopted with a view to protecting consumers' interests, the purpose of Article 3[52] of the Directive was to ensure that suppliers of services in certain sectors were not disproportionately affected by the application of any regulations made under the Directive. In the court's opinion, car hire undertakings constituted an activity that the Directive had intended to exempt from the application of the Directive.

By contrast, online car dealers are caught by the DSRs. In May 2005 the OFT issued guidance on compliance with the DSRs in relation to cars and other vehicles sold by distance means.[53] In the past a distinction had been made between selling brand new cars and used cars. The argument was that a brand new car required the purchaser to choose not only the model and make, but also the colour of the vehicle and various other optional extras. The motor industry had argued that this amounted to customization of the car and as such was outside the scope of the DSRs.[54] Not so, according to the guidance published by the OFT. Merely selecting optional extras from a list of standard options did not amount to customization. In order to be taken outside of the scope of the DSRs, something far more imaginative is necessary. The same regulation also provides an exception for goods that deteriorate quickly.[55] The OFT made it clear that this related to the physical deterioration of the goods and not just the loss of financial value. The fact that a car has been sold and registered to a new user does not amount to any deterioration in the goods even though there is a marked decrease in the value of the vehicle.

However, the consumer is under an obligation to take reasonable care of the vehicle. The OFT made it clear that it would be unlikely to object to suppliers pointing out to a consumer what they considered to be reasonable care by suggesting an acceptable mileage limit. However, if consumers did not follow such guidance, it would be a question of fact as to whether they had taken reasonable care. Any excess mileage in itself would not take away a consumer's statutory right to cancel.

Ecommerce Regulations

The EU Ecommerce Directive on certain legal aspects of information society services, in particular electronic commerce, in the Internal Market (Directive on Electronic Commerce)[56] is transposed into English law by the provisions of the Electronic Commerce (EC Directive) Regulations 2002[57] ('Ecommerce Regulations').

The Ecommerce Regulations regulate the provision of 'information society services'. These are services that are normally provided for remuneration at a distance by means of electronic equipment at the individual request of a recipient.

The requirement that the services are provided for remuneration includes websites whose only form of remuneration is payment for advertisements on them. The DTI's guidance notes indicate that the definition catches all ecommerce sites including those of businesses providing free information on a website as well as all online ads, email etc.

There are a number of matters that are excluded from the application of the Ecommerce Regulations and these are set out in Regulation 3. The Regulations do not apply to tax, data protection, cartel law or betting, gaming or lotteries nor do they regulate information society services provided by public notaries or in relation to the defence of a court case.

The key point to note is that the Ecommerce Regulations do not apply 'in relation to any Act passed on or after the date these Regulations are made or in exercise of a power to legislate after that date'.[58] This is especially important in relation to the defences provided to information society service providers ('service providers') in respect of liability for third-party materials.[59] This means that every time a new Act of parliament is passed, a statutory instrument extending the scope of the Ecommerce Regulations must be made if that Act is to come within the ambit of the Regulations.

The Ecommerce Regulations can be divided into three broad parts. The first deals with information that has to be provided by all service providers, the second deals with information that has to be provided when contracting online and the third deals with the liability of service providers for third-party material stored on their systems.

Country of origin principle

Before considering the information and liability provisions of the Ecommerce Regulations, there is a further aspect of the Regulations that needs to be considered, namely the country of origin principle. The EU Directive adopted a 'country of origin' approach. The aim of the Directive was originally to ensure that anyone providing services over the web need only be concerned with the laws of the country in which it is established.

Unfortunately, Recital 23 of the Directive made it clear that the Directive did not override the existing conventions dealing with questions of forum and choice of laws. This means that the Brussels Regulation 2000[60] and the Rome Convention 1980 both still apply.

The country of origin principle is transposed into English law by Regulation 4 of the Ecommerce Regulations. In its simplest form, this means that as long as a UK business complies with UK laws, it can 'ignore' the laws of other member states. If this rule applied throughout the EU, it would be good news for businesses, because it allows them to target consumers in all member states without needing to follow the rules of all of the member states. However, this basic rule is qualified.

The country of origin principle applies to requirements within the 'Coordinated Field', which is defined as:

> requirements applicable to information society service providers or information society services, regardless of whether they are of a general nature or specifically designed for them, and covers requirements with which the service provider has to comply in respect of:
>
> (a) the taking up of the an information society service, such as requirements concerning qualifications, authorization or notification, and
>
> (b) the pursuit of the activity of an information society service, such as requirements concerning the behaviour of the service provider, requirements concerning the quality or content of the service including those applicable to advertising and contracts, or requirements concerning the liability of the service provider,
>
> but does not cover requirements such as those applicable to goods as such, to the delivery of goods or to services not provided by electronic means.

However, there are some specific exceptions. Regulation 4(4) provides that the provisions of Regulations 4(1) – 4(3) do not apply to those fields set out in the Schedule, namely:

- copyright and industrial property rights;
- freedom of parties to choose the applicable law;
- contractual obligations concerning consumer contracts;
- real estate; and
- unsolicited commercial communications or spam by email.

Most significantly, the Ecommerce Regulations do not apply the country of origin principle to the terms of consumer contracts. In practical terms, this means that a UK-based ecommerce site's terms and conditions should meet the laws of every member state in which consumers can buy its products, not just UK laws. As a result of the consumer contract exception, any site selling to French consumers must provide its terms and conditions in French, otherwise they may be considered invalid. If selling into Denmark, consumers must be given a 14-working day cooling-off period during which the consumer can change his or her mind about the purchase and return the goods for a refund. In the UK, the cooling-off period is only seven working days. These are only examples, there are many other differences.

The application of the country of origin principle is extremely limited in its scope.

Information provisions

Regulation 6 sets out the general information to be provided by a service provider. The information to be provided is as follows:

(a) the name of the service provider;

(b) the geographic address at which the service provider is established;

(c) the details of the service provider, including his electronic mail address, which make it possible to contact him rapidly and communicate with him in a direct and effective manner;

(d) where the service provider is registered in a trade or similar register available to the public, details of the register in which the service provider is entered and his registration number, or equivalent means of identification in that register;

(e) where the provision of the service is subject to an authorization scheme, the particulars of the relevant supervisory authority;

(f) where the service provider exercises a regulated profession

    (i)   the details of any professional body or similar institution with which the service provider is registered;

    (ii) his professional title and the member State where that title has been granted;

    (iii) a reference to the professional rules applicable to the service provider in the member State of establishment and the means to access them; and

(g) where the service provider undertakes an activity that is subject to value added tax, [its VAT registration number].[61]

The information must be provided in a 'form and manner which is easily, directly and permanently accessible'.[62] One way of achieving this is to collate all of the information on a web page and to include a link to this page from the website's home page.

In addition to the general information to be provided under Regulation 6, there is a requirement to provide specific information when contracts are to be entered into electronically.[63] If neither of the parties are consumers, they may contract out of the obligations set out in Regulation 9.[64] The information to be provided under Regulation 9 is as follows:

(a) the different technical steps to follow to conclude the contract;

(b) whether or not the concluded contract will be filed by the service provider and whether it will be accessible;

(c) the technical means for identifying and correcting input errors prior to the placing of the order; and

(d) the languages offered for the conclusion of the contract.

In addition there must be a link to all relevant codes of conduct. By way of example, a firm of solicitors providing paid for legal advice online must include a link to the code of practice of the relevant Law Society. This obligation does not apply to contracts entered into by email.

Where terms and conditions are provided, the service provider must ensure that they are provided in a way in which they can be stored and reproduced. In other words they must be capable of being saved and printed by the customer. The requirement to make available the terms and conditions applicable to a contract in a form that allows the recipient to store and reproduce them is a mandatory requirement regardless of whether the contract is with a consumer or between two businesses.

Once an order has been placed using 'technological means' the service provider must acknowledge receipt of the order without undue delay and by electronic means. The acknowledgement of the order does not necessarily have to be given using the same electronic means by which the order was placed. It is important to note that the Ecommerce Regulations discuss the placing of an 'order' and the sending of an 'acknowledgement'. The Ecommerce Regulations do not establish a framework for creating online contracts. Rather, they provide for information to be provided both before and following the contract process. It is particularly important that any acknowledgement sent is appropriately worded so as to avoid a contract being entered into inadvertently.[65]

The service provider must provide a means of identifying and correcting input errors before the order is placed. This may be as simple as including a clear button on the page on which the order form appears.[66]

The obligations imposed on a service provider upon receipt of an order apply in relation to all of its dealings with consumers. They will also apply to dealings with another business unless the parties have contracted out of the obligation. Once again, the obligations do not apply to contracts concluded exclusively by exchange of electronic mail or by equivalent individual communications.

Failure to comply with the obligations imposed by the Ecommerce Regulations can give rise to a claim for damages for breach of statutory duty or even a right to rescind a contract.[67]

Liability of intermediaries

Regulations 17 through to 22 deal with the liability of service providers in certain circumstances. In essence the regulations deal with situations where the service provider:

- is acting as a mere conduit;
- is caching certain information; or
- is acting as a host.

If the service provider complies with the regulations then the service provider will not be liable to third parties for damages, but more importantly compliance will act as a defence to a criminal prosecution being brought against the service provider.

The Ecommerce Directive[68] specifically requires that member states should not impose a general obligation on those providers to monitor the content on their service. Generally speaking, it is normally accepted that if a service provider monitors the content on its servers then it will be at greater risk as it will be treated as an editor or a publisher of that information.

(a) Mere conduit

The mere conduit exception set out in Regulation 17 is extremely narrow. Where the information society service consists of either a transmission in a communication network of information that has been provided by a recipient of the service or where the information society service consists of the provision of access to a particular communication network then the service provider will not be liable in damages:

- if it did not initiate the transmission;
- did not select the receiver of the transmission; and
- did not select or modify the information in the transmission.

The DTI in its guidance notes makes it clear that manipulations of a technical nature that take place in the course of the transmission, for example the automatic adding of headers, does not mean that the service provider will be treated as having modified the transmission. It will only do so if it in some way modifies the information itself.

(b) Caching

Regulation 18 provides protection to service providers in respect of cached copies of websites used in the provision of their access services. The service provider will not be liable in damages where the caching is 'automatic, intermediate and temporary' for the sole purpose of providing a more efficient service.

Further, the service provider must:

- not modify the information;
- comply with conditions on access to the information. This may be difficult. For example, the copyright notice attached to a website may provide that the information on the website may not be stored in an

electronic retrieval system. If so, then on the face of it, this precludes the website being cached by the service provider in order to provide a more efficient service;

- comply with any industry rules regarding the updating of the information;
- not interfere with the lawful use of technology, widely recognized and used by industry, to obtain data on the use of the information; and
- act expeditiously to 'remove or to disable access to the information he has stored upon obtaining actual knowledge of the fact that the information at the initial source of the transmission has been removed from the network, or access to it has been disabled, or that a court or an administrative authority has ordered such removal or disablement'.

Regulation 22 provides some guidance as to what its meant by 'actual knowledge'. This includes ascertaining whether the service provider has received a notice about the data and that notice includes:

- **the full name and address of the sender of the notice;**

- **details of the location of the information in question; and**

- **details of the unlawful nature of the activity or information in question.**[69]

(c) Hosting

Regulation 19 provides a defence for a service provider in respect of hosted material. That is any information that is stored by it where that information has been provided to the service provider by someone using its service. However, the person who has posted the material must not be under the authority or control of the service provider.

In such circumstances the service provider will not be liable in damages where it does not have actual knowledge[70] that the information or material is unlawful nor does it have constructive knowledge that the information is unlawful.[71] While there is no obligation to monitor the contents of the site, it is arguably not open to a service provider to merely turn a blind eye. Once again the service provider must act immediately upon gaining knowledge that the material is unlawful by either removing or disabling access to the material.

1.2 COMMON TERMS

1.2.1 'Subject to contract'

The term 'subject to contract' is used where the parties to a negotiation wish to avoid entering into a binding agreement. On the face of it the words make it clear that the parties do not intend to be bound until such time as they have entered into a formal contract. However, where the parties have begun to perform on the basis of their discussions, then notwithstanding the use of the words 'subject to contract' a binding agreement may have been formed. The only question to be determined will be the terms on which the parties have contracted.

It is important to avoid using variations of the phrase as this may not have the intended result. In *Beta Investments SA v Transmedia Europe Inc* (2003), the words 'subject to more complete documentation' did not prevent a binding agreement coming into effect. The courts will look at all of the facts surrounding any negotiations, including the conduct of the parties, to ascertain whether there is a binding agreement. The fact that the parties have stated that the negotiations are subject to contract will be only one of the factors taken into account and may not be the determining factor.

1.2.2 'Time of the essence'

A contract term that provides in relation to the performance of an obligation that time is of the essence is extremely onerous. If the obligation is performed even 10 minutes late then the other party will be entitled to terminate the contract and, if appropriate, seek damages for breach of contract. Accordingly, the inclusion of such a provision in a contract is usually fiercely contested.

In the absence of a time of the essence obligation, failure to perform at a given time or on a given date will give rise usually to a right to claim damages and not a right to terminate the contract. Generally speaking time will not be of the essence in relation to the time of performance under a contract unless the contract includes a specific provision to that effect or it is clear from the nature or subject matter of the contract or the conduct of the parties that it was intended that time should be of the essence. Time will become of the essence if a party who has suffered an unreasonable delay gives notice to the defaulting party that the obligation must be performed by a particular time and making time of the essence.

1.2.3 'Best endeavours' and 'reasonable endeavours'

One of the most argued over phrases within a contract is whether a party should use 'best endeavours' or 'reasonable endeavours' to perform an obligation. It is sensible to consider the two phrases together.

The obligation to use 'best endeavours' is not as onerous as many believe it to be. The words do not impose an obligation to do everything possible to achieve the required result and are not akin to an absolute obligation to perform. Rather, an obligation to use 'best endeavours' imposes an obligation to do what can reasonably be done in the circumstances.[72] This means that a party that has given an undertaking to use its 'best endeavours' must take such action as is commercially practicable and incur such expenditure as is reasonable in the circumstances. However, the undertaking does not preclude the party from acting in its best interests. It is important to note that the reasonableness or otherwise of undertaking a particular course of action will be determined by reference to the circumstances existing at the time that the actions are to be performed and not at the time when the parties entered into the contract.[73]

The obligation to use 'reasonable endeavours' imposes a considerably lesser obligation than best endeavours. It is doubtful that the person undertaking to use reasonable endeavours will be required to do anything that may be financially or commercially disadvantageous.

1.2.4 'Reasonable skill and care'

The standard to which an obligation is to be performed under a contract will either be set out in the contract or may be implied by statute. In a contract for services, the Supply of Goods and Services Act 1982 imposes a duty on the service provider to use 'reasonable skill and care' in the provision of its services. The same standard of conduct is often imposed on a party by an express term of the contract.

The requirement of 'reasonableness' introduces an element of objectivity. The courts will look at all of the circumstances to determine what level of care would ordinarily be expected from a person of normal intelligence engaged in the activity in question. While the lack of experience of the person providing the services will not be taken into account, if a person professes to have a particular skill or expertise, this will be taken into account.

1.2.5 Core contract terms

It is essential that the parties to a binding contract understand and agree to the terms of that contract. The main purpose of having written terms and conditions is so that each party has a clear understanding of the terms of the agreement before entering into it and to ensure that a record of that agreement is kept.

Clauses of general application

(i) 'Entire Agreement'

The purpose of an entire agreement clause is to make it clear that all of the contractual terms are to be found in the document containing the clause and not elsewhere. In addition, a typical entire agreement clause will seek to exclude liability for any pre-contract representations that have not been repeated within the contract. The clause will also make it clear that all previous agreements entered into between the parties in relation to the matters dealt with by the contract are superseded and will seek to exclude as far as possible any terms that may be implied into the agreement by statute.

Section 3 of the Misrepresentation Act 1967 and section 8 of the Unfair Contract Terms Act 1977 provide that any exclusion of liability for misrepresentation will only be enforceable to the extent that it satisfies the reasonableness test.[74] The courts have held that on the face of it a clause that seeks to limit the liability of the parties to the four corners of the contract will be reasonable. The rationale behind this is that it makes commercial sense for parties to agree to be bound by the terms that are set out in the agreement as the commercial risks that they have agreed to accept will be reviewed in light of those commitments. However, if the clause seeks to exclude liability for fraudulent misrepresentation, then this would be unreasonable and would not be enforceable. In this respect, it is not uncommon to see words along the lines of 'nothing in this clause shall limit liability in respect of fraudulent misrepresentation' added at the end of an entire agreement provision.

(ii) 'Indemnities'

An indemnity is an express obligation to compensate by making a money payment for some defined loss or damage as opposed to contractual obligation giving a right to sue for damages for breach. The losses covered by an indemnity will be set out in a specific indemnity provision within the contract. Generally speaking, the rules relating to remoteness of damage do not apply nor is there a duty on the person receiving the benefit of the indemnity to mitigate their loss, unless there is a specific obligation to do so within the contract. It is also important to note that the provisions of the limitation of liability clause will not automatically apply in relation to any indemnity given under a contract. Rather, the provisions of an exclusion of liability clause need specifically to be expressed to extend to cover any such indemnity.

The most common indemnity in an IT context is in relation to the intellectual property rights. Typically, the indemnity will be linked to a warranty from one party that it either owns, or has been licensed all necessary rights to use any intellectual property rights that it is making available to the other party or using in the provision of its services. The rationale is to protect the receiving party against any claim brought by a third party that the intellectual property rights in question infringe those of a third party. Traditionally, such clauses have not had any cap of liability on them, although there is a move away from this trend. In any event, as it is an indemnity, unless the limitation of liability clause makes a specific provision to cap the liability for the indemnity, it will not generally be caught.

In return for indemnifying the customer, a supplier will usually expect to take control of any proceedings that were brought against the customer and will restrict the customer's ability to compromise or settle any claims.

(iii) 'Limitation of Liability'

The general position is that parties are free to contract on such terms as they see fit. However, the provisions of the Unfair Contract Terms Act (UCTA) 1977 modify this position. The Unfair Contract Terms Act 1977 is primarily a piece of consumer protection legislation. However, it also applies to business-to-business contracts. UCTA is undergoing a review at present and is likely to be extended so that it not only regulates all consumer contracts but also a large number of contracts entered into with SMEs.[75]

Section 2 of UCTA prohibits any clause within a contract that seeks to limit or exclude liability for death or personal injury resulting from the negligence of a party to the contract. This applies to all contracts, and explains why in all commercial agreements, even those unlikely to give rise to any form of liability for death or personal injury, there is always a clear statement that nothing in the agreement seeks to limit liability in this way. The reason for including such a clause is to ensure that the remaining limits on liability are not struck out by the court on the basis that they are so widely drawn they may inadvertently exclude liability for death or personal injury. Section 2 goes on to say that parties are not able to exclude liability for negligence, generally, except in so far as the term in the contract or the exclusion notice satisfies the requirement of reasonableness.

The reasonableness test requires that the term shall 'have been a fair and reasonable one to be included having regard to the circumstances which were, or ought reasonably to have been, known to or in the contemplation of the parties when the contract was made'.[76] Schedule 2 of UCTA sets out some of the matters that are taken into account in applying the reasonableness test. These include:

- the strength of the bargaining positions of the parties relative to each other;
- whether the customer received an inducement to agree to the term;
- whether the customer knew or ought reasonably to have known of the existence and extent of the term; and
- whether the goods were manufactured, processed or adapted to the special order of the customer.

Section 3 of UCTA provides that any clause that seeks to exclude or restrict liability for breach of contract will only be enforceable to the extent that it satisfies the requirement of reasonableness. The section applies only to contracts where one party is acting as a consumer or where one party is dealing on the other's standard written terms of business.

If a party wishes to exclude or limit its liability, then it must do so clearly and unambiguously. If the provision upon which it seeks to rely is not clearly drawn, then it may be ineffective. The clause must clearly identify the liability that is to be excluded or limited. However, the clause must not be so wide in its application that to enforce it would defeat the main purposes of the contract.

UCTA prohibits any clause within a contract that seeks to exclude or limit liability for death or personal injury that is caused by negligence. UCTA also provides that any exclusion for loss or damage arising due to the negligence of the party is subject to the reasonableness test as is any exclusion or limitation of liability contained within a contracting party's standard terms of business.

Until the Court of Appeal decision in *Watford Electronics Limited v Sanderson CFL Limited* [2001], there had been a series of cases where IT customers were found to have dealt on a supplier's written standard terms notwithstanding the fact the contracts had often been negotiated. In the Watford case, the court held that the reasonableness of a term should not be considered in isolation. Where experienced businessmen representing substantial companies of equal bargaining power negotiate an agreement, they may be taken to have had regard to the matters known to them. In such circumstances, the businessmen should be taken to be the best judge of the commercial fairness of the agreement that they have made, including the fairness of the terms in that agreement and whether those terms are reasonable. Unless it is clear that one party has taken unfair advantage of the other, the terms of the contract agreed between the parties should be considered to be reasonable.

A well-drafted limitation of liability clause will seek to do a number of things. It will seek to exclude liability for certain categories of loss. Typically, these losses will be in relation to indirect or consequential loss. However, it is essential that the clause is drafted to spell out the types of loss envisaged, such as loss of revenue or profits, loss of anticipated savings etc., rather than merely including a blanket exclusion of indirect consequential or special loss or damage. An exclusion clause will also seek to place a limit on the liability of each party in relation to different types of loss. For example, there may be a separate cap on liability in relation to real property or intellectual property rights and in relation to liability for breach of contract.

(iv) 'Notices'

Every contract should include a notices provision. This allows the parties to determine the point at which a notice is deemed to be sent and the point at which it is deemed to be received under the contract. This is important, as it allows the parties to alter the position under the Postal Rule and the general rule.[77] A notice provision is particularly important in relation to the use of electronic communications, as there are no general rules of law that apply.

A well-drafted notice clause will provide for the place at which notice is to be served, the method by which it is to be served and when service is deemed to take place. If a contract specifies that notices must be given in a particular form then, in order to comply with the terms of the contract, notices must be given in that form. This allows the parties to exclude certain types of notice, for example notice by email or by facsimile transmission.

(v) 'Termination'

In the absence of any provision within the contract to the contrary, all agreements can be terminated by either party giving to the other reasonable notice of termination. However, it is often commercially necessary to ensure that a contract should continue in force for a minimum period. This may be necessary so that one party is able to recoup its pre-contract expenditure. In such circumstances, a contract may include a provision that the agreement will continue in force for a minimum term. In any event, most contracts will include a provision providing a specified period of notice to terminate the agreement. This allows both parties to have certainty as to the amount of notice that they will receive upon the other party deciding to end the contract. This allows both parties to effect an orderly disengagement from the contract.

Unfortunately, things may go wrong in relation to contracts. It is usual to include provisions that allow for the earlier termination of the agreement in certain circumstances. The most common triggers give a party the right to terminate if:

- there has been a material or continuing breach of contract;
- there has been a change in control of a party;
- the other party becomes insolvent; or
- there has been a change in the circumstances of one party making it impossible for it to continue with the contract.

The termination provision will often provide that where one party to the contract is in material breach of the contract then unless it has remedied that breach within a set period, the other party may terminate the agreement. The period provided should be a reasonable one in the context of the contract and of the breach to be remedied. If the contract is of particular importance to the business of one of the parties, then the period within which the breach has to be remedied may be very short.

On the whole, businesses like to know with whom they are dealing. Often, a business will be uncomfortable if the entity that it has contracted with is subsequently taken over by another organization. This will be an issue particularly if the new owner is a competitor. Accordingly, it is not unusual for a contract to include a clause that allows a party to terminate the agreement if there is a change in control or ownership of the other party.

If one of the parties to a contract becomes insolvent, then it is important that the other party is able to terminate the agreement. The termination provision will be drafted so that the party who wishes to terminate with the insolvency of the other can do so as soon as is reasonable. This prevents any delay arising as a result of having to wait until the other party has gone into insolvent liquidation.

Finally, contracts will often include provisions that provide for the agreement to come to an end if certain events arise. Where one party requires a licence from the government in order to provide its services, then the contract will usually terminate upon that licence being revoked. Equally, if the ability to fulfil its obligations under a contract is dependant upon that party having an agreement with a third party, then the clause may provide that in the event that such third-party agreement comes to an end, the contract will also be terminated.

(vi) 'Force majeure'

Force majeure arises where events that are outside of the control of a party to a contract prevent that party from complying with its obligations under the contract. Where a contractual obligation has become incapable of being performed a contract may become frustrated. Rather than having the agreement come to an end, parties will often include a mechanism to deal with force majeure.

A force majeure clause should contain clear statements on the following.

- The events capable of bringing the clause into operation. There are two ways in which these events may be defined. First, an exhaustive list of events that will enable a party to rely on the provisions of the force majeure clause. This is a very restrictive approach and is used in circumstances where the parties wish to only allow force majeure to relieve either party of their obligations in certain specified circumstances. The second and more common approach is to have a list of events that constitute an event of force majeure but to have this open-ended so that it includes all other events that are beyond reasonable control of the party affected.
- The effect such an event must have on a party's ability to perform its contractual obligations.
- The affected party's duties in respect of overcoming the consequences on event of force majeure. This is to ensure that a party who is relying upon a force majeure event to relieve it of its obligations under contract must seek ways of either overcoming or working around the problem.
- A mechanism for bringing the clause into operation. Typically this will involve one party giving notice to the other with details of the event of force majeure that has arisen and the consequences of event of force majeure.
- A mechanism adjusting the existing contractual terms.
- A mechanism for bringing the operation of the provisions of the force majeure clause to an end.

(vii) 'Confidentiality'

There is no statutory law of confidence. It is a concept that has developed in common law, and therefore has been decided by judges in individual cases to protect a party who confides in another party. Generally speaking, in order for any information to be treated as confidential it must not be generally available, it must be clearly identifiable and it must be imparted to the recipient under a duty of confidence.

The fact that the information may be in the public domain, but is not easily or readily available in a collection, may still mean that the information itself is considered to be not generally available for the purposes of affording it protection under the law of confidentiality. Confidential information must be of a specific character, which means that the information must be clearly identifiable as a class of information that is being treated as confidential. This does not necessarily mean that everything needs to be labelled 'private and confidential'. However, marking information as confidential does ensure that that information falls within a clearly identifiable class of information, which is to be treated as confidential. That being said, the fact that a document is marked 'private and confidential' does not mean that it is confidential in nature.

So when does the duty of confidentiality arise at common law? A duty of confidentiality may be accepted contractually or it may be implied where the nature of the information of itself is such that it is clear that it is intended that it should be kept confidential. A good example of this would be credit card details, which are provided for the express purposes of payment for services or goods. It is clear that the intention is that that information should be kept confidential and not provided to any third party other than the payment company.

More obviously, where information is disclosed to someone under a specific duty of confidence the obligation to keep that information confidential will be imposed. This applies equally to information that has been obtained in breach of a duty of confidence. The rule relating to privity of contract means that only those who are party to the contract or are clearly identified as being subject to provisions of the contract may be caught by the obligations of confidentiality.[78] However, if the recipient has actual or constructive notice that the information was subject to a duty of confidence originally, then the same duty will be imposed on the recipient. Certain relationships, such as lawyer, accountant, priest, professional persons, etc., will give rise to what is known as a 'fiduciary' relationship. This means that the persons concerned are in a position of trust and are required to keep information disclosed to them confidential.

With the above in mind, it is important to avoid using blanket confidentiality statements that provide that all information will be treated in confidence. In the first instance the information may not have the necessary quality of confidentiality and second such a clause may impose an obligation in respect of certain information that the parties do not wish to be kept confidential.

A well-drafted confidentiality clause will provide that the information in question is clearly identified and that it has a specific character of confidentiality. The clause should then limit what can be done with the confidential information. A typical confidentiality provision will specify a purpose for which the information may be used and will permit the confidential information to be used only for that purpose. Equally, it may restrict those parties to whom the information may be divulged and the purpose for which it may be divulged to such third parties.

One of the key remedies in relation to a breach of confidentiality is an ability to seek a court order preventing the person who is using that information from using it or making it further publicly available. It is not unusual to see clauses that provide that damages alone would not be an adequate remedy and reserving the right to seek equitable remedies such as injunctions or orders for specific performance.[79] However, such a clause in itself does not mean that the parties seeking to rely on it will automatically be granted an injunction. This does not of course mean that damages cannot be sought as well.

In general, information given or received in confidence for one purpose may not be used for a different purpose, or passed to anyone else, without the consent of the provider of the information. There are some exceptions to this, for example where the disclosure is in compliance with a court order or where circumstances give rise to a public duty of disclosure. A well-drafted confidentiality clause should deal with the circumstances where the information may be disclosed to third parties.

(viii) 'Governing law and jurisdiction'

On the whole, it is open to the parties to a contract to determine the law that will apply to the contract and which courts will have jurisdiction. However, there are specific rules that apply in relation to consumers.

If both parties are based in England and the services to be provided under the contract are to be performed in England, then English law will apply and the English courts will have the necessary jurisdiction to deal with any dispute. While in such circumstances the parties may elect for the contract to be subject to the laws of the State of New York, such an election will be ineffective if it has been made to get around a mandatory requirement under English law.[80]

Where the parties to the contract are based in different countries or the services or goods are to be performed or delivered in a different country, it is preferable for the parties to ensure that the contract includes a governing law and jurisdiction clause. In addition to providing which country's law will govern the contract, the clause will provide which courts will have jurisdiction. This will be either on an exclusive or non-exclusive basis. If the contract provides that the courts of a particular country will have exclusive jurisdiction, then any action for breach of contract must be brought in those courts. This is attractive because it ensures that a business will not have to defend itself against actions brought in foreign courts. However, if the other party to the contract is based in another country then any award of damages may need to enforced in that other jurisdiction. This means that first there would have to be a case to determine whether there had been a breach and to determine the appropriate remedy, and then a separate enforcement action in respect of the court's award. If the clause provided for the non-exclusive jurisdiction of the courts in question, then each party would have the option to make its claim in the courts in the country in which the party being sued is located. This would not affect the choice of law and would cut out the need for separate enforcement proceedings.

1.3 LETTERS OF INTENT

There are occasions where the parties involved in a transaction need to provide each other with some comfort as to their intention to enter into a contract in the future. This may arise where the negotiation of the terms of the contract are ongoing, but one party needs to place orders for materials in order to be able to fulfil its obligations under the contract once it has been agreed, or the parties wish to set a timetable for the transaction and the negotiations. In such circumstances the parties may decide to enter into a letter of intent or a memorandum of understanding. Quite often, such agreements are not intended to be contractually binding and are often marked 'Subject to Contract'. However, the letter of intent will often set out the main terms on which the parties hope to contract in future.

The term 'letter of intent' has no legal significance and the courts have found so-called letters of intent to be binding contracts. The problem is that there is no requirement under English law for contracts to take a particular form. The conduct of the parties by relying upon the terms set out in a letter of intent may in itself lead to a binding contract on the terms set out in the letter of intent. Equally, on occasions there are parts of a letter of intent, such as those relating to confidentiality or lock-in arrangements, which the parties require to be binding in any event. This means that careful thought needs to be given to the way in which the letter of intent is drafted and the way in which the parties will act following signature. If it is not intended to be binding then the letter of intent must only reflect the intentions of the parties. Under English law, an agreement to agree something at a later date does not create a binding agreement.

It is important to bear in mind that the usual contract rules in relation to offer, acceptance and consideration will all apply. This means that in order to protect the parties, the letter of intent needs to deal with some of the issues ordinarily dealt with in a contract.[81] The problem with this is that the inclusion of such terms tend to make the letter more akin to a contract and may tip the balance in deciding whether it has created a binding agreement.

1.4 IT SPECIFIC ISSUES

1.4.1 Software specific clauses

(i) Licences

IT contracts often involve the licensing of intellectual property rights. An obvious example is a software licence. A 'licence' is permission to do something that would otherwise be unlawful. It is not lawful to make copies of any works that are protected by copyright without the copyright owner's permission to do so. A software program is protected by copyright and so either the copyright has to be assigned or a licence needs to be granted in order for the software to be used lawfully.

Typically, a licence will grant to the licensee the right to use the software for a particular purpose in return for the payment of a licence fee. The licence may contain restrictions in relation to the number of people who may use the software or may be limited to the use of the software at a particular location or on particular equipment.

It is important that the licence provision deals with such issues clearly and sets clear parameters as to the way in which the software can be used. Generally speaking the owner of the intellectual property rights in the program may determine how the program may be used and impose such restrictions as it sees fit. However, the Copyright Designs and Patents Act 1988 provides that certain restrictions relating to the making of back-up copies and reverse engineering the software will be treated as void in certain circumstances.[82]

(ii) Acceptance testing provisions

There are a number of issues that need to be considered in relation to acceptance testing. The most important point to bear in mind is that the acceptance criteria need to be agreed at an early stage. All too often this is left until too late in the process and disputes arise as to what the acceptable level of functionality and performance is to be.

A well-drafted acceptance clause will do the following:

- specify what is going to be tested and at what stage;
- specify how the acceptance criteria are going to be determined, by whom and by when;
- provide the other party an opportunity to review and comment on the proposed test criteria;
- specify where the testing will take place and by whom;[83]
- set parameters for passing the test;[84]
- provide a mechanism for correcting the errors and submitting the program to further tests. It is essential that the timescales for undertaking corrective work are realistic; and
- provide each party the opportunity to break the cycle.[85]

You will often see 'deemed acceptance' provisions in acceptance testing clauses. These provisions are designed to protect the developer against customers who either delay implementing or commenting on the acceptance tests or having rejected the software go ahead and use it in a live environment. It is important that these provisions are clearly drawn so that there can be no argument as to when the customer will be deemed to have accepted the software.

There is a clear correlation between the ability for the software to pass acceptance testing and properly drawn up functional and technical specifications. These documents are the yardstick against which the performance of the software will be measured.

(iii) Warranties in IT contracts

In addition to any express warranties within an IT contract a number of warranties may be implied into it. As a result, most forms of IT contract will seek to exclude all implied warranties 'to the fullest extent permitted by law'. The words 'to the fullest extent permitted by law' are used to ensure that the contract does not fall foul of any statutory provisions prohibiting the exclusion of certain implied warranties.

The most important implied warranty to exclude is that of 'fitness for purpose' or 'satisfactory quality'. In this respect clauses are often inserted into software licences to the effect that the customer is responsible for the selection of the software for its processing needs. This is particularly the case in respect of package software.

Commercial imperatives dictate that a software developer must provide its customers with some form of protection. The typical warranties provided are as follows:

- the developer will provide its services with reasonable skill and care;
- the software delivered will, for a period, comply in all material respects with its technical specification; and
- ownership of intellectual property rights. This is the most important warranty. The developer is asserting that it has the right to provide the software to the customer.

Where bespoke software is being developed, the customer will often wish to take an assignment of the intellectual property rights in all or parts of the software. There are a number of points for the software developer to bear in mind:

- Does the software being developed use any code that will be reused by the developer? If so, then such code needs to be excluded.
- If part only of the rights in a program are to be assigned, then have the parts that are being kept and being assigned been adequately defined? Too often the descriptions are too vague or, worse, overlap.
- Does the agreement actually assign the intellectual property rights? Often the wording is such that a further assignment is needed. It may be preferable for the rights to be assigned as they are created subject only to receipt of payment.

A well-drafted clause will provide what is to happen if the agreement is terminated early. Any assignment of any intellectual property rights should be coupled with what is known as a 'further assurance clause', which imposes an obligation on the assignor to do such additional acts as may be necessary to perfect the assignment of the intellectual property rights to the assignee.

If the licence is of package software the warranties will be limited in scope. If the licence is merely a trial licence then there will be little or nothing in the way of warranties, which will be supplied on an 'as is' basis.

(iv) Service levels

In addition to an undertaking to use reasonable skill and care in the provision of services, it is becoming increasingly common to see the inclusion of service levels in contracts for services. A service level is a statement of the way in which, or the standard to which, a particular service is to be provided. Service levels must be:

- capable of objective measurement. If they are not, then the parties will end up arguing over whether a particular service level has been met; and

- realistic. The service level obligations can be used to set the expectations of both parties as to the way in which the services will be provided.

If a contract includes specific service levels, it will often include a mechanism for enforcing such service levels. Typically, this will involve either an obligation to pay liquidated damages or service credits if the required service standard is not met. It is important that the amount payable does not amount to a penalty, which will be unenforceable.[86] At the very least, the continued failure to meet the required standard should give rise to a contractual right to terminate the contract. Although, in so far as remedies are concerned, this represents a blunt instrument as opposed to a rapier.

(v) Intellectual property rights indemnity

This is one of the most important clauses in an IT contract. In essence the software developer is being asked to stand behind its product.

A well-drafted intellectual property rights indemnity will be linked to a definition of intellectual property rights. It is important for the party giving the indemnity that this definition is limited to those intellectual property rights that it knows that it owns. Equally, it may be sensible to seek to exclude particular jurisdictions, for example the USA, and this is often done by limiting the definition of intellectual property to the intellectual property rights arising within a particular jurisdiction.

From the software developer's perspective, a well-drafted intellectual property rights indemnity will provide for the developer to control the defence of any claim brought and will prevent the customer from settling or compromising the claim without the consent of the developer. This is reasonable because the software developer is the party being asked to provide the indemnity and will have to pay out if a successful claim is made.

The software developer will want to limit its liability under the indemnity. Accordingly, it will often seek the right to amend the software so that it becomes non-infringing, to obtain a licence for the use of the infringing elements or to terminate the software agreement. The latter option is designed to reduce the amount of damages the developer may have to pay to the third party.

(vi) Source code escrow

Customers often ask for source code to be put in escrow. A source code escrow clause usually requires that within a certain period after the date on which the agreement is signed the party enters into a source code escrow agreement[87] with an escrow agent and deposits a copy of the source code with the agent. It is possible to set up a one-to-many escrow, so that the same source code deposit is used for all customers. Costs tend to be borne by the customer, but this is really a question of negotiation.

1.5 ANATOMY OF MAIN IT AGREEMENTS

1.5.1 Software development agreement

(a) Purpose

As businesses use information technology more and more, there is a growing trend to have the software used by them customized to fit their specific business needs. Often this will involve the customization of an existing software package by adding functionality or varying the existing functionality. On occasion, it is necessary to start from scratch and create a completely new software program. In either case, the parties will need to enter into a software development agreement, which is primarily an agreement for the provision of services, namely software development services. As with any services agreement it is essential that the services to be provided are clearly set out.

The developer needs to know exactly what it is being asked to develop. This is usually achieved by reference to a functional specification drawn up by the customer. However, often the first task for the developer is to scope the development work to be undertaken by it. The developer will need to tell the customer if there are any elements of the functional specification that it will not be developing or that need to be changed.

In theory the developer's first job should be to create a technical specification from the functional specification. In practice, the specification is often created at the same time as the software is developed. It is important that the development agreement is drafted so that it reflects the way in which the developer operates.

(b) Key provisions

In addition to the clauses that may be found in all contracts, the key provisions of a software development agreement will deal with the following issues:

- provision of the services;
- timetable for the project;
- ownership of the intellectual property rights;
- acceptance testing;[88]
- payment terms; and
- changes to the specification or services.

The software development agreement will need to set out clearly the services to be provided by the developer. This will become the yardstick against which the developer's performance will be measured. The contract will set out the standard of care to be adopted by the developer and may include specific provisions relating to the methodology to be adopted and even the personnel to be used in providing the services.

In addition, the contract will usually incorporate a project plan or timetable. There will be occasions where the customer will have a legitimate need to complete a project by a certain date and it is common to agree a longstop date by which the work has to be completed. Failure to meet this date can give rise to a claim for damages and/or termination of the contract. When agreeing to any form of timescales, whether it is in relation to a project timetable or in respect of certain actions to be taken under the agreement,[89] it is essential that the timescale is realistic. This is especially important when agreeing a longstop date. Where the developer will be dependent on input from the customer, then it is important for the developer to ensure that the agreement makes it clear that any slippage in the timetable due to a failure by the customer to fulfil its obligations will lead to a consequential extension of the project timetable.

Where software is developed on behalf of a business, it will often seek to ensure that it owns the copyright in the program. This can be done by means of an assignment provision within the agreement. However, the developer may not be willing or able to do this. The developed software may be based on the developer's existing software, which it uses for other products or which may incorporate software developed by third parties. In such circumstances the developer will only be willing to grant a licence to use the software.[90] Regardless of whether there is an assignment or a licence, the agreement should include a specific warranty from the developer that it has all of the rights necessary to enable it to perform the services and that the program will not infringe the intellectual property rights of any third party. This should be backed up by an indemnity.

There are two basic payment models that are commonly adopted in relation to development agreements, namely:

- time and materials model, where the customer pays on the basis of the time spent developing the programs; and
- fixed price model, where the developer is required to produce the software for a fixed fee.

Customers are keen on fixed prices for obvious reasons and may wish to phase the payment of the fee so as to provide the developer with an incentive to fulfil its obligations under the software development agreement in a timely manner. In practice, the payment provisions often mix the two types of payment models with a fixed fee for part of the work such as the scoping exercise and with a time and materials basis for other parts – albeit sometimes subject to an overall cap.

If payment is late under a contract then the payee is entitled to receive interest under the terms of the Late Payment of Commercial Debts (Interest) Act 1998 at a rate of 8% above the Bank of England rate. It is possible to contract out of this obligation 'where the parties agree a contractual remedy for late payment of the debt that is a substantial remedy. . .'[91]

During a software development project, either of the parties may wish to change the scope of the work. Accordingly most software development agreements have what is known as a change control procedure. In essence these all work in the same way. One party makes a suggestion for change, which the other party is required to review, comment on and either accept or reject the proposed change. A well drawn clause will provide sufficient time to review the proposal, amend it and cost the work and allow additional time to be added to the timetable to complete any phase of the project that has been delayed as a result of the review of the change control request.

1.5.2 Software licence agreements

(a) Purpose

Software programs are protected by copyright. The owner of the software program will have invested time and money in the development of the program. Accordingly, the owner will want to ensure that it protects those rights so that it can exploit the software with a number of different customers. The way in which this is achieved is by using a software licence. The aim of a well-drafted software licence should be to achieve a balance between the rights granted to the user and the rights retained by the software owner.

(b) Key provisions

In addition to the clauses that may be found in all contracts, the key provisions of a software licence agreement will deal with the following issues:

- licence of the software;
- acceptance testing;[92]
- warranties;[93] and
- intellectual property rights indemnity.[94]

The key provision in a software licence is the licence itself. The licence must identify clearly what is being licensed. This will usually be done by setting out details of the software including its release and version number either in a schedule or in the definition of the software. The licence grants the licensee permission to use the software. In this respect, the licence will establish what the software can be used for, by whom it may be used and where it may be used.

The licence may also contain other restrictions or conditions as to the use that may be made of the software. Often the use of the software is limited to the licensee's 'own internal business purposes'. This is intended to differentiate between a licensee using the software to process its own data and the licensee using the software to process a third-party's data or to provide some kind of computer bureau service.

Software may be licensed on a number of different models. These include:

- site licences, where the software can be used only at a particular location and sometimes only on specified hardware;
- seat licences, where the licence permits the software to be used by a specified maximum number of concurrent users. This model is often

linked with an ability to increase the number of seats and the payment of a recurring licence fee. In the past software companies have sought the names of the individual licensees to be provided, but the current trend seems to be to limit it solely to number of users or to allow the customer to change details of registered users so long as the total in use does not exceed the maximum; or

- enterprise licences, which may permit use of the software by an entire company, division or group of companies.

Typically the grant of a licence will be non-exclusive. This means that the licensor is free to use the software itself and to licence others to do so. There is no limitation on the way in which the licensor can exploit the software. An exclusive licence prevents the licensor from granting any further licences or from using the software itself. This is often the case where the licensor has developed a bespoke software program that is based on its underlying core software. As such the licensor cannot assign its intellectual property rights in the software, but it may grant an exclusive licence of the bespoke parts.

The duration of the licence will be driven by the pricing model and will depend on whether a one-off licence fee is payable or a recurring licence fee is payable.

In the past typical restrictions contained within a licence included an absolute bar on:

- reverse engineering;
- incorporating the program into other programs; and
- making copies of the software.

However, it is no longer permissible to include absolute prohibitions on these activities as the licensee has certain inalienable rights.[95] It is important that any restriction on the licensee in relation to the above is expressed to be subject to the licensee's statutory rights.

1.5.3 Software maintenance agreement

(a) Purpose

Once a business has acquired its new software, it will want to ensure that the software continues to work and that the business is able to benefit from any upgrades made to the software. Unless the intellectual property rights in the software have been assigned, it is probable that the software developer will provide maintenance services.

There are two separate elements to be considered. First, the licensee may need support in its use of the software. This may take the form of the provision of help desk services and may require the developer to fix any bugs or errors in the software. Second, the licensee may wish to benefit from any improvements made by the developer to the software that make it easier to use or add functionality.

(b) Key provisions

In addition to the clauses that may be found in all contracts, the key provisions of a software maintenance agreement will deal with the following issues:

- provision of maintenance services;
- provision of upgrade services;
- exclusions from the services;
- service levels; and
- payment terms.

It is essential that the software maintenance agreement sets out the precise scope of the services to be delivered. This will include identifying exactly what is to be maintained. This is particularly important where the software to be maintained incorporates third-party software or relies on the simultaneous use of third-party software in order to operate. The actual services to be provided also need to be clearly set out. The types of maintenance services[96] and the times when they will be available all need to be established in the software maintenance agreement.

In addition to support services, the software maintenance agreement may provide for the licensee to be supplied with upgrades. This may be limited to releases and exclude new versions that add functionality.[97] A software maintenance agreement may specify that only the latest version of the software will be maintained and will specifically exclude the maintenance of any third-party software. This is important as the software company will not wish to be required to maintain old versions of the software, just because the customer has decided not to take any upgrades. In these circumstances, the maintenance fee usually includes the provision of the latest versions of a program backed with a requirement for the licensee to implement the upgrade.

In order to limit the scope of the maintenance services to be provided by the software company, software maintenance agreements often set out a list of exclusions. Typically maintenance services will:

- only be available in relation to the current and previous release of the software; and
- not cover any faults arising from:
  - modifications made to the software by the user or any third party;
  - user error;
  - third-party software faults;
  - unauthorized configuration; or
  - failure to implement previous recommendations made by the software company.

Most software maintenance agreements will include service levels, which set the parameters for the way in which the services are to be provided. The typical service levels in a software maintenance agreement relate to the time that it will take the software company to respond to a request for support and the time that it will take to either fix or find a work around to the problem.

The time allocated to resolving an issue may depend on the severity of the issue and the importance of the software to the licensee.

Failure to meet a service level may lead to certain remedies specified in the contract such as liquidated damages, service credits or a right of termination.

The payment provisions in a software maintenance agreement normally require payment of an annual or quarterly fee in advance. This fee is often calculated by reference to the amount of the licence fee and subject to annual increases.

1.5.4 ASP agreement

(a) Purpose

Software and the infrastructure needed to support it can be extremely costly. One way of reducing this cost is to use software on an ASP basis. 'ASP' stands for application services provider. An ASP is a business that makes its software available on a subscription basis typically via the internet. The software is not downloaded by the end-user but is accessed via an internet browser. This means that the end-user does not have to store the software or, for that matter, the data that is being processed on its own servers or laptop and, therefore, can reduce the specification of the hardware it uses. This is particularly attractive to users in relation to expensive software or when they have large amounts of data to process and store.

The important thing to bear in mind is that the ASP model usually adopted is a one-to-many model. The same service is provided to many end-users and the level of customization is either non-existent or minimal.

(b) Key provisions

In addition to the clauses that may be found in all contracts, the key provisions of an ASP agreement will deal with the following issues:

- provision of the services;
- exit management;
- service levels; and
- security.

Under an ASP model the software is run on the servers of the ASP provider. The end-user does not need to download the software onto its systems. As such, all that is being provided is a service. In exactly the same way as it is important to ensure that the software being licensed is clearly identified in a software licence, so it is important to ensure that the services to be provided by the ASP are clearly defined.

With regard to payment the main issue to consider is whether the person using the system is paying a one-off fee for the privilege, or whether the fee is payable either on a periodic basis or based on the amount of use made by the end-user. Whether the periodic model or the pay per use model is adopted will depend on the nature of the software being provided and the expected use that the end-user is going to make of that software. In fact there is nothing new about this. Periodic licence fees, often tied to the provision of maintenance services and upgrades, have been used by the software industry for some time, as have run-time licences based on the usage of the licensee.

The ASP has to provide or lease the infrastructure necessary to enable it to make the software readily available to end-users and to store and process the end-user's data. This will often involve the ASP in up front costs. The term for which the agreement is entered into then becomes of critical importance. The ASP does not want to be put in a position whereby it incurs expenditure creating the necessary infrastructure only for the end-user to terminate the ASP agreement after a couple of months.

As the ASP is processing and storing data on behalf of the third parties it needs to ensure that it does not become liable for any unlawful content that it may be storing. In many respects, an ASP needs to take account of the same considerations as an information society service provider.[98] In this respect, most ASPs require their users to adhere to an authorized use policy, which sets out the basis upon which the service can be used. This needs to be linked to a right of the ASP to either suspend or terminate the provision of the services if the authorized use policy is breached and if necessary to delete data.

Unlike a typical software licence, an ASP agreement should include an exit policy. The end-user will have access only to the software and its data by using the service. If the ASP agreement is terminated, then the end-user will no longer be able to access that data nor use the software. The ASP agreement must deal with the handover of the data. Unless the data files are stored in standard formats, the ASP agreement needs to provide the end-user with continued access to the software to the extent that this is necessary to enable the end-user to access the data. One way around the obligation to provide continued access to the software would be to convert the data into a form that can be accessed and processed by commercially available software.

Because the ASP is providing services, end-users will be looking to impose service levels on the ASP. In relation to an ASP agreement the key service levels relate to the availability of the service in terms of access to the service and the functionality provided by the service.

The ASP may wish to exclude certain items from the calculation of availability. The obvious exclusions relate to the situation where the service is not available due to third-party network failure. This is particularly important in relation to the use of mobile technology because the availability of the service may depend upon the network coverage in any particular area of the mobile communications service provider used by the end-user. Equally, there will be occasions when the service has to be suspended so that the ASP can undertake maintenance of its systems. While an ASP will, no doubt, endeavour to ensure that any maintenance does not affect the service that it is providing, it should exclude any service loss that results due to routine maintenance. This is usually tied in to an obligation to undertake routine maintenance at certain times only and also to give notice of planned maintenance to the end-users.

When considering the period over which the service level is to be calculated, it should be remembered that the longer the period the better it is for the ASP. If the ASP says that its service will be available for 99.8 per cent of the time and this is calculated over a period of one year, then at any one time during the year the service can be unavailable for a period of up to 17½ hours. If the same calculation is made on a monthly basis, the amount of permissible downtime is reduced to 1.5 hours for that month.

As with any form of service levels, the ASP agreement may specify certain contractual remedies. However, because the ASP has to invest in infrastructure or commit to third parties to lease infrastructure, the termination of the agreement has a considerable cost consequence for the ASP. Also the ASP model is a one-to-many model, which means that if the ASP is unable to provide its service, then this is likely to be the case for all of its end-users. It is, therefore, essential for the ASP that a cap is placed on the liability of the ASP to its end-users under the service level arrangements.

One of the most important issues for anyone using software on an ASP basis is that of security. The ASP will need to be able to demonstrate that its systems are secure and to guarantee the integrity and confidentiality of the data stored and processed on its systems. This is especially important if personal data is to be processed using the ASP. The Data Protection Act 1998 imposes obligations on data controllers to ensure that personal data is kept secure and to ensure that any third parties processing data on their behalf are contractually bound to have appropriate security measures in place.[99]

1.5.5 Escrow agreements

(a) Purpose

A software program is a set of instructions to a computer. These instructions are recorded in a human readable form, know as source code, and a machine readable form known as object code. Software companies are extremely jealous of their source code as it can be used to recreate the software and so, generally speaking, they do not make it available to third parties. In certain situations, the source code may be needed to maintain the software. This is why the party providing maintenance services is usually the software developer.

However, what is the licensee to do if the software developer fails to provide adequate support services or goes into liquidation? Without the source code the licensee may not be able to maintain the software. In order to get around such issues, the software industry has developed the use of source code escrow agreements, where the source code is held by a trusted and independent third party, known as the escrow agent and is released to the licensees on the occurrence of certain events.

In selecting an escrow agent, it is essential to ensure that the agent is truly independent. It should not be the solicitors or accountants of either party. Also, it is important to ensure that the escrow agent has the necessary storage facilities, especially if the source code is stored on tape or disk.[100]

(b) Key provisions

In addition to the clauses that may be found in all contracts, the key provisions of a source code escrow agreement will deal with the following issues:

- escrow services;
- release triggers; and
- payment terms.

An escrow agreement involves three parties: the software owner, the licensee and the escrow agent. The agreement will impose obligations on both the software owner and the escrow agent. The software owner will be required to deposit with the escrow agent a copy of the source code together with such other documentation as may be necessary to enable a competent software engineer to maintain the software. The software owner will be required to update the information deposited with the escrow agent regularly and whenever a change is made to the source code. The escrow agent will be obliged to hold the source code safe and to release it only on the occurrence of certain events. In addition to the core escrow services, the escrow agent may offer a verification service. This involves a review of the source code and other materials deposited to ensure that they are sufficient for the purpose for which they have been deposited. Both the software owner and the escrow agent are answerable to the licensee if they fail in their obligations under the agreement.

The escrow agent is required to keep the source code deposited with it safe until either the escrow agreement comes to an end or a release event occurs. In most cases, the release events will be the insolvency of the software owner or the failure of the software owner to provide maintenance services in accordance with the terms of a maintenance agreement. From the escrow agent's perspective, the release events should be drafted in such a way that the escrow agent does not need to make a decision as to whether to release the source code. In other words, the escrow agent does not have to determine the relevant merits of a dispute between the parties, but merely to go through a set procedure.

The escrow agreement will set out what the licensee can do with the source code if it is released to it. Typically, this will be no wider than the original licence granted to the licensee, although it may allow the licensee to provide the source code to third parties for the sole purpose of providing maintenance services.

The escrow agreement will normally provide for the payment of a fee to the escrow agent for setting up the escrow arrangements followed by an annual fee. It will be for the software owner and the licensee to determine which of them is responsible for paying these fees or, if both of them are to pay, the amount each has to contribute.

REFERENCES

Acts of Parliament and Regulations

Acts of Parliament and Statutory Instruments may be found at http://www.opsi.gov.uk. However, bear in mind that the documents linked to are as the Acts or Statutory Instruments were originally enacted and do not take account of any amendments made by subsequent Acts or Statutory Instruments.

The chapter refers to the following:

Legislation

- Misrepresentation Act 1967
- Unfair Contract Terms Act 1977
- Sale of Goods Act 1979
- Contracts (Rights of Third Parties) Act 1999
- Consumer Protection (Contracts concluded by means of a Distance Communication) Regulations 2000
- Electronic Commerce (EC Directive) Regulations 2002
- The Consumer Protection (Distance Selling) (Amendment) Regulations 2005

Cases

The following cases are referred to in the chapter:
- Pinnel's Case (1602)
- *Adams v Lindsell* (1818)
- *Hadley v Baxendale* [1854]
- *Currie v Misa* (1875)
- *Derry v Peek* (1889)
- *Carlill v Carbolic Smoke Ball Co.* [1891–94]
- *Terrell v Mabie Todd & Company Limited* [1952]
- *Pharmaceutical Society of Great Britain v Boots Cash Chemists* [1953]
- *Fisher v Bell* [1961]
- *Partridge v Crittenden* [1968]
- *Beta Computers (Europe) Limited v Adobe Systems (Europe) Limited* (1995)
- *Hotmail Corporation v Van Money Pie* (1998) US Case
- *Sprecht and others v Netscape and AOL* (2001) US Case
- *easyCar (UK) Limited v Office of Fair Trading* (Case C-336/03) [2005]

Useful Web Resources

- http://www.out-law.com
- http://www.dti.gov.uk
- http://www.oft.gov.uk
- http://www.lawcom.gov.uk

2 Privacy

ADRIAN ROBERTS-WALSH

2.1 INTRODUCTION: PRIVACY, ANONYMITY AND IDENTITY

While the chapter is titled privacy, added to this should be anonymity and identification because the three are interrelated. Anonymity represents the freedom from identification and possibly scrutiny or monitoring by others, with identification representing those methods or techniques that are used to undermine an individual's anonymity.

Privacy or the right to privacy represents the ability of an individual to be able to control what others are able to know about them. Where an individual has control there is privacy, where not there is identification and therefore a loss of anonymity.

The concept of privacy and the right to privacy has opponents as well as proponents: there are competing aims and some line has to be drawn between these aims; the question that arises is where exactly does one draw that line between anonymity and privacy as a legitimate aim of a citizen and the competing aim of wanting information: by security or policing authorities, commercial organizations, political parties, etc. Arguments have been made both in favour and against anonymity. Anonymity raises many problems with regard to issues such as libel, intellectual property issues such as the distribution of pirated software, DVDs, CDs, etc., IP spoofing, spamming, electronic hate mail and stalking. It should be noted that what is not legal in one state may be not illegal in another; further while an activity may not be illegal, it may be deemed immoral or unethical. Issues of inter state legality raise a number of issues when questions of transferring data or information arise.

There are arguments in favour of anonymity or privacy. Anonymity allows people to communicate information that may be personally sensitive or commercially sensitive but nevertheless in the public interest to know. Here it may be possible to separate privacy and anonymity in that in some circumstances persons may seek anonymity while in others persons adopt a pseudonym, nevertheless in both there may be a desire for non-traceability. Privacy is also concerned with the issue of confidentiality, which is the entrustment of information to another party in the belief that it will, without permission, go no further. There are numerous examples in everyday life where individuals seek confidentiality with regard to their personal data, for example health records, employment or personal records, banking or credit details.

The issue of privacy and anonymity has been impacted upon by terrorist attacks such as 9/11 and bombings in London on 7 July 2005, which have given new impetus for some states to consider legislating for greater data retention. The material here is aimed to be as accurate as possible at the time of writing in 2007.

It should be borne in mind that efforts to control privacy and anonymity predate these recent terrorist events. The state has a dual role in both promoting and restricting an individual's privacy through legislation. The state also has the role of repository of data and thus often has a self-interest in keeping data private. There is sometimes a perceived dichotomy between keeping information private and making it available. At the same time as governments offer individuals access to state information they also want to have access to individuals' information, for example through controls on encryption technology that enhances privacy and also through data retention laws.

Issues of data privacy and anonymity relate not just to text-based data but also to the use of, for example, mobile phone location technology, biometric identification technology, face-recognition technology, CCTV and digital cash payments systems.

Given the global nature of information technology, issues of privacy, anonymity and identity necessarily involve issues of jurisdiction. This may arise, for example, in matters regarding the traceability of internet originated communications that are encrypted and transmitted by remailers especially via chain remailing.

While this chapter is based on privacy legislation pertaining to the UK, particularly England and Wales, there may be occasions where overseas legislation will have either a direct or indirect impact. The nature and scope of privacy legislation in part is dependant on the socio-economic culture from which it has derived; in the USA for example the prime driving force has been the 'market', whereby commercial interests have been key in promoting or holding back privacy developments, while in Europe it has been far more politically and socially inspired. It is possible to see in the development of privacy legislation historical similarities with the development of legislation in a previous Industrial Age to protect workers and members of the public from pollution, unsafe working practices, etc. In a post-Industrial or Information Age, the issue of protection has again arisen but this time it is to protect the vast amounts of information about individuals – or commercial interests – either in a direct or indirect form.

2.1.1 The development of privacy protection in the UK

Traditionally there has been no right to privacy at English common law. In English law privacy has had to be protected more circuitously, for example by means of actions for defamation or malicious falsehoods. Privacy may also be protected by means of obligations of confidence. There are many examples where a person owes an obligation of confidence: for example employees to their employers, doctors to their patients, consultants to their clients. Obligations of confidence cover many commercial transactions and may be implied even if there is no express or explicit agreement regarding confidentiality. While privacy through defamation may have been approached via tort, breach of confidence has traditionally been within the equitable jurisdiction. A notable case in the nineteenth century referring to privacy proceeded along the lines of breach of trust; in *Prince Albert v Strange*[101] the prince obtained an injunction to prevent the unauthorized exhibition of royal etchings – see also more recent cases such as *Kitechnology BV v Unicor GmbH Plastmaschinen*[102] and *Douglas, Zeta-Jones and Northern & Shell v Hello, Hola and EduardoSanchez Junco.*[103]

Breach of confidence has also been given statutory recognition (see section 171(1) of the Copyright, Designs and Patents Act 1988 and the former section 2 of the 1911 Official Secrets Act – replaced by the narrower section 1 1989 Official Secrets Act). The law of breach of confidence seeks to protect information or data not in the public domain and where appropriate preventing via injunction that information or data being made public.

In an up-to-date case, *HRH The Prince of Wales v Associated Newspapers Ltd*,[104] the Prince of Wales sought to prevent publication by the *Mail on Sunday* of extracts from a Hong Kong travel journal, which had been leaked to the press by his former secretary. The secretary, Ms Sarah Goodall, had signed a confidentiality agreement at the time she had been employed in 1988. She had left royal employment in 2000. The Prince of Wales won the privacy claim against the *Mail on Sunday*. Lawyers for the Prince had argued that he was entitled to the same degree of privacy as an ordinary citizen while the newspaper had argued that publication was in the public interest and an appropriate exercise of their freedom of expression. In the High Court Mr Justice Blackburne in a summary judgment held that the newspaper had breached both Prince Charles' confidence and his copyright awarding the Prince costs and damages. Mr Justice Blackburne stated that: 'There is reason for concluding that the claimant establishes . . . a reasonable expectation of privacy in respect of their contents.'[105] An appeal by Associated Newspapers Limited against the judgment of the Court of Appeal was dismissed. The Prince's victory relates to one journal, with the newspaper in possession of seven other journals that the Prince seeks to be returned.[106]

Contrast may be made with the development of privacy protection in other common law jurisdictions. In the USA for example, privacy protection was given an intellectual foundation in Warren and Brandies' 'The Right to Privacy' (1890). New York put privacy protection on the statute book in 1902; the Supreme Court of Georgia accepted the right to privacy in *Pavesich v New England Life Insurance Co*[107] with most US states subsequently recognizing the right to privacy.

Given the extent to which data or information is stored and processed by technology it is not surprising that legislation has been deemed necessary to control its storage, access, use and distribution.

Attempts to cope with the issue of data privacy are not, however, new; the issues involved were considered in the Younger Report and the Lindop Report, both in the 1970s.

While much of the legislation referred to in this chapter is that of England and Wales, it is increasingly difficult to escape from the fact that much of the legislation in relation to privacy, while badged 'made in the UK', has been sourced or originated in Europe and arguably implemented because of pressure from Europe.

In some respects the UK has lagged behind in the implementation of data privacy legislation when compared with examples such as the Swedish Data Act 1973, the United States Privacy Act 1973 and the Hesse Data Protection Act 1970; the United Kingdom's first major piece of data protection legislation being the 1984 Data Protection Act.

2.1.2 The influence of Europe and wider

Some of the developments in the field of data privacy have the been result of legally binding agreements between states and some from less formal means from which member states may or may not opt out of. Examples of the latter may include the guidelines for data protection outlined by the Organisation for Economic Co-operation and Development (OECD) in 1980 but which have no formal means for adoption; the UK, Ireland, Australia, Canada and Turkey did not at the time adopt the guidelines while the USA did.

The decisions of the Council of Europe are more formal and treaty based. The Council of Europe has responsibility for the European Court of Human Rights and the European Convention for the Protection of Human Rights and Fundamental Freedoms; privacy is a key area of the Convention. The Council of Europe drew up Treaty 108, the Convention for the Protection of Individuals, with regard to the automatic processing of personal data, containing eight principles to govern data processing to protect the respect for privacy while allowing for the flow of information to assist trade.

The eight principles are:

(i)   fair and lawful obtaining and processing of personal data;

(ii)   storage of data only for specified purposes;

(iii)   personal data should not be used in ways that are incompatible with the specified purposes;

(iv)   personal data should be adequate, relevant and not excessive in relation to the purposes for which the data is stored;

(v)   personal data should be accurate and where necessary kept up to date;

(vi)   personal data should be preserved in an identifiable form for no longer than is necessary;

(vii)   adequate security should exist for personal data; and

(viii) personal data should be available for individuals to access with these individuals having rights of rectification and erasure.

Amendments to the Treaty adopted in June 1999 allow for states to apply the Convention to non-automated – for example, manual or paper-based data – and also to the data relating to legal persons in addition to living individuals. Additional protocols were added in November 2001 for states to accede to; these included provisions for the establishment of independent supervisory authorities and that personal data was not to be passed to non-Convention signatories unless adequate protection was in place.

Similar with respect to data legislation passed by the UK, the treaty was signed by the UK and came into force in January 1985. Treaty 108 was subsequently amended to bring it into line with EU Directive 95/46.[108]

While states may seek to avoid adherence to international guidelines and treaties there is a risk particularly for states without a great degree of economic muscle to succumb to trade pressures to adopt such measures sooner or later.

2.1.3 The European Convention on Human Rights and the Human Rights Act (HRA) 1998

Of importance with regard to the issue of privacy are the provisions of the European Convention for the Protection of Human Rights and Fundamental Freedoms (ECHR), specifically Article 8. The Convention was adopted by the Council of Europe on 4 November 1950 with the UK ratifying it in 1951 but without incorporating it into domestic law. This was done by means of the Human Rights Act 1998, which came into force on 20 October 2000, with public bodies and the courts required to apply the rights stated in the Convention.

Article 8

Article 8 refers to the right to respect for private and family life. It states:

> (1) Everyone has the right to respect for his private and family life, his home and correspondence.
>
> (2) There shall be no interference by a public authority with exercise of this right except such as in accordance with the law and is necessary in a democratic society in the interests of national security, public safety or the economic well-being of the country, for the prevention of disorder or crime, for the protection of health or morals, or for the protection of the rights and freedoms of others.

2.1.4 The application of the ECHR

Article 8 has been extended beyond a narrow definition of 'home'. The ECHR has adopted a broad approach to the concept of 'private life' to cover private, business and public.

In *Niemietz v Germany*[109] the Court extended the concept of privacy to include certain workplaces. This case concerned the search of a lawyer's office by a police officer. It was held that Article 8 protected the lawyer's office space, the Court accepting that a person's private life was carried out both at home and sometimes at other places, which included an office. The Court stated:

> respect for private life must also comprise to a certain degree the right to establish and develop relationships with other human beings. It is after all, in the course of their working lives that the majority of people have a significant, if not the greatest opportunity of developing relationships with the outside world.[110]

The right to privacy in correspondence and the right to uncensored and uninterrupted communications was outlined in the case of *Malone v United Kingdom*.[111] Here the Court held that the British Government had violated Article 8 when it intercepted the phone calls of the applicant who was an antiques dealer convicted of receiving stolen goods. The Court held that the British Government had not been acting in accordance with the law as it did not have at the time statutory procedures in place in order to monitor the phone calls of private citizens. The Court stated in paragraph 79:

> In view of the attendant obscurity and uncertainty as to the state of the law in this essential respect, . . . the law of England and Wales does not indicate with reasonable clarity the scope and manner of exercise of the relevant discretion conferred on the public authorities. To that extent, the minimum degree of legal protection to which citizens are entitled under the rule of law in a democratic society is lacking.

This led to subsequent legislation to overcome this defect. Interesting is the emphasis that is applied on Article 8(2)'s concept of 'in accordance with the law', not only that there must be domestic legislation to cover a possible infringement but that legislation must be consistent with the concept of the 'rule of law', i.e. there should be some objective non-arbitrary basis for the law to exist in the first place, thus just simply to allow for the convenience of an authority in question is insufficient justification.

An interesting case with regard to the keeping of personal records and databases is to be found in *Rotaru v Romania*.[112] The applicant, Rotaru, was a Romanian citizen. In 1948 the applicant had been imprisoned for a year for criticizing the communist regime established in 1946. In 1992 the applicant brought an action seeking the rights granted to those who had been persecuted under the former regime under Decree 118 of 1990. One of the defendants in the proceedings, the Interior Ministry, submitted to the Barlad Court of First Instance a letter sent to it by the Romanian Intelligence Service (RIS) on 19 December 1990 containing information regarding the applicant's political activities during the period 1946–1948. It also contained information that the applicant had been a member of an extreme right wing movement in 1937.

The applicant claimed that some of the information contained in the letter of 19 December 1990 was inaccurate and defamatory, particularly the allegation made that he had in the 1930s been a member of the right wing 'legionnaire' movement. The applicant brought proceedings against the RIS, seeking compensation and the amendment or destruction of the file that he claimed contained false information. The applicant's claim was rejected by the Romanian courts claiming that it did not have the power to order the amendment or destruction of the information that had been contained in the 1990 letter. The information had not been obtained by the RIS but by its predecessor the 'Securitate', the RIS was simply the depositary for such information.

The applicant lodged a complaint with the European Commission on Human Rights in 1995.

Subsequently in 1997 the RIS accepted that the information referring to membership of the 'legionnaire' movement had been in error and had in fact referred to another person with the same name. The applicant sought a review of the Romanian Court of Appeal's judgment of 1994 and claimed damages. The Romanian Court of Appeal quashed the earlier judgment and declared the information about membership of the legionnaire movement to be null and void.

Referring back to the complaint lodged with the ECHR, the applicant claimed that the RIS held and could make use of information relating to his private life some of which he claimed was inaccurate and defamatory. The applicant claimed that as such there was a violation of Article 8.

The Court considered that keeping information in secret registers fell within the scope of Article 8(1). The Court stated that:

> public information can fall within the scope of private life where it is systematically collected and stored in files held by the authorities. That is all the truer where such information concerns a person's distant past.

The Court further noted that:

> the RIS's letter of 19 December 1990 contained various pieces of information about the applicant's life, in particular his studies, his political attitudes and his criminal record, some of which had been gathered fifty years earlier. In the Court's opinion, such information, when systematically collected and stored in a file held by agents of the State, falls within the scope of 'private life' for the purposes of Article 8(1) of the Convention. That is all the more so in the instant case as some of the information has been declared false and is likely to injure the applicant's reputation.

The Court considered that:

> the storing by a public authority of information relating to an individual's private life and the use of it and the refusal to allow an opportunity for it to be refuted amount to interference with the right to respect for private life secured in Article 8(1) of the Convention.

The Court considered that there was interference with the right to respect to private life and insufficient justification, safeguards or supervision and thus a violation of Article 8.

The ECHR has considered that the simple storing of personal information, whether or not there is to be any further processing of the information, to be an interference with the right to privacy stated in Article 8. In *Amman v Switzerland*,[113] the case related to the interception of phone calls and maintaining a card record of an individual. The Court held that there had been a violation of Art 8 by intercepting the phone calls; creating and storing the information was also a violation of Art 8. The Court considered telephone calls received on private or business premises to come under the notion of 'private life' and 'correspondence' under Art 8(1). The interception was an 'interference' by a public authority under Art 8(2). The Court stated:

> ...the storing by a public authority of data relating to the private life of an individual amounts to an interference within the meaning of Article 8. The subsequent use of the stored information has no bearing on that finding.[114]

It is possible for consent to be given such that no breach of Article 8 will occur although it is open to debate to what extent consent has been freely given and not given through direct or indirect pressure.

Bearing in mind that breaches may be justifiable under Art 8(2), note may be taken of cases involving the collection of personal information. In *McVeigh, O'Neill and Evans v UK*[115] the taking of fingerprints without consent was a justifiable breach. The applicants had been held under prevention of terrorism legislation; they were searched, questioned, photographed and fingerprinted. No charges were made. The fingerprints and photographs were retained. It was held that the taking of fingerprints was not a breach of Art 8.[116] The Court stated: 'Whilst they may have involved interference with the rights guaranteed by Art 8(1), they were justified under 8(2).'[117] The denial for the applicants to speak with their wives was a breach of Article 8.

Covert listening and phone tapping have been found to be breaches of Article 8. Brief mention is made here of *Malone v United Kingdom*[118], which resulted in legislation, the Interception of Communications Act 1985, to legalize the interception of telephone calls on public lines; it was also held that keeping a register of numbers called from a phone except for billing purposes was a breach of Article 8. Comparison should be made with the new EU data retention directive.

In *Halford v United Kingdom*[119], which concerned calls over private lines, Article 8 was again breached and has had to be remedied by legislation, the Regulation of Investigatory Powers Act (RIPA) 2000. Drilling holes in walls to listen from an adjoining property was found to be a breach in *Govell v United Kingdom.*[120] The interception of private mail or telephone calls has been found to be a breach of Art 8 in terms of private life and correspondence. In *Hewitt and Harman v United Kingdom*[121] the applicants were prominent members of the National Council for Civil Liberties, which MI5 tended to consider 'subversive'. The applicants Patricia Hewitt and Harriet Harman, now prominent New Labour politicians, complained that secret surveillance of their private lives by MI5 violated Article 8 and other articles. It was held that storing information in a secret police register interfered with the right to respect for private life under Article 8(1). The interception of private mail or telephone calls was a breach of Article 8 in terms of private life and correspondence.[122]

Contrast may be made with Canada, which introduced a legal framework with regard to the interception of private communications via the 1973 Protection of Privacy Act.

Compulsory blood testing[123] and random drug testing using a urine test[124] have been found to breach Article 8.

Central to the ECHR as we have seen is the rule of law and legitimacy, restrictions of an individual's freedom are permitted where there are legitimate reasons for the restrictions. Nevertheless where restrictions are imposed those must be in proportion to the legitimate aim that is being sought.

In *Klass v Germany,*[125] the Court stated that:

> One of the fundamental principles of a democratic society is the rule of law, which is expressly referred to in the Preamble to the Convention...The rule of law implies, inter alia, that an interference by the executive authorities with an individual's right should be subject to an effective control.[126]

It should be noted that there are differences between Article 8 and Treaty 108; while Treaty 108 has been amended so as to allow for the privacy rules to be extended to non-legal persons, Article 8 remains primarily geared toward the protection of individual privacy rights. Companies and government department and bodies do not as far as Article 8 is concerned have a family life. This may be seen in the case of *Derbyshire County Council v The Times Newspapers*[127] where the House of Lords held that a local authority was unable to sue with regard to its reputation.

Article 8 is in two parts: while part 1 establishes the right to privacy, it should have been noted that the rights are not absolute; they are qualified and as such part 2 provides the basis upon which breaches of the right to privacy may be justified. Thus while someone may bring and succeed in claiming that their rights under Article 8(1) have been breached, the breach may be found to be justified. The previously mentioned case of *Peters v Netherlands*[128] while breaching Article 8(1) was held to be justified under Article 8(2). Similarly in *Chare nee Julien v France*[129] the Court held that there was justification in continuing to record details of an individual's previous psychiatric treatment.

Linked with the right to privacy under Article 8(1) and justification of breaches under Article 8(2) are issues relating to disclosure of information and rights of access; these must be considered alongside access rights granted under the Data Protection Act (DPA) 1998 and the Freedom of Information Act 2000 with regard to public bodies.

Again it is worth considering some relevant European Court of Justice cases. In *Leander v Sweden*,[130] the applicant had been refused permanent employment at the Naval Museum because of certain information that made him a security risk. The dossier maintained by the Swedish National Police Board Security Service was held by the Court to be a breach of Article 8(1). It was held that:

> both the storing and release of such information, which were coupled with a refusal to allow Mr Leander an opportunity to refute it, amounted to an interference with his right to respect for private life as guaranteed by Article 8(1).[131]

However, the Court further held that the applicant did not have an entitlement to receive the information.

In contrast with this is the decision in *Gaskin v United Kingdom*.[132] The applicant had been in care from 1959 to 1977, mainly with foster parents. The applicant considered that he was ill-treated in care and had tried to obtain his records. Some files were released. He claimed that the failure to release all files was a breach of Article 8 and his right to receive information under Article 10. It was held that Article 8 was breached. It stated, citing Leander: 'the right to freedom to receive information basically prohibits a government from restricting a person from receiving information that others wish or may be willing to impart to him',[133] nevertheless there was no obligation on the state under Article 10 to impart the information.

Protection of family life may be invoked to find out information about environmental risks. In *Guerra and Others v Italy*,[134] 40 applicants claimed that the state had failed to provide information about risks related to a chemical factory, under Article 10, claiming also that the right to respect to family life under Article 8 had been infringed because of the failure to provide the information. Article 10 was held not applicable but Article 8 was applicable and infringed. The court held: 'The direct effect of toxic emissions on the applicants' respect for their private life and family life means that Article 8 is applicable.'[135] Further it held that the 'State may have "positive obligations" to fulfil Article 8.'[136]

In *McGinley and Egan v United Kingdom*,[137] the applicants had been stationed near to nuclear tests on Christmas Island. They claimed that documents linking their health problems to radiation had been withheld and affected a pensions' appeal and were a breach of Article 8. The Court held that that while no breach occurred, governments engaging in hazardous activities, under Article 8 had a requirement to 'provide an effective and accessible procedure...which enables...persons to seek all relevant and appropriate information'.[138]

There may be instances where individuals attempt to prevent the disclosure of information. In *MS v Sweden*[139] the disclosure of medical records from a clinic to the Swedish Social Insurance Office, i.e. from one point to another, was held to be a breach of Article 8(1), nevertheless it was considered justified and therefore there was no breach of Article 8(2).

In *TV v Finland*[140] the disclosure of a prisoner's HIV status was held by the Court to be valid as it was necessary for the protection of prison staff. In *Z v Finland*[141] the issue involved the seizure and disclosure of a Swedish woman's (Z's) medical records and identity in court proceedings and its judgment. She was married to X who had been tried for sexual offences/attempted manslaughter. It was held that the seizure did not breach Article 8; but release to the public would, as would disclosure by the court of the applicant's identity and medical condition. It held that:

> the protection of personal data, not least medical data, is of fundamental importance to a persons enjoyment of his or her right to respect for family and private life as guaranteed by Article 8.[142]

It is also necessary to bear in mind that Article 8 does not exist in isolation. While there may be a claim to privacy there may well be an equally valid claim to have information made available via Article 10, which like Article 8 is the qualified right to freedom of expression.

There is some overlap between the provisions of the ECHR and Directive 95/46 – which has had an influence on the 1998 DPA, to be looked at later – whereby 'Member States shall protect the fundamental rights and freedoms of natural persons, and in particular their right to privacy with respect to the processing of personal data' (Article 1). The rights established by Article 8 are also somewhat ameliorated by section 12 of the Human Rights Act 1998.

Many of the cases mentioned have been related to states other than the United Kingdom. The reader may be wondering why there is the need to include overseas cases brought before the European Court of Human Rights in Strasbourg.

Not only does the HRA 1998 section 3(1) require that so far as is possible legislation both primary and secondary is 'read and given effect in a

way which is compatible with the Convention rights' but also section 2(1) requires that Courts or Tribunals determining questions that have arisen in connection with a Convention right 'must take into account' judgments, decisions or rulings of the European Court of Human Rights or the opinions of the Human Rights Commission.

It has been previously been stated that the HRA 1998 came into force on 20 October 2000; it is worth considering some cases that have been brought since 2000 and the effect of the HRA.

In *R v City of Wakefield Metropolitan Council & another ex parte Robertson*[143] issues relating to a breach of Article 8 were linked with breaches of the DPA and Article 3 of the Protocol 1 of the HRA. The case concerned the sale of names and addresses from an electoral register. To be able to vote requires entry on an electoral register. Electoral registration officers were at the time obliged to sell copies of this register if someone wanted to buy a copy, and many were bought for marketing purposes. Robertson objected to the sale of his details on the roll but the electoral registration officer refused to omit his name on the grounds that there was a statutory obligation to include names etc. on the lists. The claimant succeeded under each of the grounds claimed. The court held that the sale of names and addresses from electoral registers was capable of being protected by Article 8 and that despite legislation to provide an opt-out, which had not been effectively introduced by the Representation of the People Act 2000 and the subsequent Representation of the People (England and Wales) Regulations 2001, there was insufficient opt-out in place to allow justification under Article 8(2). There was a breach of the DPA and local authorities were bound by the Act.

In *Campbell v Mirror Group Newspapers*,[144] Naomi Campbell claimed that the newspaper had breached the DPA 1998 and sought compensation. The High Court found for Ms Campbell, the Court of Appeal found in favour of the newspaper and finally the House of Lords found again for Ms Campbell though not on the grounds of a breach of the DPA but for a breach of Article 8.

2.1.5 The Computer Misuse Act 1990

This Act while not directly aimed at securing privacy nevertheless has a bearing on the privacy of data through the prevention of unauthorized access and modification of data, i.e. through the attempt to prevent and curtail 'hacking'. The Act creates three offences: section 1, unauthorized access to a computer program or data, those found guilty are liable to a maximum sentence of six months imprisonment; section 2 unauthorized access with a further criminal intent, those found guilty are liable to a maximum sentence of five years imprisonment; and, section 3 unauthorized modification of computer material, for example programs or data, those found guilty are liable to a maximum sentence of five years imprisonment.

2.2 DATA PROTECTION LEGISLATION

2.2.1 Introduction

The UK's first Data Protection Act came became law on 12 July 1984. It has subsequently been updated by the Data Protection Act 1998, which came into force on 1 March 2000, although there are elements that are to be phased in up to 24 October 2007. To be aware of the most up to date requirements with regard to data protection, it would be advisable to visit the official website of the Information Commissioner (formerly the Data Protection Registrar). While the 1998 DPA builds on elements of the first 1984 DPA, it is important to note that the basis or foundation for the Act is Directive 95/46.

In simple terms, the 1998 DPA concerns the holding of personal data relating to living identifiable individuals and aims to prevent the misuse of personal data. The revised act had been necessary to bring the UK in line with other European states who had commonly agreed sets of data protection rules; based on the Council of Europe's Data Protection Convention, Treaty 108, which the UK had in part adopted in the 1984 Act, the provisions of Directive 95/46 included new rules applying restrictions on passing data to non-participating states.

2.2.2 Key Definitions in the 1998 Act

The 1998 Act introduced a number of key concepts or definitions.

(i) 'Data'

It is wise to be aware of what the Act defines as 'data'. Section 1 states that it is information that:

    (a) is being processed by means of equipment operating automatically in response to instructions given for that purpose;

    (b) is recorded with the intention that it should be processed by means of such equipment;

    (c) is recorded as part of a relevant filing system or with the intention that it should form part of a relevant filing system; or

    (d) does not fall within paragraph (a), (b) or (c) but forms part of an accessible record defined by section 68.

Section 68 refers to health records, educational records and other accessible public records.

Directive 95/46, while mentioning in Article 2 the processing of personal data, does not give a definition as such.

(ii) 'Processing'

Section 1 of the DPA defines processing to mean:

> obtaining, recording or holding the information or data or carrying out any operation or set of operations on the information or data, including:

(a) organization, adaptation or alteration of the information or data,

(b) retrieval, consultation or use of the information or data,

(c) disclosure of the information or data by transmission, dissemination or otherwise making available, or

(d) alignment, combination, blocking, erasure or destruction of the information or data.

(iii) 'Relevant filing system'

The 1984 Act applied to automated filing systems, i.e. kept on some form of computerized equipment and then accessed. The new Act goes further, to include not only data kept within an IT system, so that it could now cover sales, customer or personnel files kept manually. 'Relevant filing system' is defined in Part I of the 1998 Act to mean:

any set of information relating to individuals to the extent that although the information is not processed by means of equipment operating automatically in response to instructions given for that purpose, the set is structured, either by reference to individuals or by reference to criteria relating to individuals, in such a way that specific information relating to a particular individual is readily accessible.

This should be compared to the definition contained in Article 2 of Directive 95/46 whereby a

'personal data filing system' ('filing system') shall mean any structured set of personal data which are accessible according to specific criteria, whether centralised, decentralised or dispersed on a functional basis.

The key term in both definitions would seem to be 'structured'; a list of names and addresses in a word-processed document may not appear to be as structured as a database perhaps but can it not be accessed by a using a command like 'find' to search on the basis of address or name. Similarly the Act would now apply to data kept on any paper-based system, for example a filing card system that can be accessed by specific criteria such as alphabetically, by date of birth, payroll number etc.

(iv) 'Personal data' and 'data subjects'

Those about whom data is kept are known as 'data subjects', these have the right, with exceptions, to know who holds data about them, what data is being held, that the data being held is held for an appropriate or specified purpose and is being used properly.

While the 1998 DPA defines a 'data subject' as 'an individual who is the subject of personal data', Directive 95/46 does not directly define what a data subject is but refers to it in the definition of 'personal data' in Article 2, which states that:

> Personal data shall mean any information relating to an identified or identifiable natural person (data subject); an identifiable person is one who can be identified, directly or indirectly, in particular by reference to an identification number or to one or more factors specific to his physical, physiological, mental, economic, cultural or social identity.

The definition in the 1998 DPA is a little more precise in some ways and broader in others; section 1(1) states:

> Personal data means data which relate to a living individual who can be identified
>
> (a) from those data; or
>
> (b) from those data and other information which is in the possession of or is likely to come into the possession of the data controller, and includes any expression or opinion about the individual and any indication of the intentions of the data controller or any other person in respect of the individual.

In the 1998 Act we can see that personal data thus refers to data that can be used, possibly alongside other data held by the data controller to identify a living individual. Examples of personal data would therefore include a person's name or a name and address. It would be debatable whether an address or telephone number by itself would be classified as personal data. Email addresses that clearly identify the user, for example Gordon.Brown@gov.uk would classify as personal data; leader@conservative.co.uk may well not, although put with other information it may well be. Data held about the dead is not personal data, therefore data held about Robin Cook, Mo Mowlam and Ronnie Barker would not be covered. It should also be noted that the section refers to 'opinion' and therefore does not just restrict itself to 'quantitative' data but also to arguably less objective qualitative data. Thus while incidental information in a text may not be sufficient to classify data as personal, where the data subject is the focus, for example, in a job application reference that would suffice; see for example *Durant v Financial Services Authority*.[145]

The DPA definition is narrower than the Directive in the sense that there is an element to which the information is possessed or potentially possessed by the data controller. Were a conflict to arise between the two, given that courts are required to give effect to the Directive, the Directive definition would presumably take precedence over the DPA.

Data held about companies is not personal as these are not classed as individuals for data purposes, information about individual company employees or directors, however, would be classified as personal; in the case of sole traders or partnerships where there is not a legal identity separate from the individual then data or information is likely to relate to the individual and therefore come under the DPA.

Personal data is not restricted to data in text format; an image of person in a traditional photograph or video or its digital equivalent, for example on a shopping centre CCTV, could therefore come under the classification of personal data. Other items possibly coming within the scope of the DPA could include: voice patterns that can be digitized such that a voice can be unique to an individual or DNA information. Less straightforward might be internet usage: an email address arguably can be used to identify an individual or can it? What about an IP address? It may identify the source computer but not necessarily the individual using it especially if there is a general logon name, for example ITLawbooksales@bcsmarketing.co.uk (not a real address). This is an issue of interest because with the use of cookies and spyware, internet users can be targeted for marketing purposes based on their user profiles; an individual email address may result in a profile to target that individual. In the case of multiple users and profiling based on IP address or terminal usage, identity may be less clear-cut. This also raises issues of preventing spam, which is discussed later.

(v) 'Data controller' and 'data processors'

The 1984 Act refers to 'data users'; the 1998 Act is more specific in defining data controllers and data processors. Section (1) defines a 'data controller' as 'a person who (either alone or jointly or in common with other persons) determines the purposes for which and the manner in which any personal data are, or are to be, processed'. The same section defines a 'data processor' as 'any person (other than an employee of the data controller) who processes the data on behalf of the data controller'.

Those who have a responsibility for keeping data, for example database administrators, have obligations to ensure that the data is kept secure and that there is no disclosure to unauthorized persons.

The DPA is enforced by the Information Commissioner who is appointed by the Queen and reports to Parliament; the Information Commissioner's Office is not a government department.

That is the basic overview, let's now look at it in a bit more detail.

2.2.3 The eight data protection principles

These are set out in Part I of Schedule 1. In detail these are that:

(1) Personal data shall be processed fairly and lawfully and shall not be processed unless:

(a) one of the conditions contained in Schedule 2 is met; and

(b) in the case of sensitive personal data, at least one of the conditions contained in Schedule 3 is met.

(2) Personal data must be obtained for only one or more specified and lawful purpose(s), and shall not be further processed in any manner incompatible with that purpose or purposes.

(3) Personal data must be adequate, relevant and not excessive in relation to the purpose or purposes for which they are processed.

(4) Personal data must be accurate and, where necessary, kept up to date.

(5) Personal data that is processed for any purpose or purposes must not be kept for longer than necessary for that purpose or those purposes.

(6) Personal data must be processed in accordance with the rights of data subjects under the Act.

(7) Appropriate technical and organizational measures shall be taken against unauthorized or unlawful processing of personal data and against accidental loss or destruction of, or damage to personal data.

(8) Personal data must not to be transferred to a country or territory outside the European Economic Area, unless that country or territory ensures that there is an adequate level of protection for the rights and freedoms of data subjects in relation to the processing of personal data.

While being similar to the requirements of the 1984 Act and Treaty 108 of 1981, they go a little deeper. This is most noticeable in Principle 1, which further requires that one of the conditions of Schedule 2 is met and if sensitive information is involved one of the conditions of Schedule 3 is met.

Schedule 2 concerns the conditions relevant for processing data under Principle 1 and these are:

(i) That the data subject has provided their consent to the processing.

(ii) That the data processing is necessary:

(a) for the performance of a contract to which the data subject is a party, or

(b) for the taking of steps at the request of the data subject with a view to entering into a contract.

(iii) The data processing is necessary in order to comply with any legal obligations to which the data controller is subject, other than an obligation imposed by contract.

(iv) The processing is necessary in order to protect the vital interests of the data subject.

(v) The data processing is necessary for:

(a) the administration of justice,

(b) the exercise of any function conferred by or under any enactment,

       (c) the exercise of any functions of the Crown, a minister of the Crown or government department, or

       (d) the exercise of any other function of a public nature exercised in the public interest by any person.

  (vi) The processing is necessary for the purposes of legitimate interests pursued by the data controller or by the third party or parties to whom the data are disclosed, except where the processing is unwarranted in any particular case by reason of prejudice to the rights and freedoms or legitimate interests of the data subject. The Secretary of State is empowered to state whether this condition is or is not being satisfied.

On the face of it the sixth condition would seem wide enough to allow most data processing.

Principle 1 also referred to the processing of 'sensitive personal data'. Schedule 3 covers the conditions relevant for the processing of sensitive personal data. Such data is defined in Section 2 of the Act and consists of information as to:

(i)   the racial or ethnic origin of the data subject;

(ii)   the political opinion(s) of the data subject;

(iii)   the religious beliefs or other beliefs of a similar nature of the data subject;

(iv)   whether the data subject is a member of a trade union (within the meaning of the Trade Union and Labour Relations (Consolidation) Act 1992).

(v)   the physical or mental health or condition of the data subject;

(vi)   the data subject's sexual lifestyle;

(vii)   the commission or alleged commission of any offence by the data subject; and

(viii) any proceedings for any offence committed or alleged to have been committed by the data subject, the disposal of such proceedings or the sentence of the court in such proceedings.

In addition to at least one of the conditions for processing contained in Schedule 2 being satisfied, one of the following Schedule 3 conditions must be satisfied for the processing of sensitive personal data to be legal.

The Schedule 3 conditions include:

(1)   the explicit consent by the data subject to processing the personal sensitive data;

(2)   the processing is necessary to exercise or perform any right or obligation conferred or imposed by law upon the data controller in connection with employment;

(3)   the processing is necessary:

     (a) to protect the vital interests of the data subject or to protect the interest of another person where

(i) consent cannot be given by or on behalf of the data subject, or

(ii) the data controller cannot reasonably be expected to obtain the consent of the data subject.

(b) to protect the vital interests of another person, in a case where consent by or on behalf of the data subject has been unreasonably withheld.

(4) the data processing is carried out in the course of its legitimate activities by a body or association, which exists for trade union, philosophical, political or religious purposes, and is not established or conducted for profit; where the processing is carried out with safeguards for the rights and freedoms of the data subjects; the processing relates only to individuals who are members of such bodies or have regular contact with it connected to its purposes and there is no disclosure to third parties without permission;

(5) the information contained in the personal data has been made public through deliberate steps by the data subject;

(6) the processing is necessary for the purpose of or in connection with any legal proceedings or prospective proceedings; is necessary for the purpose of obtaining legal advice; or is necessary for the purpose of establishing, exercising or defending legal rights;

(7) the processing is necessary for the administration of justice or for a function of the Crown, a minister of the Crown or a government department;

(8) the processing is necessary for medical purposes and to be carried out by a health professional; and

(9) if the data processed is of a racial or ethnic nature, it must be necessary for the purpose of identifying or reviewing the existence or absence of equality of opportunity or treatment ensuring that these groups are treated fairly.

2.2.4 Exemptions from the Act

Exemptions to the Act are contained in Part IV. Exemptions are provided for the purposes of protecting national security,[146] the prevention and detection of crime,[147] the apprehension or prosecution of offenders[148] and for purposes of assessment and collection of taxes.[149] There are also exemption provisions where the information concerns health, education and social work.[150] Further exemptions relate to journalism, literature and art together with research and statistical purposes and for regulatory activity.[151] Domestic personal data is exempt.[152] Data is exempt where there is a requirement for disclosure by a data controller pursuant to an enactment or where it is required by law or in connection with legal proceedings.[153] The Secretary of State can further exempt data by order.[154]

2.2.5 Procedures to legally process data: notification

Section 17(1) of the 1998 DPA requires that: 'personal data must not be processed unless an entry in respect of the data controller is included in the register maintained by the Commissioner'. This process is called 'notification'. However, there is a difference between the 1984 requirements and that of the 1998 Act: under 1984, registration could be refused if the Registrar – the forerunner to the Information Commissioner – considered that an application did not meet with the Principles set out in the Act; under the 1998 Act no properly made application can be refused.

Section 21(1) states that: 'If section 17(1) is contravened, the data controller is guilty of an offence.' Notification currently costs £35 and is required annually (section 19(4)) – and if the nature for which the data is kept changes, section 20. A data controller can notify via the Information Commissioner's website, by email, by post or by phone. The Information Commissioner's website provides advice and proforma templates for common types of organization required to notify. Note that Part III on notification refers to data controllers not data processors.

There is a requirement under section 16(1) to provide certain information when notifying, which includes:

(a) the name and address of the data controller;

(b) the name and address of the data controller's nominated representative, if any;

(c) a description of the personal data being or to be processed by or on behalf of the data controller and also the category or categories of data to which they relate;

(d) some description of the purpose(s) of the data processing;

(e) a description of the intended recipient(s) of the data;

(f) names of countries outside the EEA to which the data controller directly or indirectly transfers, or intends to transfer or may wish directly or indirectly to transfer the data; and

(g) if appropriate a statement as to which data is exempt from notification.

Where notification is being undertaken by a business it is necessary that the correct company address is used;[155] this is either its registered office or for a non-registered company its principal place of business in the UK. Where a company consists of several smaller separately registered companies each of these will have to be notified to the Information Commissioner. In addition where different sub-companies use differing permutations of data for varying purposes these will also have to be notified in order that intra-company – within the overall company – transfers are compliant with the DPA.

In line with Principle 7 of the DPA, notification requires data controllers to indicate what methods have been put in place to safeguard the security of data from unauthorized or unlawful processing and from accidental damage, destruction or loss.

There are exemptions from the need to register with the Information Commissioner, the consequence for data subjects being that they then no longer have the right to scrutinize the data held or to have the data amended or to claim compensation where incorrectly held data causes loss or distress.

Exemptions

Exemptions from notification include:

(i)   data held in connection with personal, family or household affairs or for recreational use, for example non-profit making clubs;

(ii) data being used for preparing the text of documents;

(iii) data required for use in payroll, pensions and accounts purposes such as purchases and sales;

(iv) data required to be held in the interest of national security;

(v)   data held for mailing/distribution purposes where the data subject has given consent; and

(vi) under section 17(4) 'any processing whose sole purpose is the maintenance of a public register'.

While there may be an exemption from a requirement to notify, this does not mean that there is an exemption from any of the other provisions of the DPA.

Penalties under the DPA for non-notification

There are penalties for not notifying. Failure to undertake notification may result in a fine currently of up to £5000 in a magistrates' court or an unlimited fine in the High Court. Under section 21(3) it is a defence when charged with an offence to show that due diligence to comply has been exercised.

2.2.6 The rights of data subjects

The rights of data subjects are contained in Part II. Under sections 7–9 data subjects have the right of subject access; this means that a person has a right to obtain information held about him from a data controller. The request for information must be made in writing, [156] which includes email, and must have included the required fee. [157] Under section 7(1)(a) an individual is entitled to be informed by a data controller whether personal data about the data subject is being processed. Where such data is being processed under section 7(1)(b) the data controller is required to give a description of the personal data, the purpose for which it is being processed and the recipients or classes of recipients to whom the personal data is or may be disclosed. Section 7(1)(c) entitles the data subject to have communicated in an intelligible form the personal data of which that individual is the data subject and any information available to the data controller as to the source of the data.

The data controller is entitled to charge a fee for processing the data subject's request. This is currently £10. The data controller has to reply to a data subject access request within a specific time period; this is within 40 days of the request or on receipt of suitable identification required to locate the requested information and/or the fee, whichever is later.

Dealing with inaccurate data

Under section 14, a data subject may make an application to a court and if that court is satisfied that the personal data of which the applicant is subject is inaccurate, that he would be entitled to compensation under section 13 and that if there is a substantial risk of further contravention, the court may order the data controller to rectify, block, erase or destroy such personal data. The court may further order under section 14(3) that the data controller inform third parties to whom the data has been disclosed of the rectification, blocking, erasure or destruction where reasonably practicable.

Compensation to data subjects

Where a data controller has contravened the requirements of the DPA such that a data subject has suffered damage or distress, under section 13 he is entitled to compensation from the data controller. A data controller has a defence if he can prove that he took all reasonable steps to comply with requirements.

Data protection and records obtained under a data subject's right of access: enforced subject access

There are times when a data subject seeks for his own interest to obtain data held regarding himself. There are also times where data subjects may be expected to reveal data held about themselves, which may be referred to as enforced subject access. Under section 56(1) of the DPA, a person must not require another person or a third party, in connection with recruitment, continued employment or the provision of services, to supply or produce 'relevant records'. Contravention is an offence under section 56(5). Relevant records are defined in the table in section 56(6); these include convictions, cautions, certain details under children and young persons legislation, details under prison legislation and social security legislation.

The prohibition on requiring the production of relevant records does not apply under section 56(3) where 'the requirement was required or authorized by or under any enactment, by any rule of law or by the order of a court' or 'the imposition of the requirement was justified as being in the public interest'. Under section 56(4) the detection and prevention of crime is insufficient to come under the category of public interest. The Police Act 1997 introduced the Criminal Records Bureau (CRB) to allow employers/potential employers to seek knowledge of a person's criminal records.

2.2.7 The Information Commissioner and the Tribunal

The 1984 Act established the Data Protection Registrar, this person was renamed the Data Protection Commissioner; he is appointed by the Queen, but neither he or his officials are Crown servants or agents. He is now known as the Information Commissioner. Under the DPA the Commissioner is tasked with:

(i)   promoting good practice by data controllers;

(ii) ensuring compliance and observance of the Act by data controllers;

(iii) the development and publication of Codes of Practice;

(iv) the maintenance of a register of data controllers, required under the DPA to notify the Commissioner that they are involved in the processing of personal data; and

(v) the enforcement of data protection legislation.

Enforcement of DPA legislation by the Information Commissioner

The Information Commissioner has a number of methods to ensure compliance.

(i)   Assessment: A data subject who thinks he is affected by the processing of personal data can request that the Information Commissioner assesses whether the DPA principles are being complied with by the data controller concerned. The Commissioner is required to notify the data subject of the assessment and any action taken or to be taken.

(ii) Information Notices: requested of the data controller within a specific period of time. Failure to comply with such a request is an offence.

(iii) Warrants: These are available, under Schedule 9, to enter and search premises where the Commissioner considers that DPA legislation has been breached or is being breached. The Commissioner does not issue the warrant, it is issued by a Circuit Court judge. Premises are defined in Schedule section 13 to include 'any vessel, vehicle, aircraft or hovercraft'.

(iv) Enforcement Notices: Where the Commissioner considers that a breach in the DPA has occurred, an enforcement notice can be issued requiring a certain course of action to be taken or refrained from. Failure to comply with a notice is an offence.

The 1998 Act also establishes a Data Protection Tribunal with a legally qualified chair and deputy and other members who may be non-legally qualified. Where a notice is issued by the Commissioner, the person subject to the notice can appeal to the Information Tribunal with a further avenue of appeal on points of law against a decision of the Tribunal being to the High Court.

2.2.8 Manual records

The Data Protection Act 1998 incorporates manual records within its coverage. However, there were two transitional relief periods allowed for manual records pre-dating 1998, when the Act came into force in 2000. The expiration date for this second transitional period is midnight 23 October 2007:

effective from 24 October 2007 the DPA 1998 applies to all personal data and information.

2.2.9 Data protection and websites

As has been previously stated the 1998 DPA has its derivations in Directive 95/46. Cases with reference to this directive come before the European Court of Justice (ECJ), the decisions of which the UK and other states of the EU have to take notice, thus reinforcing a point made earlier that while being primarily concerned with UK legislation it is no longer possible to view such legislation in isolation especially when initiated from Europe. The ECJ has as one of its roles to ensure that EU law is applied uniformly and with consistency across the EU. The ECJ has effectively provided a corpus of law that has fleshed out the provisions of the various treaty articles, directives and regulations. It has also adapted where necessary the customs and practices of the member states' legal systems where appropriate to its ends; one such practice is the development of using a body of case law to aid future decisions, widely used in common law systems, less so in civil law systems.

At the time of writing possibly the most up-to-date case concerning data protection and websites is *Bodil Lindqvist v Aklagarkammaren i Jonkoping*.[158] Mrs Lindqvist had posted information on a website for her church that contained personal information regarding some of the congregation, for example first names, full names, telephone numbers, including information that one of the congregation had had a foot injury and was working part-time on medical grounds. Mrs Lindqvist had not obtained permission from any of those whose details she posted on the website. She later removed the details.

Mrs Lindqvist was subsequently taken to court for breaches of Sweden's data protection legislation, which was based on Directive 95/46. She was fined for processing personal data by automatic means without notifying the supervisory authority in writing, transferring data without authority to third countries and processing sensitive (medical) personal data. She appealed to the Swedish Court of Appeal, which referred to the ECJ for guidance with regard to: the scope of Directive 95/46; the definition of the term 'sensitive data'; the transfer of personal data to countries outside the EEA; the ability of member states to apply stricter rules than the Directive; and the principles of the Directive versus the principles of freedom of expression.

Of particular interest is the ECJ's decision that data protection legislation does apply to non-profit making organizations including churches, especially when publishing personal information via a website on the internet. Such an activity could not be classified as being exclusively personal or domestic and therefore was not exempt. Identifying individuals by, for example name or telephone number on an internet page, was processing personal data wholly or partly by automatic means. With regard to the issue of 'sensitive data', medical data is sensitive data and therefore requires more care and diligence when being processed. The ECJ held that special rules

applied to transfer data outside the EEA, however, this was not directly applicable here as the website was hosted within the EEA and required a conscious
access attempt by those seeking the information rather than simply being a
blanket transmission of the data.

2.2.10 The DPA and electronic voting

Governments in the UK and elsewhere have been interested in finding ways
of extending voter participation in various elections and possibly reducing
the costs of traditional voting. One such way is the use of electronic voting systems through a variety of media such as telephones, text messaging,
the internet, interactive television, ATM machines and dedicated e-voting
machines in, for example banks, supermarkets, airports or petrol stations. A
number of issues arise when considering an effective and efficient election
system, some of which include personation, secrecy, multiple voting and
corruption of voters and officials. These questions affect electronic systems
as well, but we might want to add issues that may come under the scope of
the Computer Misuse Act such as hacking and tampering with the election
system.

The obligation to ensure voter secrecy and privacy is contained in both
the European Convention on Human Rights and the Representation of the
People Act 1983. Secrecy and privacy involve issues such as undue influence
and intimidation or fear of reprisal where voting is contrary to the wishes of
another. In 2002 the Communications –Electronics Security Group report to
the Office of the e-Envoy considered that an electronic voting system required
the following safeguards: voter anonymity and data confidentiality, i.e. that
votes are secret. Here there is some linkage with the DPA. Under section
55 of the DPA regarding the unlawful obtaining of personal data, a person
must not knowingly or recklessly without the consent of the data controller
obtain or disclose personal data or information contained in personal data.
In addition they must not procure the disclosure to another person of the
information contained in personal data. Therefore it is possible that where
e-voting systems are broken into, not only will offences under the Computer
Misuse Act be committed but also there will be breaches of the DPA if voter
data is obtained and/or passed on.

2.2.11 Data sharing and data transfer

The second principle sets out that personal data is obtained for one or more
specified purposes and shall not be further processed in a manner incompatible with the specified purposes. This might seem to prevent data sharing,
which may be of importance particularly to government departments that
wish to combine individual strands of personal data into a larger 'picture'. It
may also be of interest to businesses for marketing or commercial purposes.
There are ways in the Act in which the second principle can be circumvented so as to share data with exemptions applying to safeguard national
security, for crime and taxation issues and for personal data covering health,

education and social work. While these are reasonably broad it has been necessary to pass specific legislation in order to share personal data. One such example has been the Television Licences (Disclosure of Information) Act 2000. The BBC grants free licences to those over 75. Applicants had to apply and prove eligibility, time-consuming for both the BBC and the applicant. The Department of Social Security stored data on individuals which would have quickened the process, however, there was a conflict with DPA principle 2.

The Television Licences (Disclosure of Information) Act was enacted to allow the sharing of specific personal data by means of the ministerial order. The Television Licences (Disclosure of Information) Act 2000 (Prescription of Information) Order 2000 (SI 2000/1955) provides that information regarding name, date of birth, address and national insurance number of individuals over 74 may be passed. The Act specifies that the sole purpose is to ascertain eligibility for free licences and not for other uses.

The DPA restricts the transfer of data outside the EEA. The eighth principle refers to an 'adequate level of protection', which is expanded upon in Schedule 1 Part II para 13. Regard must be made 'in all circumstances' as to:

(a) the nature of the personal data;
(b) the country or territory of origin of the information contained in the data;
(c) the country or territory of final destination of that information;
(d) the purposes for which and period during which the data are intended to be processed;
(e) the law in force in the country or territory in question;
(f) the international obligations of that country or territory;
(g) any relevant codes of conduct or other rules that are enforceable in that country or territory (whether generally or by arrangement in particular cases); and
(h) any security measures taken in respect of the data in that country or territory.

The eighth principle does not apply where one of conditions contained in Schedule 4 apply and therefore a transfer outside the EEA is allowed. The Schedule 4 conditions are:

(1) consent by the data subject;
(2) transfer is necessary for the performance of a contract or a proposed contract with the data subject;
(3) transfer is necessary to conclude a contract between the data controller and third party at the data subject's request or the performance of such a contract;
(4) transfer is necessary for reasons of substantial public interest;
(5) transfer is necessary in relation to legal proceedings, or obtaining legal advice, or defending legal rights;

(6) transfer is necessary to protect the vital interests of the data subject;

(7) personal data is held on a public register and the transfer is in compliance with the register being open to inspection;

(8) transfer is undertaken on terms approved by the Information Commissioner; or

(9) transfer is authorized by the Information Commissioner.

2.3 FREEDOM OF INFORMATION ACT 2000

Much has been said as to the requirement of data controllers to store personal data responsibly and be subject to request by data subjects for details of the information and where appropriate for amendments or deletions to erroneous data held.

Less easy, traditionally, has been a person's ability to find out what information is held by public bodies. This has to some extent been alleviated by the Freedom of Information Act (FOIA) 2000; this has opened to public scrutiny all recorded information held by the public sector, except in so far as exemptions apply. The requirement to provide responses to requests by the public came into force on 1 January 2005. The Freedom of Information Act applies in England, Wales and Northern Ireland, with a separate Freedom of Information (Scotland) Act 2002.

While FOIA initially seems to affect public bodies it can also apply to information pertaining to the private sector where it performs functions for a public body. Therefore it is important that those responsible for data in the private sector are aware that they could be subject to the provisions of the FOIA.

Any person may make a request for 'information recorded in any form'.[159] The request must be in writing but this includes electronically, for example by email. Requests must include the requestor's name, address and a description of the information sought.[160]

When a request is made, public bodies are required to inform the requestor whether or not it holds the information specified in the request – except where absolute exemptions apply – and if such information is held to supply the requestor with the information except where exemptions apply. The public body may make a reasonable charge for ascertaining if it has the information, its costs of retrieval and any costs of putting the information in a suitable format. There is a maximum that can be charged and the proposed fee must be notified to the requestor with the requestor allowed a three-month period to decide whether to proceed with his request for the information.

Once the requestor agrees the fees and decides to proceed, the public body has 20 working days to respond, although longer periods may apply where the public body is considering an application for exemption.

Exemptions apply to the FOIA, some are referred to as 'absolute exemptions' and others as 'non-absolute'. Examples of absolute exemptions include:

information obtainable by the public by other means, information about the security services and information that the public body is prevented by legislation from disclosing. Non-absolute exemptions may include information for future publication, non-disclosure of information that may be prejudicial to either international relations or the UK's defence. Exemptions may also include exemptions from even confirming or denying the existence of the information requested.

Oversight of the FOIA comes under the responsibility of the Information Commissioner. Section 19(1)(a) of FOIA states that:

> **It shall be the duty of every public authority to adopt and maintain a scheme which relates to the publication of information by the authority and is approved by the Commissioner.**

If a request is made that a public body does not accede to, an application is to be made to that public body's internal complaint handler; if this is unsuccessful the requestor of the information can apply to the Information Commissioner to decide if the requested information should be supplied. The Information Commissioner can order a public body to disclose the information requested. Schedule 3 of FOIA provides the Information Commissioner with powers to enter and inspect premises, to inspect and seize relevant documentation and to inspect, examine, operate and test any equipment that may have stored the relevant information of concern. The warrant to enter and inspect is issued by a Circuit Judge satisfied by information on oath provided by the Information Commissioner that:

    (a) a public authority has failed or is failing to comply with:
        (i)   any of the requirements of Part I of FOIA,
        (ii) so much of a decision notice as requires steps to be taken, or
        (iii) an information notice or enforcement notice; or
    (b) that an offence under section 77 has been or is being committed.

Public bodies and applicants can appeal to the Information Tribunal if dissatisfied with the decision to order disclosure or to refuse disclosure.

2.4 THE ENVIRONMENT INFORMATION REGULATIONS 2004

2.4.1 Objectives of the Regulations

The Environmental Information Regulations 2004 (SI 2004/3391) came into force on 1 January 2005. The Regulations implement EU Council Directive 2003/4/EC on public access to environmental information.

The Regulations apply to environmental information held by public authorities. Environmental information is deemed to be held by a public authority if that information is in the authority's possession and has been produced or received by the authority, or if it is held by another person on behalf of the authority (Reg 3). The Regulations do not apply to any public authority when acting in a judicial or legislative capacity (Reg 3(3)); in addition the Regulations do not apply to either of the Houses of Parliament (Reg 3(4)).

Environmental information has the same meaning as given in Article 2(1) of the EU Directive. Such information may be kept in 'written, visual, aural, electronic or any other material form'. Regulation 2(1) (paragraphs a–f) provides information on what constitutes environmental information.

2.4.2 Duties under the Regulations

Under Regulation 4(1) public authorities are required to progressively make available to the public environmental information that it holds 'by electronic means which are easily accessible' and to 'take reasonable steps to organize the information relevant to its functions with a view to the active and systematic dissemination to the public of the information'. This requirement to provide information in electronic form is not required of information collected prior to 1 January 2005 (Reg 4(2)).

Further under Regulation 5(1) public authorities holding environmental information are to make such information available on request. This is restricted by 5(3) such that 'to the extent that the information requested includes personal data of which the applicant is the data subject, paragraph (1) shall not apply to those personal data'. It is important to note that under Regulation 5(6): 'Any enactment or rule of law that would prevent the disclosure of information in accordance with these Regulations shall not apply.'

2.4.3 Exceptions to the duty to disclose environmental information

Regulation 12(2) imposes upon public authorities an obligation to apply a presumption in favour of disclosure. However, Regulation 12(1)(a) allows a public authority to refuse to disclose environmental information where exceptions under Regulations 12(4) and (5) apply and potentially more wide-ranging under Regulation 12(1)(b) where 'in all the circumstances of the case, the public interest in maintaining the exception outweighs the public interest in disclosing the information'. Regulation 12(4) covers refusal where the information requested is not held, the request is unreasonable, the request is too general, the information relates to incomplete data or unfinished documentation or requests the release of internal communications. Regulation 12(5) refers to refusal on the grounds of defence, security, justice, intellectual property rights, confidential commercial or industrial information where confidentiality is provided by law or to protect the interests of the person providing the information and finally to protect the environment to which the information relates.

There are restrictions on the disclosure of personal data (Reg 13).

Where a public authority refuses to provide information under Regulations 12 or 13, under Regulation 14 it must put the refusal in writing, giving reasons as soon as possible and no later than 20 working days after the receipt of the request for information. If the information is being prepared by another authority under (Reg 12(4)(d)), the applicant is to be provided with its name or under Regulation 10 have the request transferred.

2.4.4 Time limits and charging

Public authorities have a duty to make available environmental information upon request as soon as possible and no later than 20 working days after the receipt of the request (Reg 5(2)).

Public authorities may make a charge for making the information available (Reg 8(1)), such a charge shall not exceed an amount that the public authority is satisfied is reasonable (Reg 8(3)). Public authorities are required to publish a schedule of charges and circumstances under which a charge may be made or waived (Reg 8(8)). A public authority may require an advance payment before making information available, where it does it must notify the applicant of the requirement and the amount required no later than 20 working days after the date of receipt of the request for information (Reg 8(4)). Where a charge is to be made a public authority is not required to provide the requested information unless the charge has been paid no later than 60 working days after the date it gave notification of the charge (Reg 8(5)). The period between notification and receipt of payment is in addition to the 20-working-day period for a public authority to provide information (Reg 8(6)).

Public authorities can not charge for an applicant accessing public registers or lists held by the public authority or for examining requested information at the place that it makes available for that examination (Reg 8(2)).

2.4.5 Form and format of information to be supplied

The information made available and compiled by public authorities or on their behalf 'shall be up to date, accurate and comparable' (Reg 4(4)).

An applicant seeking information can request that information is made available in a particular form or format unless it is reasonable for the authority to make it available in another format or if the information is already publicly available and easily accessible to the applicant in another form or format (Reg 6).

Where the information is not made available in the form or format requested by the applicant, the public authority (Reg 6(2)) shall:

(a) explain the reason for its decision as soon as possible and no later than 20 working days after the date of receipt of the applicant's request for information;

(b) provide an explanation in writing if the applicant so requests; and

(c) inform the applicant of the provisions of Regulation 11 and of the enforcement and appeal provisions of the Act applied by Regulation 18.

Regulation 11 provides that where a person has made a request for environmental information from a public authority that person may make representations to that authority if it appears that the authority has not complied with the requirements under the Regulations with regard to the request. Representations must be considered by the authority free of charge. The public authority must make a decision on these representations as soon as possible and no later than 40 working days after the date of receipt of such representations.

2.4.6 Enforcement of the Regulations

Regulation 18 applies the enforcement and appeals provisions of the Freedom of Information Act 2000 to the Regulations. A complaint may be made to the Information Commissioner by a person who has made a request for environmental information if that person considers that the public authority has not dealt with the request, or representations to the authority about the request, in accordance with the Regulations. The Information Commissioner has powers to enforce the Regulations. These include the powers of entry and inspection. Obstruction of the Information Commissioner in the execution of a warrant is liable on summary conviction to a fine.

There is a further offence of altering records with the intent to prevent disclosure. Under Regulation 19 where a person alters, defaces, blocks, erases, destroys or conceals any record held by the public authority, with the intention of preventing the disclosure by that authority, on summary conviction such a person is liable to a fine.

2.5 REGULATION OF INVESTIGATORY POWERS ACT 2000

Previous mention has been made of the Malone and Halford cases. The former gave rise to the Interception of Communications Act (ICA) 1985 while the latter gave rise to the Regulation of Investigatory Powers Act (RIPA) 2000. The 1985 ICA related to the interception of communications via a public telecommunications network; anyone intentionally intercepting, without authority, a communication being transmitted via a public telecommunication network was guilty of a criminal offence. A public telecommunications network was at that time defined by the 1984 Telecommunications Act and would have been quite limited to, for example, British Telecom, Kingston Communications operating around Hull, and Mercury Limited. Interceptions were permitted, for example the Home Secretary could permit phone taps. The ICA 1985 did not, however, cover non-public telecommunications networks, for example internal phone systems or the, at the time, relatively new ideas of local area networks (LANs) etc. The consequence of this non-private coverage was that employers were relatively free to monitor telephone calls and internal emails within their organizations. This was the position up to the case of *Halford v United Kingdom* in 1997. A senior police officer, Ms Alison Halford, claimed that both her home and office telephone had been tapped. The office system was part of a private network and therefore beyond the scope of the ICA 1985. Ms Halford nevertheless brought a case against the British Government at the European Court of Human Rights claiming that there had been a breach of Article 8 of the European Convention on Human Rights, namely her right to privacy and also Article 13, the right to a domestic remedy. The ECHR while finding that there had not been an unlawful phone tap nevertheless held that conversations on her office phones did come within the definition of the terms 'private life' and 'correspondence' contained within Article 8 (1). Ms Halford could reasonably have expected to have had privacy in her calls. The ECHR further held that there had been a breach of Article 8(2), which states that any derogation from Article 8(1) must be 'in accordance with the law'. The ECHR held that a breach of Article 13 had occurred as there was no means at that point by which an individual could complain about interceptions over a private network.

RIPA 2000 was a consequence of the Halford case.

RIPA is broadly divided into four areas:

(i)   the interception of communications (Part I Chapter I) including:

    (a)   provisions covering monitoring by businesses,

    (b)   the use of interception warrants;

(ii) the acquisition and disclosure of communications data (Part I Chapter II);

(iii) surveillance and covert human intelligence sources (Part II); and

(iv) the investigation of electronic data that has been protected by encryption (Part III).

RIPA attempts to provide a clear framework for dealing with the lawful interception of postal, telecommunication and digital-based communications. RIPA widens the scope and repeals the 1985 Interception of Communications Act, the Act also implements Article 5 of the EU Directive 97/66/EC, which relates to the processing of personal data and the protection of privacy within the telecommunications sector. RIPA covers the interception of communications via public postal systems, public and private telecommunications systems. The definition of a telecommunications system has been broadened to include not only fixed/landline providers such as BT but also mobile phone providers and internet service providers (ISPs). A private telecommunications system is any non-public telecommunications system that is connected to a public system; thus it includes not only internal phone systems but also internal IT networks and would cover communications via a company's intranet email.

In the same way as a breach of ICA 1985 was a criminal offence, interception intentionally and without lawful authority under RIPA can be a criminal offence; it can also give rise to a civil action.

Section 1(1) makes it an offence to intercept in the UK without lawful authority communications by post, public telecommunications systems and under section 1(2) private telecommunications systems.

Under Section 1(3) any interception of a communication in the UK by, or with the express or implied consent of, a person having the right to control the operation or use of a private telecommunications system shall be actionable by the sender or recipient or intended recipient, if it is without lawful authority. The interception of that communication must have been in the course of its transmission by a private telecommunications system or by a public telecommunications system to or from apparatus in a private system.

Under RIPA an interception is not actionable where it has been carried out with lawful authority. Lawful authority is defined in sections 3 and 4. Under section 3(1) interception by a person is authorized where the communication is one which, or which that person has reasonable grounds for believing, is a communication sent by a person who has consented to the interception and a communication the intended recipient of which has consented.

Under section 4(2) lawful authority may arise where the Secretary of State, by way of regulations, authorizes any such conduct that appears to him to constitute a legitimate practice reasonably required for the purpose, in connection with the carrying on of any business, of monitoring or keeping a record of communications of transactions entered into in the course of that business or other communications relating to that business.

The regulations mentioned are the Telecommunications (Lawful Business Practice) Regulations 2000, which came into force on 24 October 2000. These set out the conditions under which it is permissible for a business to monitor its private telecommunications network.

Regulation 3(a) sets out the five instances whereby communications may be both monitored and recorded:

(i)   monitoring for standards purposes, for example to ensure compliance with regulatory or self-regulatory practices;

(ii) in the interests of national security;

(iii) to prevent or detect crime;

(iv) to investigate or detect unauthorized use of a telecommunication systems; and

(v)   to ensure the effective use of the system.

There are two purposes whereby the communications may be monitored but not recorded. These are:

(i)   to ascertain whether the communication is related to the systems controller's business; or

(ii) to monitor the use of confidential phone lines.

The Secretary of State may issue interception warrants although these are mainly limited to issues of national security and criminal investigation.

In order to assist businesses in being compliant with the provisions of RIPA, the Information Commissioner has produced a 'Code of Practice, Monitoring at Work', which is available from the Information Commissioner's website.

2.6 THE PRIVACY AND ELECTRONIC COMMUNICATIONS (EC DIRECTIVE) REGULATIONS (SI 2003/2426)

Direct marketing may have a number of terms: 'junk (e)mail', 'unsolicited (e)mail' or 'spam'. Whatever name is used, for the recipient they are at the very least an annoying waste of time; contrasting with this is cheapness and ease of marketing products and services from the point of view of the originator. In addition to time wasted reading and deleting junk mail, an opportunity cost occurs, because persons could be productively engaged on other tasks. Electronic junk mail can result in extra resources of the receiver being used such as memory space, with spam even overloading a person's memory allocation. Junk mailing through faxes can increase business costs through the extra usage of paper and printer ink. Junk (e)mailing may also be of an offensive nature. While some mailing is random, originators often need to source their targets' data and this is directly relevant to the issue of privacy. Much of this mailing originates beyond UK and European jurisdictions; of concern here is the legislation in place that affects direct marketers in Europe.

There is a variety of legislation with regard to direct marketing. Here we will briefly consider some parts that deal with aspects of privacy.

Section 11(3) of the Data Protection Act 1998 refers to direct marketing as 'communication (by whatever means) of any advertising or marketing material which is directed to particular individuals', a wide enough definition to cover unsolicited email. Section 11(1) provides that:

> an individual is entitled at any time by notice in writing to a data controller to require the data controller at the end of such period as is reasonable to cease, or not to begin, processing for the purposes of direct marketing personal data in respect of which he is the data subject.

The Electronic Commerce (EC Directive) Regulations (SI 2002/2013), which came into force on 21 August 2002, implements Directive 2000/31/EC of the European Parliament and Council dated 8 June 2000 on certain legal aspects of information society service, in particular electronic commerce in the internal market. Information society services are those provided normally for remuneration over distance through electronic media by a request from the intended recipient of that service, Recitals 18 and 19 of the Directive extend the coverage beyond remunerated services.

The Regulations have an impact on website content, the promotion and sale of goods and services online and the transmission, storage and provision of electronic communications. Regulation 8 requires that unsolicited commercial email is identifiable. Article 7(1) of the Directive states:

> Member States shall take measures to ensure that service providers undertaking unsolicited commercial communications by electronic mail consult

regularly and respect opt out registers in which natural persons not wishing to receive such commercial communications can register themselves.

The Telecommunications (Data Protection and Privacy) Regulations (SI 1999/2093) Regulations 11 and 12 required that telecommunications providers offered an anonymizing facility to hide caller identification numbers.

Directive 2002/58/EC concerning the Processing of Personal Data and the Protection of Privacy in the Electronic Communications Sector (the (e)Privacy Directive) replaces the Telecomunications Directive 97/66/EC, which had included automated calling machines and faxes but not emails. The Privacy Directive is implemented by the Privacy and Electronic Communications (EC Directive) Regulations 2003/2426, effective 11 December 2003.

The Regulations cover 'unsolicited messages' by email, text, pictures, video, phone and fax, i.e. communications by electronic means. It also covers traffic data and cookies. Regulation 22 allows that unsolicited communications could be sent with previous consent (an opt-in), reflecting Article 13(1) of the Directive. For existing customers there was an 'opt-out' provision, so messages could still be sent.

The soft opt-in implying consent can apply where details have been obtained through a sale or negotiation for sale, without the sale being completed. Until the person opts out further marketing is permissible. Senders of marketing messages must not conceal their identity and must provide valid addresses for opt-out requests. The Information Commissioner has issued guidance: 'Electronic Mail Marketing'.

Under Regulation 6 those using tracking devices, for example cookies must notify information users or subscribers as to the purpose/extent and a chance to refuse them, i.e. opt-out; although without specifying what that information consists of. Tracking devices that process personal data must be DPA compliant.

The Regulations require that traffic data no longer required for billing or communications must be anonymized or erased. The use or processing of traffic data for further marketing requires consent. The use of location data requires consent for value-added services.

In terms of uninvited personally addressed postal mail, individuals can seek to have this prevented by registering with the Mailing Preference Service, similar services apply to telephone marketing through the Telephone Preference Service and fax marketing through the Fax Preference Service.

Other jurisdictions have introduced legislation against spam, for example, the Controlling the Assault of Non-Solicited Pornography and Marketing Act 2003 (the US Can-Spam Act), effective 1 January 2004. This, like the EU Privacy Directive, is restricted i.e. only applicable to ISPs/mailers within its jurisdiction.

This is not the case with Australian Spam Act 2003, effective 10 April 2004. Section 14 states that the Act 'extends to acts, omissions, matters and things outside Australia'. The Act refers to messages with an 'Australian Link', under section 7(c) messages have an 'Australian Link' where a 'computer, service or device that is used to access the message is located in Australia'. This is indicative that the Australian state is prepared to extend anti-spam legislation in theory if perhaps not in actual practice beyond its borders.

2.7 INDIRECT PROTECTION OF PRIVACY

Section 85 of the Copyright, Designs and Patents Act 1988 provides a limited right to privacy with regard to certain photographs and films. This right is applicable to someone who has for private and domestic purposes commissioned the taking of a photograph or the making of film. The Act gives them the right not to have: copies of the work issued to the public; or, the work exhibited or shown in public; or the work broadcast or included in a cable programme service. It is important to note the requirement, that the work be commissioned for private and domestic purposes, which does little for celebrities whose images appear in the media. It may, however, be of concern for those who are professional photographers using digital storage of material.

2.8 RECENT LEGISLATIVE DEVELOPMENTS

Possibly the most wide-ranging new legislation is the new EU Directive on Data Retention 2006/24/EC, which was approved by the European Parliament at the end of 2005, coming into force 20 days after appearing in the *Official Journal of the European Union*. The Directive has aimed to amend and extend the provisions of Directive 2002/58/EC on Privacy and Electronic Communications. Under this Directive traffic and location data had to be erased or made anonymous when no longer required for the purpose of the transmission except in so far as it was required for billing or interconnection purposes. With the expansion of pre-paid mobile, flat rate tariff billing and developments such as Voice over Internet Protocols (VoIP), the need to keep information for billing purposes has often become redundant. This means that public authorities would not be able to have access to data on traffic and location data in order to carry out their duties preventing and combating crime and terrorism. Restrictions with regard to erasure and anonymity were available to states via Article 15(1) for reasons of national security and for the prevention, investigation, detection and prosecution of crime. There was not, however, a uniform approach across the EU.

The new directive aims to harmonize requirements regarding the retention of certain types of data by providers of electronic communications services. Are there implications for a person's right to privacy? The EU itself acknowledges in the draft to the Directive that it 'will have an effect on the privacy right of citizens under Article 7 of the Charter (of Fundamental Rights), as well as on the right to protection of personal data as guaranteed under Article 8 of the Charter, the interference with these rights is justified in accordance with Article 52 of the Charter' (p3) whereby the limitations are necessary and proportionate to prevent and combat crime and terrorism. Personal data that is processed under the directive is covered by the data protection provisions of Directives 95/46/EC and 2002/58/EC such that it is claimed that 'additional provisions on general data protection principles and data security are not necessary', the processing of such personal data 'will be under the full supervisory powers of the data protection authorities in all Member States'.[161]

This legislation establishes mandatory requirements for telecommunications operators and ISPs with regard to the collection, retention and retrieval of communication records. The Directive requires that operators retain details of the following:

(i)   data necessary to trace and identify the source of a communication;
(ii)   data necessary to trace and identify the destination of a communication;
(iii) data necessary to identify the date, time and duration of a communication;
(iv)   data necessary to identify the type of communication; and
(v)   data necessary to identify the location of mobile communication equipment.

The term 'data' is defined in article 2 of the Directive to mean traffic data and location data together with any related data necessary in order to identify the subscriber or user. A user is defined as 'any legal entity or natural person using a publicly available electronic communications service, for private or business purposes, without necessarily having subscribed to this service'.

Article 6 deals with retention periods: 'Member States shall ensure that the categories of data specified in Article 5 are retained for periods of not less than six months and not more than two years from the date of communication.' The draft Directive required fixed and mobile telecommunications providers to retain data for 24 months while ISPs must retain data for at least six months. Article 12(1) allows a state to extend the maximum period for a limited amount of time; under Article 12(2) the Commission approving or rejecting such a measure within six months.

When requested by a competent authority, these providers must provide the specific information without unnecessary delay. At present the requirement is for details of a transaction to be logged but not the content, for example for a text, message details would be kept for the sender and recipient but not the actual text itself. The draft states that the: 'Directive is not applicable to the content of communications – this would amount to the interception of telecommunications, which falls outside the scope of this legal instrument'.[162]

Member states have it seems about 18 months to introduce legislation to implement the Directive. Under Article 15(1) member states have until 15 September 2007 to implement the Directive. However, under Article 15(3) each member state may postpone application of this Directive to the retention of communications data relating to internet access, internet telephony and internet email until 15 March 2009. The UK has made such a Declaration pursuant to Article 15(3).

With regard to each of the requirements under Article 4 of the new directive, the types of data to be retained are:

(a)   Data needed to trace and identify communication sources:
  (i)   fixed network telephony:
    (a)   calling telephone number;
    (b)   name and address of subscriber or registered user;
  (ii)   mobile telephony:
    (a)   calling telephone number;
    (b)   name and address of subscriber or registered user;
  (iii)   internet access, internet, internet email and internet telephony:
    (a)   internet protocol (IP) address, whether dynamic or static, allocated by the internet access provider to the communication;
    (b)   user ID of the source of the communication;
    (c)   connection label or telephone number allocated to any communication entering a public telephone network;
    (d)   name and address of the subscriber or registered user to whom the IP address, connection label or user ID was allocated at the time of the communication.

(b)   Data required to trace and identify the destination of communications:
  (i)   fixed network telephony:
    (a)   called telephone number(s)
    (b)   name(s) and address(es) of subscriber(s) or registered user(s);
  (ii)   mobile telephony:
    (a)   called telephone number(s);
    (b)   name(s) and address(es) of subscriber(s) or registered user(s);
  (iii)   internet access, internet email and internet telephony:
    (a)   connection label or user ID of intended recipient(s) of the communication
    (b)   name(s) and addresses of the subscriber(s) or registered user(s) who are the intended recipient(s) of the communication.

(c)   Data required to identify the date, time and duration of a communication:
  (i)   fixed network and mobile telephony:

(a) the date and time of the start and end of a communication;

(ii) internet access, internet email and internet telephony:

(a) the date and time of the log-in and log-off of the internet sessions on a certain time zone.

(d) Data required to identify the type of communication:

(i) fixed network telephony:

(a) telephone service used, for example voice, conference call, fax and messaging services;

(ii) mobile telephony:

(a) telephone service used, for example voice, conference call, short message service (SMS), enhanced media service or multi media service.

(e) Data required to identify communications devices or what purports to be a communications device:

(i) mobile telephony:

(a) the international mobile subscriber identity (ISMI) of the calling and called party;

(b) the international mobile equipment identity (IMEI) of the calling and called party.

(ii) internet access, internet email and internet telephony:

(a) the calling telephone number for dial-up access;

(b) the digital subscriber line (DSL) or other end point identifier of the originator of the communication;

(c) the media access control (MAC) address or other machine identifier of the originator of the communication.

(f) Data required to identify the location of mobile communication equipment:

(i) the location label (Cell ID) at the start and end of the communication;

(ii) data mapping between Cell IDs and their geographical location at the start and end of the communication.

The new directive is called EU Directive 2006/24/EC on the retention of data generated or processed in connection with the provision of publicly available electronic communications services or of public communications networks.

2.9 NON-STATUTORY PRIVACY REGULATION: COMMERCIAL REGULATION

While much of privacy protection is now statute based, one should not forget various industrial or commercial initiatives to establish industry-wide standards.

The World Wide Web Consortium (W3C) has developed the Platform for Privacy Preferences Project (P3P), which allows websites to inform users of a site's privacy policies. P3P covers nine aspects of online privacy. Five relate to the data tracked by the site; they inform the user as to:

(1) who is collecting the data;

(2) what information is being collected;

(3) the purpose of collection;

(4) what information is shared with others;

(5) who are the data recipients.

Four further aspects relate to:

(6) whether users can make changes as to how their data is used;

(7) how disputes are resolved;

(8) an explanation of the policy for retaining data; and

(9) where these policies can be found in a 'human readable' form.

P3P allows websites to put their privacy policies in machine-readable format, which can be searched by a user's browser and compared to the user's preferences or regulatory guidelines. This allows users to make an informed decision as to whether to use a site or not.

The Institute of Quality Assurance has introduced the global W-Mark certification for websites. Websites are assessed in terms of accessibility, consistency and appearance, navigation, service commitment, security and privacy and data protection. In terms of privacy, W-Mark considers whether sites have a privacy policy detailing how data is gathered, how data is used, whether data is passed or sold on to others and compliance with regulatory requirements.

The law on privacy is constantly evolving; an attempt has been made here to briefly highlight some of the important influences that affect those who deal with personal data.

REFERENCES

- Australia: Spam Act http://www.dcita.gov.au/communications_and_technology/policy_and_legislation/spam (date accessed 19/08/07)
- Center for Democracy and Technology: http://www.cdt.org (date accessed 19/08/07)
- Computer Misuse Act 1990: http://www.opsi.gov.uk/acts/acts1990/Ukpga_19900018_en_1.htm (date accessed 19/08/07)
- Controlling the Assault of Non-Solicited Pornography and Marketing Act 2003 (The Can-Spam Act) USA: http://frwebgate.access.gpo.gov/cgi-bin/getdoc.cgi?dbname=108_cong_public_laws&docid=f:publ187.108.pdf (date accessed 19/08/07)
- Data Protection Act 1998: http://www.opsi.gov.uk/acts/acts1998/19980029.htm (date accessed 19/08/07)
- Electronic Privacy Information Center (EPIC): http://www.epic.org (date accessed 19/08/07)

- Electronic Voting: Interesting list of references on the topic: http://www.social-informatics.net/evoting.htm (date accessed 19/08/07)
- Environmental Information Regulations 2004: http://www.opsi.gov.uk/si/si2004/20043391.htm (date accessed 19/08/07)
- EU Directive 95/46/EC on the protection of individuals with regard to the processing of personal data and the free movement of data. 24 October 1995. (Data Protection Directive): http://europa.eu.int/comm/justice_home/fsj/privacy/law/index_en.htm (date accessed 19/08/07)
- EU Directive 97/7/EC on the protection of consumers in respect of distance contracts. 20 May 1997. (Distance Selling Directive): http://europa.eu.int/comm/consumers/cons_int/safe_shop/dist_sell/index_en.htm (date accessed (19/08/07)
- EU Directive 97/66/EC concerning the processing of personal data and the protection of privacy in the telecommunications sector. 15 December 1997. (Telecommunications Directive): http://europa.eu.int/ISPO/infosoc/telecompolicy/en/9766en.pdf
- EU Directive 2000/31/EC on certain legal aspects of information society services in particular electronic commerce in the internal market. 8 June 2000. (Electronic Commerce Directive): http://ec.europa.eu/internal_market/e-commerce/directive_en.htm (date accessed 19/08/07)
- EU Directive 2002/58/EC concerning the processing of personal data and the protection of privacy in the electronic communications sector. 12 July 2002. (Privacy Directive): http://europa.eu.int/eur-lex/pri/en/oj/dat/2002/l_201/l_20120020731en00370047.pdf (date accessed 19/08/07)
- EU Directive 2006/24/EC on the retention of data generated or processed in connection with the provision of publicly available electronic communications services or of public communications networks: http://europa.eu.int/eur-lex/lex/LexUriServ/site/en/oj/2006/l_105/l_10520060413en00540063.pdf (date accessed 19/08/07)
- Fax Preference Service: http://www.fpsonline.org.uk/fps/ (date accessed 19/08/07)
- Freedom of Information Act 2000: http://www.opsi.gov.uk/acts/acts2000/20000036.htm (date accessed 19/08/07)
- Information Commissioner's Office: http://www.ico.gov.uk (date accessed 19/08/07)
- Information Commissioner: Electronic Mail Marketing: http://www.ico.gov.uk/upload/documents/library/data_protection/practical_application/electronic_mail_marketing_good_practice_note.pdf (date accessed 19/08/07)
- Information Commissioner: Freedom of Information Act: http://www.ico.gov.uk/Home/what_we_cover/freedom_of_information.aspx (date accessed 19/08/07)

- Information Commissioner: Monitoring at Work: http://www.ico.gov.uk/upload/documents/library/data_protection/practical_applicatio coi_html/english/supplementary_guidance/monitoring_at_work_1.htm (date accessed 19/08/07)

- Information Commissioner: Privacy and Electronic Communications: http://www.ico.gov.uk/Home/what_we_cover/privacy_and_electronic_communications.aspx (date accessed 19/08/07)

- Information Commissioner: spam: http://www.ico.gov.uk/Home/for_the_public/topic_specific_guides/spam_emails.aspx (date accessed 19/08/07)

- Institute of Quality Assurance (IQA) (since 01/01/07 known as the Chartered Quality Institute): http://www.thecqi.org (date accessed 19/08/07)

- Mailing Preference Service: http://www.mpsonline.org.uk/mpsr/ (date accessed 19/08/07)

- Privacy and Electronic Communications (EC Directive) Regulations 2003: http://www.opsi.gov.uk/si/si2003/20032426.htm (date accessed 19/08/07)

- Regulation of Investigatory Powers Act 2000: http://www.opsi.gov.uk/acts/acts2000/20000023.htm (date accessed 19/08/07)

- Telephone Preference Service: http://www.tpsonline.org.uk/tps/ (date accessed 19/08/07)

- Warren, S and Brandeis, L: 'The Right to Privacy'. Vol. IV December 15, 1890 No. 5 http://www-swiss.ai.mit.edu/6805/articles/privacy/Privacy_brand_warr2.html (date accessed 19/08/07)

- World Wide Web Consortium (W3C): http://www.w3.org (date accessed 19/08/07)

3 Evidence

LOUISE TOWNSEND

This chapter introduces the concept of evidence and in particular electronic evidence. It explains when documents may be admitted as evidence and, if they are, what weight might be given to them by a court or tribunal.

Once legal proceedings are contemplated, it is important to have a basic understanding of the rules of evidence so as to be properly prepared for the proceedings. However, this is a complex area of law that has developed through both statute and case law over many years and specialist legal advice should always be sought. This chapter is intended as a basic overview and cannot go into the specific rules and exceptions in detail.

Nevertheless, organizations should not wait until court or tribunal proceedings are contemplated before considering evidential issues. It is important to build evidence as a consideration into, for example, document retention policies, security policies and investment in technology to ensure that, if required, the evidence that an organization has will be available and reliable.

While this chapter touches on information security and encryption, these issues are discussed in more detail in Chapter 6.

3.1 BASIC CONCEPTS

3.1.1 What is evidence?

Evidence is the way that a fact is proved or disproved in a court or tribunal. There is a whole body of law, referred to as the law of evidence, which dictates whether something can be introduced as evidence in legal proceedings and the status accorded to it if it is introduced. Some of this law is statutory, for example the Civil Evidence Act 1995 in relation to hearsay. Some of this law, known as common law, has been developed over the years by judges in court cases.

There are a wide range of courts and tribunals that assess evidence. Evidential issues arise not just in criminal courts but also in civil courts, employment tribunals, adjudications and other legal forums.

In a commercial context an organization may require evidence to refute a claim of unfair dismissal from an employee, evidence to prove that it has intellectual property rights in an invention, evidence that it is insured if its factory burns down and evidence to show that its customer agreed to pay it a certain amount for the goods that it supplied. All of this evidence is unlikely to be held in the same place in an organization and it is important to develop an understanding of what may be required, when and in what circumstances so that an organization can ensure that this is available for evidential purposes.

3.1.2 Types of evidence

Evidence comes in many different forms, for example oral testimony is where a witness gives oral evidence in court, real evidence is evidence in a material form such as 'the bloody knife'.

It is important to consider that evidence can be primary or secondary evidence. Secondary evidence suggests that there is other and better evidence available. This other and better evidence is the primary evidence – evidence of the best or highest kind. For example, history sources are often referred to as primary and secondary – an eyewitness account of a battle is a primary source, a report in a newspaper is a secondary source because it is not necessarily as reliable. The same applies to legal evidence – primary evidence could be the signed original contract, secondary evidence could be a draft of the contract or a witness statement saying what the contract contained. Neither of these are as good as seeing the original contract.

Electronic evidence can be primary or secondary; simply because it is held in electronic format does not relegate it to the status of secondary evidence. However, issues of weight and credibility may be particularly relevant to electronic evidence and this is discussed below.

Hearsay is another form of evidence. This is evidence given by one person as to what another person said. It is easy to see how this may not be as reliable as evidence given by the person themselves. For example, rather than John, the IT Manager, standing up in court and explaining how he monitors business communications on the company systems, the reasons for this and so on, Jo, the HR Manager, stands up and explains what John told her he does. Hearsay evidence can also be contained in a written document or statement.

Although potentially less reliable, in civil cases hearsay is generally admissible as the Civil Evidence Act 1995 section 1(1) states that evidence shall not be excluded on the ground that it is hearsay and section 1(2) defines hearsay as 'a statement made otherwise than by a person while giving oral evidence in the proceedings which is tendered as evidence of the matters stated'.[163] A party must give reasonable notice of its intention to adduce hearsay evidence.[164] The court then considers what weight should be given to such evidence and this is discussed below.

In criminal cases, the law of hearsay has recently been codified in the Criminal Justice Act 2003. Criminal hearsay is generally only admissible if it is covered by this Act – for example where a witness has died – if all parties agree or if the court is satisfied that it is in the interests of justice.

3.1.3 Relevance of evidence

Whatever the evidence, it must be sufficiently relevant to the particular case in dispute. Relevant evidence is something that proves or disproves something else or makes something more or less probable. For example, the fact that you change your health and safety policies after an accident is irrelevant as to whether you were negligent in causing the accident in the first place.[165] Similarly, if you are trying to prove the terms on which a contract was entered into, the fact that you have entered into other contracts on particular terms is not relevant to the contract in issue.[166]

3.1.4 Burden and standard of proof

The burden of proof in a civil case will normally lie with the claimant as it is the claimant who is asserting that something is the case. For example, if you sue another party for breach of contract then you must prove that a contract was in place and that the other party has breached it.

In some cases you may not need to prove everything, for example if you sue for breach of contract and the other party admits that there is a contract in place between you then you will not need to prove that there is a contract, just that it has been breached.

A defendant to a claim may also need to prove certain facts. For example, if the basis of a party's defence raises new facts and assertions, then these must be proved by the defendant as it is now the defendant that is asserting that something is the case.

The standard of proof in civil cases is the balance of probabilities – that it is more probable than not that what is asserted is correct.

In a criminal matter it is the prosecution that bears the burden of proving their case and the standard is that they must, subject to some exceptions, do this beyond reasonable doubt.

3.2 DIGITAL EVIDENCE

Evidence will not always be given by witnesses as oral testimony. Much evidence may be documentary and in light of the increased use of document management systems and other electronic systems, much documentary evidence may now be in digital format.

Evidence in digital format is legal evidence and is as equally acceptable as any other form of evidence. This can be seen by looking at some of the legal definitions.

The Civil Evidence Act 1968, which has now been repealed, defined a document as including:

> any disc, tape, soundtrack or other device in which sounds or other data (not being visual images) are embodied so as to be capable (with or without the aid of some other equipment) of being reproduced therefrom.[167]

Although this definition was widely drafted, the courts had to look at how it applied in the light of new technologies. In *Grant v Southwestern and County Properties Ltd*[168] Walton J stated that:

> **The mere interposition of necessity of an instrument for deciphering the information cannot make any difference in principle. A litigant who keeps all his documents in microdot form could not avoid discovery because in order to read the information extremely powerful microscopes or other sophisticated instruments would be required. Nor again, if he kept them by means of microfilm which could not be read without the aid of a projector.**

This case held that a tape recording was capable of being a document within this definition.

In *Derby & Co. Ltd v Weldon (No 9)*[169] it was held that a computer database that formed part of the business records of an organization was a document within this definition where information can be retrieved and converted into readable form.

The Civil Evidence Act 1995 also contains a wide definition. This states that a document is:

> **anything in which information of any description is recorded, and 'copy', in relation to a document, means anything onto which information recorded in the document has been copied, by whatever means and whether directly or indirectly.[170]**

Defining a document by reference to 'information' leaves this technology neutral and open to new forms of storing information and what is clear is that the definition of a document is not just intended to cover paper information.

The Civil Procedure Rules (CPR) dictate how civil litigation should be carried out in the High Court. Part 31 of the CPR covers the disclosure of documentary evidence from one party to the other. A party to legal proceedings must, subject to certain exceptions, disclose all documents on which he relies, documents that adversely affect his own case, adversely affect another party's case or documents that support another party's case.[171]

Rule 31.4 of the CPR defines a document as 'anything in which information of any description is recorded'. Again, the reference to 'information' leaves the definition open to be interpreted widely and so could include emails, photographs, multimedia files and other electronic information as long as there is information and it is recorded in some way. There is a positive duty on an organization to search for documents as Rule 31.7 CPR requires a party to make a reasonable search for documents having regard to the number of documents involved, the nature and complexity of the proceedings, the ease and expense of retrieval and the significance of any documents likely to be located.

The Practice Direction accompanying Part 31 was amended in October 2005 to deal more specifically with the disclosure of electronic documents. This states that:

> The parties should, prior to the first Case Management Conference, discuss any issues that may arise regarding searches for and the preservation of electronic documents. This may involve the parties providing information about the categories of electronic documents within their control, the computer systems, electronic devices and media on which any relevant documents may be held, the storage systems maintained by the parties and their document retention policies.

Each party is required to sign a disclosure statement that sets out whether it has searched electronic documents and if so what categories. For example, the statement to be signed refers to PCs, portable data storage media, databases, servers, back-up tapes, PDA devices etc. A party may be found in contempt of court if it signs a disclosure statement without believing it to be true.

In practice, these are important points to consider because, if litigation or proceedings are contemplated, all potential evidence must be searched for and, for example, as part of the disclosure process in civil litigation, all relevant evidence must be disclosed to the other side, not just any paper records that are held. An organization should also consider the preservation of electronic documents when litigation is contemplated or pending. Once litigation has commenced and a disclosure order has been made, a party can be held in contempt of court for deliberately destroying computer-based documents.[172] In the USA in 2004 Philip Morris was fined $2.75 million for destroying potential email evidence after a disclosure order was issued by the court because it failed to suspend its email deletion policy.[173] The position is not clear prior to a disclosure order being made, it appears that there needs to be an intention to subvert or pervert the course of justice in destroying documents.[174]

Organizations should therefore have regard to the potential for litigation when considering their document retention policies and again need to understand what information they hold and in what format well before litigation is contemplated.

Finally, the Electronic Signatures Directive 1999[175] makes it clear that electronic signatures should be accepted by courts and tribunals in the same way as pen and ink signatures. This states that an electronic signature is not to be 'denied legal effectiveness and admissibility as evidence in legal proceedings solely on the ground that it is in electronic form'.[176] This means, for example, that if a contract is signed electronically there is no reason that the court should not treat this as proper evidence. However, the fact that the signature is admissible does not necessarily mean that it will be given the same weight as a pen and ink signature, for example if it can be shown to be unreliable. Electronic signatures are discussed in more detail below.

3.2.1 What is in 'writing'?

The legal definition of 'writing' can be found in the Interpretation Act 1978. This may be relevant, for example, if a piece of legislation specifies that something must be done 'in writing'. The legal definition is that writing:

> **includes typing, printing, lithography, photography and other modes of representing or reproducing words in a visible form, and expressions referring to writing are construed accordingly.**[177]

It was previously thought that this definition may not cover electronic documents as it was argued that the phrase 'words in a visible form' could not apply to electronic documents, which are made up of a series of electronic bits that are not visible. However, in December 2001, the Law Commission of England and Wales published a report entitled 'Electronic Commerce: Formal Requirements in Commercial Transactions', which examined the current legal status of electronic documents and electronic signatures in English law.

This report is discussed in more detail below in the section on electronic signatures. However, in summary, the Law Commission took the view that electronic documents can fulfil the definition of 'in writing' because where there is some human intervention, an electronic document can be seen on screen.

In practice, a contract may require certain forms of notice to be given 'in writing'. Reference may also be made in the contract to what this means. For example, it may say that where notice is to be given in writing this must be done by fax or post. Other contracts will allow for notice by email. In the absence of any restriction it is likely that the court will interpret this widely if there is a dispute and allow for notices served electronically to be classed as in writing. The parties to a contract should therefore consider how they would like any notices to be served and agree this in the contract itself.

3.3 ADMISSIBILITY, WEIGHT AND CREDIBILITY

We have seen that digital or electronic evidence can be available in many forms, from emails to photographs and databases. It is acceptable as evidence in courts and tribunals in the same way as oral testimony or more traditional forms of documentary evidence.

However, just because it is acceptable, does not mean that it will always be admissible. Nor does it mean that it will always be classed as primary evidence or given the same weight as other pieces of evidence. And, as discussed above, to be admissible a document must be sufficiently relevant. It cannot be too remote to the case at hand.

It is important to realize that the admissibility of evidence is at the discretion of the court or tribunal in question. For example, in the criminal courts a judge can exclude evidence that would otherwise be admissible on the basis it would be unfair to adduce it.[178]

In the High Court, Rule 32.1 of the CPR states that the court may control evidence by giving directions as to the issues on which it requires evidence, the nature of the evidence and the way in which the evidence is to be placed before the court. It states that 'the court may use its power under this rule to exclude evidence that would otherwise be admissible'. In doing so, the court will have regard to the overriding objective of the CPR, which is in Rule 1.1. This states that the Rules have the 'overriding objective of enabling the court to deal with cases justly'. In doing this, a court will have regard, for example, to ensuring that the parties are on an equal footing, saving expense, the amount of money involved and the financial position of each party.[179]

Conversely, a judge also has discretion to allow evidence that would otherwise arguably be inadmissible. In the case of *Jones v University of Warwick*[180] the claimant had dropped a cash box on her wrist at work and made a claim against her employer for damages. The employer admitted liability but did not agree that the claimant had an ongoing disability. The employer's insurers engaged an enquiry agent who, posing as a market researcher, filmed the claimant using a hidden camera. The Court of Appeal held that the evidence was admissible, even though there was likely to have been a breach of the Human Rights Act 1998 when the enquiry agent gained access to the house meaning that the evidence had potentially been unlawfully obtained. While not excluding the evidence, the court said that because the conduct of the insurers was improper and unjustified they should be made to pay the costs of the hearing to determine admissibility. Again, the court in this case had regard to the overriding objective of the CPR.

In relation to business and other documents, section 117 of the Criminal Justice Act 2003 contains provision for their admissibility in criminal cases so that a statement contained in a document is admissible where, for example, it was created or received by a person in the course of a trade, business, profession or other occupation and the person supplying it had personal knowledge of the matters dealt with. In civil cases this is dealt with in section 9 of the Civil Evidence Act 1995, which says that:

> (1) A document which is shown to form part of the records of a business or public authority may be received in evidence in civil proceedings without further proof.
>
> (2) A document shall be taken to form part of the records of a business or public authority if there is produced to the court a certificate to that effect signed by an officer of the business or authority to which the records belong.

In criminal cases it used to be necessary to prove that a computer was operating properly and was not being used improperly before any statement made in a document produced by the computer could be admitted in evidence in a criminal court.[181] The current position is that a presumption will exist that the computer producing the evidential record was working properly at the time in question and is therefore admissible. The presumption can be rebutted if evidence to the contrary is collected – if this occurs it will be the party wanting to rely on the evidence who has to disprove.

Crown Prosecution Service evidential guidelines state that CCTV cameras, in-store security systems, photographs and media releases are today all presented as routine aspects of evidence. Provided the origin and authenticity of any given item is proved such evidence is admissible. Courts do still retain the discretion not to admit if unclear or if there is a suggestion of tampering but are willing to deal with technological advances in evidence.

Once evidence is admitted, a court or tribunal may accord different weight to different evidence. As discussed above, primary evidence may be given more weight than secondary evidence. The Civil Evidence Act 1995 also sets out factors that a court may consider when deciding what weight to give to documents. For example, in relation to hearsay the court should consider whether it would be reasonable and practicable to produce the maker of the original statement rather than adduce hearsay, whether the hearsay statement was made contemporaneously and whether any person involved has a motive to conceal or misrepresent matters.[182] In this way, although the evidence is admitted, other relevant factors are considered when deciding what weight to place on it.

In relation to electronic documents there is a British Standards Institution Code of Practice for Legal Admissibility and Evidential Weight of Information Stored Electronically (the BSI Code). This describes how to prove that evidence has not been altered since its creation and how to prove that a digitized image of a physical source document contained in a data file is a true copy of that source document. One of the objectives of the BSI Code is to 'maximise the evidential weight which a court or other body may assign to presented information'. In addition, following the BSI Code can also improve reliability of information, provide confidence in inter-company trading and provide confidence to auditors and regulators.

For example, if an insurance company scans all original application forms into an electronic system and destroys the originals, it will only have the electronic copies to submit as evidence if it needs to. How can the organization show that this is a true copy of the original and that it has not been tampered with or altered since it was scanned in? Compliance with the BSI Code will be persuasive when a court is establishing the weight that should be given to evidence stored on a system but in this example the company will also have commercial and regulatory reasons for wanting to ensure that the information is reliable.

The BSI Code notes that digital evidence is more likely to be accepted and given proper weight where it can be shown that it is authentic, accurate and complete and sets out considerations as to how to be able to show this. For example, an organization should have an information management policy, processes for data capture, retention, security and so on.

Key to being able to show the reliability of a document is having an audit trail. An audit trail can show that evidence has not been altered since it was created, prove the integrity of the evidence and provide a historical record of all significant events associated with the information. The BSI Code advises that audit trails must be managed, inclusive and secure.

If an organization does not comply with the BSI Code then its evidence could be attacked by the other party to proceedings as unreliable; if an organization does comply with the BSI Code then it may be better able to show the credibility of its evidence.

Of course, an organization does not necessarily have to comply with the BSI Code for all of its records. It may wish to take a risk-based approach and consider the likelihood of information being required in legal proceedings. For example, the insurance company that electronically scans in application forms and destroys the originals may need to take more care with such a system than it does with some of its internal systems. Companies should again consider evidential issues well before a document is ever needed as evidence and should build such considerations into their information management policies and when considering technology investment.

3.4 RETENTION, DELETION AND RETRIEVAL

An organization will only be able to submit and rely on evidence if it actually has this in the first place. An organization must therefore carefully consider its document management policies, including a consideration of the management of electronic information. In the USA, Morgan Stanley suffered an adverse inference for failing to produce relevant emails and their attachments in legal proceedings, leading to a jury awarding $1.45 billion damages against Morgan Stanley to Perelman and an investigation by the Securities and Exchange Commission.[183]

Of course, there are other reasons why an organization needs to keep records. These can be broken down into legal reasons, regulatory reasons and best practice.

3.4.1 Legal reasons

When considering document retention policies, an organization should first consider whether there are any legal requirements to retain information. This section looks at examples of such legal requirements in the UK but an organization operating globally should consider its requirements in other jurisdictions and whether these are more onerous than the UK. For example, the US Sarbanes-Oxley Act 2002 has requirements in relation to the retention of accounting and audit records.[184]

In the UK there are many requirements for companies to retain information for specified periods or purposes. For example, the accounting records of a company must be kept for six years from the date on which they were made for a public company and three years for a private company,[185] tax returns and records must be kept for six years, or longer if there is an enquiry into the return,[186] certificates of employers' liability insurance must be kept for 40 years[187] and records of sickness payments must be kept for three years following the year to which they relate.[188]

In some cases there can be criminal penalties for failure to retain records. Under section 450 of the Companies Act 1985 an officer of a company who destroys documents relating to the company's property or affairs is guilty of an offence punishable by a fine and/or imprisonment unless he can show that he had no intention to conceal the state of affairs of the company.

In the public sector, a public authority subject to the Public Records Acts 1958 and 1967 has responsibilities in relation to selecting records for permanent preservation and transferring these to the National Archives or other designated place of deposit.

Limitation periods should also be considered in relation to document retention. The Limitation Act 1980 sets out the time limits for the commencement of a claim – an action for breach of contract must be started within six years of the date of the breach of contract (or 12 years if made under deed) and an action in tort – such as negligence – must generally be brought within six years of the date upon which the cause of action arose – for example the date of an accident. The Limitation Act 1980 does not dictate how long records must be kept but it is sensible to take this into account and consider when documents may be required as evidence when deciding how long to keep information.

3.4.2 Regulatory reasons

As well as strict legal requirements, there are a number of regulatory authorities that govern different sectors and many of these have their own rules and guidance on document retention. Again, global organizations will need to consider global compliance, for example with the rules of the Securities and Exchange Commission in the USA.

In the UK, the *Financial Services Authority Handbook* states that insurance companies must keep copies of policy documents provided to customers for three years after the information has been provided and should consider longer retention periods.[189] Other regulators include the Civil Aviation Authority and the Food Standards Agency. In some cases regulatory rules may require information to be retrieved and produced within a specified time period and this should be factored into any document retention system.

In relation to the public sector, there is a Code of Practice on the Management of Records[190], which has been issued under the Freedom of Information Act 2000 (the section 46 Code). While not setting out retention periods, it does provide a basic set of records management requirements that all public authorities must follow. This includes ensuring that records management is recognized as a specific corporate programme with proper organizational support, a requirement to have a records management policy in place that is endorsed by senior management and regularly reviewed, and having appropriately trained and resourced staff to manage records. In relation to records themselves, an authority should have a policy of active records management, taking account of the whole life cycle of a record from creation to final disposal and this should include consideration of electronic records. The section 46 Code recommends that authorities comply with the BSI Code especially for records likely to be required as evidence and states that:

> **audit trails should be provided for all electronic information and documents. They should be kept securely and should be available for inspection by authorized personnel.**

Failure to comply with the section 46 Code can result in a practice recommendation from the Information Commissioner.

3.4.3 Best practice

For documents not subject to legal or regulatory requirements, an organization will need to consider any best practice guidance issued in relation to particular documents and carry out a risk analysis as to how long to keep information for. Questions should be asked such as 'how likely are we to need the information and for how long?', 'what will happen if we don't have the information?', 'what is good business practice?'. Organizations will also need to consider the cost involved in retaining information and whether this is justified in relation to the consequences of not having the information.

An organization should also consider the expectations of its users, customers or whoever else may expect it to retain information.[191]

3.4.4 Document retention policy

Simply retaining all documents is not the answer. Keeping everything is unlikely to be practical or cost-effective and may even lead to a breach of other legislation. The Data Protection Act 1998, for example, states that personal data should only be kept for as long as necessary for the purposes for which it was obtained[192] so if a company hangs on to customer or employee information indefinitely, it may fall foul of this. The Freedom of Information Act 2000 allows requests to be made to public authorities for information that they hold and authorities may find themselves in difficulty dealing with requests if all information was retained indefinitely – although destroying information once a request has been received is a criminal offence.[193]

Organizations need to understand what requirements they are subject to and there is a range of guidance available to assist with legal, regulatory and best practice retention periods. For example, there is guidance from the National Archives for the public sector,[194] from the Chartered Institute of Personnel and Development for HR records[195] and from the Institute of Chartered Secretaries and Administrators for company-related documents.[196]

Using appropriate guidance, together with its risk analysis, an organization should create a document retention policy – or review any existing policy. This will not just achieve legal compliance but will facilitate access to and use of information within an organization, allow an organization to protect its legal rights – for example by knowing what intellectual property it has as a business – and facilitate the disclosure process in litigation. Having a document retention policy that an organization can demonstrate is appropriate and is properly followed may also assist in showing the authenticity and reliability of electronic evidence if needed in a court or tribunal.

3.4.5 Storage, archiving and destruction

Organizations must consider how documents are stored to ensure that these are available when needed. For example, consideration must be given to security, access and how documents are retrieved, back-ups and disaster recovery. Again, a risk analysis should be undertaken.

Compliance with ISO 17799, the security standard, will help to demonstrate the integrity of stored information and this is increasingly being seen as the accepted security standard for organizations. It contains best practice guidance on areas such as information security policies, compliance, access controls and business continuity management, taking a risk management approach. This is discussed in more detail in Chapter 6.

There is also ISO 15489 on Information and documentation – Records Management. The scope of this standard is to ensure that 'adequate records are created, captured and managed'. Again, as part of compliance with this standard, an organization is advised to identify the regulatory environment that it works within and to:

> establish, document, maintain and promulgate policies, procedures and practices for records management to ensure that its business need for evidence, accountability and information about its activities is met.

It defines the necessary characteristics of a record as being something that is authentic, reliable, has integrity and is useable. A record that can be shown to have these characteristics may attract more weight as evidence than a record that cannot.

Once retention periods have been identified, disposal arrangements should be considered. First, is there a need for archiving before documents are destroyed permanently? Second, what disposal arrangements should be adopted? Again regard must be had to the security and confidentiality of disposal arrangements.

3.5 ELECTRONIC SIGNATURES

It is important to consider the function of electronic signatures, the different types of electronic signatures and their validity. This is because an electronic signature can be used as evidence – if the validity of the electronic signature can be proved, then this can help to prove the validity of the document it is attached to. For example, if two companies enter into a contract but rather than signing a hard copy of a contract, the chief executive of each company sends an email to the other using an electronic signature, attaching a copy of the contract and agreeing to the terms of the contract then is this a valid contract and what weight can be given to the electronic signatures if there is any dispute that the contract has been agreed?

In this section the term electronic signature is used as an umbrella term for any type of electronic signature. The term digital signature is generally used to refer to a specific type of electronic signature sent using public key infrastructure or PKI. In simple terms a digital signature involves a private key and a public key, together with a certificate – usually provided by a certification service provider. The person sending the message uses their private key. The message goes via the certification service provider who authenticates the key, attaches a certificate and forwards the message to the intended recipient. The recipient unlocks the message using a public key. All of this in practice is carried out by computer using algorithms.

3.5.1 Common law

Prior to any legislation specifically relating to electronic signatures and the Law Commission Report, discussed below, the courts have been prepared to consider electronic means of communication.

In *Re a Debtor*[197] a faxed signature was accepted as valid and in *Hall v Cognos*[198] it was held that the act of typing a name into an email was sufficient to constitute a signature.

3.5.2 Electronic Signatures Directive

In 1999 the European Union issued the Electronic Signatures Directive.[199] Recital 4 of the Directive states that:

> divergent rules with respect to legal recognition of electronic signatures and the accreditation of certification-service providers in the Member States may create a significant barrier to the use of electronic communications and electronic commerce; on the other hand, a clear Community framework regarding the conditions applying to electronic signatures will strengthen confidence in, and general acceptance of, the new technologies.

Its aim was first to ensure that electronic signatures were legally recognized and second to regulate certification-service providers although it recognized that certified digital signatures were not the only form of electronic signature that should be accepted as valid.

The Directive defines an electronic signature as: 'data in electronic form which are attached to or logically associated with other electronic data and which serve as a method of authentication'.

An advanced electronic signature is defined as meeting the following requirements:

(a) it is uniquely linked to the signatory;

(b) it is capable of identifying the signatory;

(c) it is created using means that the signatory can maintain under his sole control; and

(d) it is linked to the data to which it relates in such a manner that any subsequent change of the data is detectable.

This is intended to refer to a more secure form of signature than other electronic signatures although in practice it is difficult to establish that a signature is uniquely linked to a signatory because even a certified digital signature can be open to abuse if a person other than the intended signatory has access to the private key used to send the message – for example because the key is stored on the signatory's computer and someone else gains access to this.

Article 5 of the Directive deals with the legal admissibility of electronic signatures and states that advanced electronic signatures that are based on a qualified certificate – discussed below – and created by a secure signature creation device will satisfy the legal requirements of a signature in the same manner as a handwritten signature and should be admissible as evidence in legal proceedings. In relation to other electronic signatures these should not be denied legal effectiveness and admissibility solely on the grounds that they are:

- in electronic form, or

- not based upon a qualified certificate, or

- not based upon a qualified certificate issued by an accredited certification-service provider, or

- not created by a secure signature-creation device.

In other words, all forms of electronic signature should be admissible as evidence. What the Directive does not do is define the weight that should be given to different forms of electronic signature, this remains a matter for the courts.

The Directive also defines the requirements for qualified certificates and certification-service providers. For example, a qualified certificate must contain the name of the signatory or a pseudonym, signature verification data that corresponds to signature creation data under the control of the signatory and the identity code of the certificate. As a member state, the UK was required to implement the Directive into national law by 2001.

3.5.3 Electronic Communications Act 2000

The Electronic Communications Act 2000 (ECA) is the first UK piece of legislation dealing specifically with electronic signatures. It is titled 'An Act to make provision to facilitate the use of electronic communications and electronic data storage...'. It was designed to implement certain of the Directive's provisions.

Section 7(2) defines an electronic signature as:

So much of anything in electronic form as:

(a) is incorporated into or otherwise logically associated with any electronic communication or electronic data; and

(b) purports to be so incorporated or associated for the purpose of being used in establishing the authenticity of the communication or data, the integrity of the communication or data, or both.

Section 7(1) states:

In any legal proceedings:

(a) an electronic signature incorporated into or logically associated with a particular electronic communication or particular electronic data; and

(b) the certification by any person of such a signature,

shall each be admissible in evidence in relation to any question as to the authenticity of the communication or data or as to the integrity of the communication or data.

What the ECA was aiming to ensure was that an electronic signature, which was attached to some other communication or document, was admissible in court as evidence of the validity of that communication or document. However, like the Directive, it does not address the legal weight to be given to such evidence, this remains for the courts to decide.

The ECA also contains an enabling power to allow any other piece of legislation to be amended to allow for the use of electronic communications or storage instead of other forms of communication or storage where, for example, the legislation required something to be done in writing or delivered by post.[200]

3.5.4 Law Commission Report

The Law Commission Report of 2001, referred to above, looked at the legal status of electronic documents and electronic signatures in English law. It reviewed the UNCITRAL Model Law on Electronic Signatures, which considered that handwritten signatures were used for the following purposes:

> (1) to identify a person;
>
> (2) to provide certainty as to the personal involvement of that person in the act of signing;
>
> (3) to associate that person with the content of a document.

This focuses on an electronic signature being able to identify the signatory and to indicate their approval of the contents of the message, rather than trying to find an electronic equivalent to various types of paper documents or signatures. In other words, the format of the electronic signature does not necessarily matter, it is the intention behind it that matters.

Under English law, the Law Commission noted that there are few statutory signature requirements. An example is a deed recording the sale of a property, which must be in writing and which requires a signature. The question to consider was whether the legal requirement for something to be in writing and for a signature would include electronic documents or signatures. If it did not then the provision referred to above in section 8 of the ECA would need to be used to amend legislation to include the possibility of electronic formats.

UNCITRAL identified the functions of paper-based documents or requirements for something to be in writing as to provide tangible evidence of the intention of the parties to be bound; to help parties to be aware of the consequences of entering into a contract; to provide a document legible to all; to provide a permanent record of a transaction; to allow a document to be reproduced and copies to be held by all parties; to allow authentication by way of a signature; to provide a document in a form acceptable to public authorities and courts; to finalize and to record the intent of the author; to allow easy storage in tangible form; to facilitate control and subsequent auditing for accounting, tax and regulatory purposes; and to create legal rights where writing is a legal requirement. Not all of these need apply in every case.

Having regard to the legal definition of writing in the Interpretation Act 1978, noted above, as well as the UNCITRAL view of the functions of something being in writing, the Law Commission came to the view that emails and website transactions fall within the natural meaning of writing without the need to amend the legal terminology.

In relation to signatures, the Law Commission noted that other forms of identification have been accepted other than a person's full name. For example, a person can use initials or even an 'X' to indicate their signature. The most important factor is that the signatory intends to authenticate the document. The Law Commission decided that in authenticating intention there is a requirement for 'something which is not purely oral and which evidences that authenticating intention'.[201] The Law Commission suggested that the test should be 'Would the conduct of the signatory indicate an authenticating intention to a reasonable person?'[202]

The Law Commission considered digital signatures (using PKI), a manuscript signature scanned into a computer, the typing of a name – for example into an email – and clicking on a website button. In each case the Law Commission concluded that these were capable of demonstrating the necessary authenticating intention of the signatory and should be enforceable under English law. Again, however, not all methods are as reliable as something like a digital signature and it is still for the courts to determine the weight to be given to an electronic signature.

For example, if the managing director of a company enters into a contract for the purchase of some new software via email and he uses his digital signature – authenticated by a certification service provider – to attach to this email, the company selling the software can be confident that the message has not been tampered with. However, it does not necessarily mean that the person using the signature is who they say they are, it simply shows that they had access to the electronic signature. Nevertheless, this may be considered more reliable than the managing director purchasing the software online where his 'signature' is his clicking on the 'I Accept' button.

3.5.5 Forms of electronic signatures – Electronic Signatures Regulations 2002

The Law Commission report was influential in the way in which the Electronic Signatures Regulations 2002 (ESRs) were drawn up. The ESRs use the Directive definitions of an electronic signature and an advanced electronic signature.

They regulate certification-service providers in relation to the issuing of qualified certificates for digital signatures and implement the parts of the Directive relating to the supervision of certification-service providers and their liability.

It is interesting to note that the European Commission is unsatisfied with the take-up of advanced electronic signatures and issued a report in March 2006[203] on the progress of the operation of the Directive. However, the report suggests that the growing use of electronic ID cards as well as the use of electronic signatures in egovernment services such as tax returns should all improve take-up and development of such signatures in the future.

3.5.6 Forms of electronic signatures – in practice

As well as digital signatures using PKI – discussed in more detail in Chapter 6 – and the typed signatures, 'I Accept' buttons and scanned signatures discussed by the Law Commission, passwords and PINs, tokens and biometric measurements are all capable of authenticating a person and, depending on the context, showing their intention to be bound. However, the status of a sender's email address as a signature on its own and automatic signatures inserted into emails is unclear.

In practice, an organization should again consider a risk-based approach to authentication. For example, a biometric measurement such as an iris scan or fingerprint has the advantage of better identifying a person than, say clicking on a website button or sending an email, both of which are open to misuse. However, it has the disadvantage of being costly to set up and, to avoid misuse, consideration still needs to be given to verifying the identity of individuals before the biometric data is collected.

If an organization asks people to sign up for a free newsletter on its website, it does not really matter who the person is. If, however, a company is entering into contracts worth millions of pounds, more thought should be given to ensuring the legal enforceability and reliability of these contracts.

Bear in mind that whatever form the electronic signature takes, the issue is the quality of evidence that shows that it is authentic, that the person intended to be bound by it and that the communication it is associated with has not been altered. Organizations should consider how to show that a document is genuine and audit trails will be important here. The advantage of digital signatures is that there is a clear, independent audit trail in place.

REFERENCES

Legislation

- Public Records Acts 1958
- Public Records Acts 1967
- Civil Evidence Act 1968
- Interpretation Act 1978
- Limitation Act 1980
- Companies Act 1985
- Civil Evidence Act 1995
- Data Protection Act 1998
- Human Rights Act 1998
- Electronic Communications Act 2000
- Freedom of Information Act 2000
- Electronic Signatures Regulations 2002
- Sarbanes-Oxley Act 2002 (US Act)
- Criminal Justice Act 2003

Cases

- *Hollingham v Head* [1858]
- *Hart v Lancashire and Yorkshire Railway Co.* [1869]
- *Grant v Southwestern and County Properties Ltd* [1975]
- *Derby & Co. Ltd v Weldon* (No 9) [1991]
- *Alliance & Leicester Building Society v Ghahremani* [1992]
- *Re a Debtor* (1996)
- *Hall v Cognos* (1998)
- *British American Tobacco v Cowell & McCabe* [2002] Australian Case
- *Jones v University of Warwick* [2003]
- *Douglas and others v Hello! and others* (No.2) [2003]

Other Resources

- Civil Procedure Rules – see May (ed) (2006) *The White Book Service,* Sweet and Maxwell, London
- Harner, A. (2004) *The ICSA Guide to Document Retention.* ICSA Publishing, London
- ISO 15489:2001 *Information and documentation – Records Management,* British Standards Institution, London
- ISO 17799:2005 *Information technology – security techniques, Code of Practice for information security management,* British Standards Institution, London
- Law Commission (2001) *Electronic Commerce: Formal Requirements in Commercial Transactions*
- www.opsi.gov.uk – for legislation referred to including Civil Evidence Act 1995
- Riem, A. & Wilkinson, C. (2006) What to e-disclose, *Solicitors Journal* (www.solicitorsjournal.com)
- Shipman, A. (2004) *Code of Practice on Legal Admissibility and evidential weight of information stored electronically,* British Standards Institution, London

4 Intellectual Property

JONATHAN EXELL

4.1 OVERVIEW OF IPR

Intellectual property (IP) and intellectual property rights (IPR) refer to the rights and property that can arise or be acquired from intellectual creations. The first recorded forms of IP existed in the 15th century and the laws and systems have evolved over time to those in existence today.

This text is intended to provide a background and some basic guidance on IP, identifying protection available and potential issues. It should not be considered a substitute for professional advice.

Intellectual property rights are national rights and are defined by national laws. This text focuses on UK law and practice, although many of the principles are common throughout the world, particularly in respect of Europe. Key non-UK law and practice is identified.

4.1.1 Non-registrable and registrable rights

There are two types of IPR: those that subsist automatically (non-registrable) and those that require registration in order to subsist. Figure 4.1 illustrates this division.

The various rights are discussed in detail in the following sections.

Intellectual property systems

In most countries, intellectual property law is implemented in a two-tier system. A national patent or IP office is responsible for accepting, processing and granting patent, trade mark and registered design applications while the courts of that country provide a forum for IPR infringement to be enforced and for IPR validity to be contested.

With a handful of exceptions that will be discussed in their relevant sections, IP rights are national rights and must be secured and enforced in their respective nation.

4.1.2 Copyright

Copyright automatically protects original works. Copyright protection extends over a wide range of artistic and business-related fields: books and other literary works, plays, paintings, music, sculptures, broadcasts and photography etc. An important point to note is that copyright does not protect an idea – it simply protects the particular way in which the idea is expressed. Where the text of a short story, say, is protected by copyright, it is not an infringement to write a story with the same 'twist' provided different words are used.

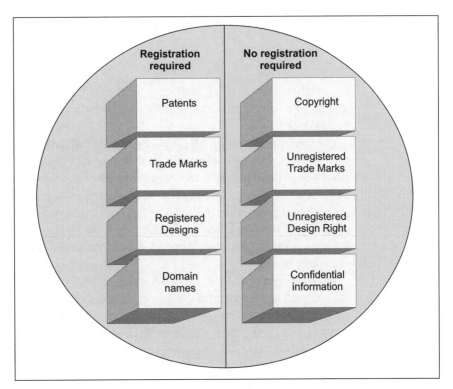

FIGURE 4.1   *The two types of intellectual property rights*

Background and origin

The scholars of Ancient Greece and the Roman Empire were the first to be concerned about being recognized for their works. However, control over works was not a great issue in view of the limited number of people able to read and write at that time.

The invention of the printing press in the 15th century resulted in the ability to print books easily and cheaply and raised the issue of piracy. Major changes in the availability of works required a form of copyright protection.

As the number of printers increased in England, the King exercised the royal prerogative to regulate the book trade and protect printers against piracy. This was the first of many decrees to control what was being printed and was probably the first form of copyright in the UK.

For a number of years, this form of 'copyright' was primarily used to seize books suspected of containing matters hostile to the Church or Government.

The 1709 Statute of Anne was the first UK Act of Parliament relating to copyright in which books and other writings gained protection. It defined an author as the owner of copyright and provided a fixed term of protection for published works.

Copyright law in the UK is set out in the Copyright, Designs and Patents Act 1988. However, this has been amended numerous times by various other Acts of Parliament – many of which enact EU Regulations in the area. If referring to specific provisions, care should be taken to ensure the text relied upon is up to date.

Works protected

Copyright is a property right that protects original literary, dramatic, musical and artistic works, published editions of works, sound recordings, films and broadcasts.

Computer programs, their preparatory materials and databases are treated as literary works. Copyright protection also covers operating manuals, instruction booklets and publicity material. No registration procedures are required, but it is wise to keep carefully signed and dated evidence of original work.

Copyright protection in the UK exists – also referred to as subsists – automatically if the work has been 'fixed' in some manner. Normally, a work must physically exist, even if encoded on a computer-readable medium, for copyright to subsist.

For copyright to subsist, the work must be original. Originality is normally understood to mean 'not copied' and is a relatively low threshold.

Generally, there is no copyright in a name, title, slogan or phrase, although these may be eligible for registration as trade marks. Similarly, copyright cannot protect an idea, it may protect the work that expresses an idea but not the idea behind it.

Although some countries require that copyright works are marked with the international © mark, followed by the name of the copyright owner and year of publication, this is not essential in the UK or most other European countries. However, it is advisable to mark the copyright work to deter copying.

As a form of intellectual property, copyright can be bought, sold or otherwise transferred. Copyright owners can choose to license others to use their works while retaining ownership over the rights themselves.

Protection provided

The copyright owner has the right of preventing others from:
- copying the work;
- issuing copies to the public;
- performing, showing or playing the work in public;
- broadcasting the work or including it in a cable programme;
- making an adaptation of the work;
- importing, possessing, selling, exhibiting or distributing an infringing copy; and
- dealing with items or providing premises used for making infringing copies.

For the last two acts, knowledge or reason to believe that the copies are infringements is usually necessary. Shutting ones eyes to the obvious is not enough to avoid infringement. Infringement is in respect of a whole or a substantial part of a work.

For most purposes, copyright lasts for the life of the author plus 70 years. For qualifying articles such as artistic works that are industrially produced, protection lasts 25 years. (This avoids anomalies with regard to articles protected by Registered Design.) These terms only apply to work originating in the UK or another state of the European Union. In all other cases the term of protection is that granted by the country of origin of the work.

Copyright exists independently of the medium on which it is recorded. Buying a copy of a book or CD does not necessarily give you the right to make further copies – even if they are for private use. Photocopying a work, scanning a work to produce an electronic copy or downloading a copy that is in electronic form all involve copying the work and will also require permission.

In the case of software, there are various additional rights. The copyright owner can prevent others from:

- permanent or temporary copying of the program, including where this is required to run, store, load or display the program – although the lawful acquirer will have the right to use a computer program for its intended purpose, including error correction, unless agreed otherwise;

- translation, adaptation, arrangement or other alteration of a program – this would catch compilation or decompilation;

- putting into circulation or possessing for commercial purposes any means the sole intended purpose of which is to facilitate the unauthorized removal or circumvention of any technical device that may have been applied to protect a computer program – device should be interpreted very broadly in this context and may include algorithms, software, hardware and possibly instructions.

The English High Court has decided on occasion in software copyright cases that copyright can be infringed by non-literal copying. Reference to the original work is required when the new work is produced but the original work need not be copied line for line. Use of architectures, algorithms or sequences underlying a computer program could be copyright infringement if a substantial part of a programmer's skill, labour and judgment has gone into them.

In *John Richardson Computers Ltd v Flanders*,[204] even though the alleged copied work was written in a different programming language, similarities at the user interface level were found to be sufficient for copyright infringement.

More recently, *Navitaire v easyJet Airline Co*[205] concerned copyright infringement of a computer-based reservation system. The source code was never made available to easyJet and it was never disputed that the languages, code and architectures used in each party's system were different. The Judge held that:

- the command set (a command language) used by the system was not protected by copyright either as individual commands – they do not have the necessary qualities to qualify as literary works – or as a whole;
- business logic implemented in the functionality of a program is not itself protected by copyright – note that the expression would most likely have been found to have been protected but copying at this level was never argued.

International copyright

Copyright is a national right and where more than one territory is involved the issues can become extremely complex. There is a principle called 'national treatment' that underpins international aspects of copyright. Countries providing such national treatment provide authors and publishers of other countries with the same rights, protection and remedies as its own authors and publishers.

Expert guidance should be sought on any issues in this area. However, as a general rule:

- the law of the nation where the work is created will determine the author and ownership; and
- the law of the nation where an infringing act takes place will determine whether copyright subsists and whether there is infringement.

Moral rights

Various moral rights are granted to authors of copyright works including:

- the right to be identified as the author or director of the work, for example when copies are issued to the public;
- the right to object to derogatory treatment of the work; and
- the right not to have a work falsely attributed to them.

Moral rights are concerned with protecting the personality and reputation of authors. The right to be identified must be asserted, i.e. the author or director must indicate their wish to exercise the right by giving notice to this effect. The right to be identified and the right to object to derogatory treatment can be waived by the author or director.

Moral rights do not apply:

- in computer programs;
- where ownership of a work was originally vested in an author's employer;
- where material is used in newspapers or magazines; and
- in reference works such as encyclopaedias or dictionaries.

Database rights

In addition to its contents – which may be copyright protected works in their own rights – a database may be protected by two copyright-based IP right: copyright and database rights. Under copyright law, a database is usually defined as a collection of data or other material that is arranged in a systematic or methodical way so that the items are individually accessible. Copyright protection covers any forms of database that fall within this definition, not just computer-based ones.

For copyright protection to apply, the database must have originality in the selection or arrangement of the contents. For database right to apply, the database must be the result of substantial investment.

There is no registration for database right – it is an automatic right like copyright and commences as soon as the material that can be protected exists in a recorded form. Database right can apply to both paper and electronic databases.

The term of protection for database right is much shorter than for copyright. Database right lasts for 15 years from creation or publication. However, whenever a database is updated, the term of protection recommences.

Database right provides the rights to control extraction and reutilization of the contents of the database. To infringe database right, a person must extract or reutilize a substantial part of the database.

It should be noted that databases are normally a collection of copyright works where copyright in the work will exist independently of the database. When compiling a database, permission should be sought from the copyright owners for use of their material. When using a database, the rights of copyright owners of the content should be considered as well as database right owners. Where a database has been delivered online, there will often be a contractual agreement between the database owner and the user setting out what use is permitted, and this will generally take precedence over any exceptions in the law.

Database rights are a relatively new type of IPR and there has only been limited guidance from the courts on their scope and effect. The most prominent case to date is *British Horseracing Board (BHB) v William Hill*.[206]

BHB claimed the publication by William Hill of data, extracted from BHB's database, concerning the runners and riders in British horse races on its website, was an infringement of its database rights. The English High Court held William Hill to have infringed the BHB's database right. However, as database rights originate from EU law, the appeal was referred to the European Court of Justice (ECJ). The ECJ held that the quoted £4 million annual cost for running the database was largely for creating the data, not the database. As the data extracted and reutilized by William Hill had not required substantial investment by the BHB, it did not constitute a substantial part of the contents of the database. BHB also argued that William Hill had infringed by the repeated and systematic extraction and reutilization of insubstantial parts of the BHB's database. The ECJ held that the reasoning behind this provision was to prevent repeated and systematic extractions of data, the cumulative effect of which would be to reconstitute or make available the whole or a substantial part of the contents of the database. As William Hill had only taken insubstantial parts of the BHB database – albeit on a daily basis – the ECJ held that there was no possibility that the cumulative effect of William

Hill's insubstantial extractions could lead to the taking and making available of the whole or a substantial part of the BHB's database.

The ECJ's decision has been followed to date by the English courts and appears to have reduced the potential scope of protection provided by database rights by focusing the requirement for a 'substantial investment' in the production of the database without taking into account costs in producing the content.

4.1.3 Patents

A patent is a monopoly right in an invention. Patents generally cover how things work, what they do, how they do it, what they are made from or how they are made. A patent can cover not only such things as an electronic circuit, a chemical product, heavy machinery or a control system, but also small household items such as a tin-opener. It can also cover processes such as a new or improved process of making a new material or a new method of navigation. In certain situations, patents can also cover software-based inventions.

Background

The origins of patents for invention are obscure and no one country can claim to have been the first in the field with a patent system. However, Britain does have the longest continuous patent tradition in the world. Its origins can be traced back to the 15th century, when the Crown started making specific grants of privilege to manufacturers and traders.

The first recorded patent was granted in England in 1449. King Henry VI awarded a patent to John of Utynam for stained glass manufacturing. This patent established the notion of a state-granted limited monopoly. There was nothing novel at the time about the art of stained glass making. However, the monarchy recognized the value of protecting certain arts and industries, including those that were imported from other parts of Europe – in this case Italy.

Starting in 1552, 'letters patents', open letters marked with the King's Great Seal, were issued by the Crown. The monarchy granted patents for its own benefit and for the benefit of officers and friends of the Court. Patents were issued on entire industries, not just inventions. For example, the Stationers enjoyed complete control over the publishing industry in England.

In an effort to curb such abuses of power, Parliament, in 1624, passed the English Statute of Monopolies, which outlawed all royally sanctioned monopolies. Realizing the importance of protecting inventors and the economic benefits associated with encouraging innovation, an exception was allowed for patents of 'new manufactures'. These patents were awarded to the inventor as long as their new devices did not hurt trade or result in price increases. Additionally, a statutory limit of 14 years was imposed on English patents.

Today's patents remain a bargain between the state and an inventor. A monopoly of 20 years is granted in return for teaching the invention to the public.

The UK Patent Office alone receives 30,000 patent applications per year. At any one time around 295,000 granted patents are in force in the UK.

Monopoly provided

A patent provides a monopoly that can be used to restrict others from making, selling or using an invention without permission.

Of course, a UK patent only restrains commercial activity in the UK. To restrain activity abroad, you must have a patent in the relevant country. Also it is important to note that you cannot initiate legal proceedings for infringement until your patent has actually been granted. To mitigate the effects of this it is possible in certain circumstances to back date a claim for damages to the date of publication of the patent application – which happens long before grant.

What is patentable?

What is, or is not, patentable is determined by national law. However, all patent systems, to some extent require:

- novelty;
- inventive step; and
- industrial applicability.

In addition, many patent systems, such as those in European countries have exclusions from patentability for certain fields.

Novelty and inventive step

To be patentable, an invention must be novel and also involve an inventive step at the time of filing. The requirement of novelty is absolute. The invention must not have been published – made available to the public in verbal or written form, by use or in any other way – anywhere in the world before the initial patent application is filed. A disclosure made under a duty of confidentiality is not considered a publication for the purposes of novelty.

Publication depends on whether the public is free and able to identify how the invention works. For example, in the case of a control system for traffic lights that has been trialled in public, operation of the traffic lights can be studied and the manner of operation identified even if the underlying programming or electronics cannot be evaluated. As such, the manner of operation will most likely be found to lack novelty. However, if the invention resided in the electronics arrangement within the traffic lights that used less power or operated more quickly for example, this would most likely remain novel assuming access by the public to the electronics was not possible. If the traffic light had actually been sold before the date of filing and there were no prohibitions on reverse engineering etc., novelty would most likely be lost for all aspects.

There are moves at an international level to introduce a 'grace period' or 'period of immunity' for those who reveal their inventions before filing a patent application. Until the law is changed one must observe the strict principle of filing before disclosure to anyone except in conditions of strict confidence. Disclosures at conferences and seminars are not exempt.

For an invention to have an inventive step, it must not be obvious to a skilled person having regard to the state of the art. In other words, to be patentable, an invention must not be obvious to someone who is skilled in the particular technology of the invention in the light of everything that was publicly known before the date on which the patent application was filed. The skilled person is assumed to have read all the relevant materials available but is not expected to be imaginative or inventive. An invention is obvious only if it follows plainly or logically from what has gone before. The nature of the problem solved, how the problem had existed, whether large numbers of people were seeking a solution and whether alternative solutions are available are all relevant when assessing inventive step. Only the prior art teachings available before the invention are considered for inventive step – hindsight is an unfair test and is not applied.

Most industrial products and processes are patentable provided they are novel and not obvious. Chemical processes, improved methods of operating already-known machinery, methods of checking parameters or product quality are all patentable. Provided a useful technical or economic result is obtained, there is generally no problem in obtaining protection. Thus for chemical processes the invention may lead to an increased yield or less pollution, or it may be cheaper to operate, or it may require a lower power input or less pure starting compounds.

For a method of operating machinery, this may lead to an improved product, or be quicker or cheaper. Methods of checking, for example inspecting the interior of pipelines, can be more reliable or quicker or require less interference with the process or product being checked.

Industrial applicability

This criterion is usually used to exclude 'impossible' inventions such as perpetual motion machines. In this context the term 'industry' includes agriculture.

Excluded subject matter

There are several areas of subject matter that UK (and European) patent law specifically excludes from being patentable. These are:
- a discovery, scientific theory or mathematical method;
- a literary, dramatic, musical or artistic work or any other aesthetic creation whatsoever – copyright or design protection is more appropriate;
- a scheme, rule or method for performing a mental act, playing a game or doing business, or a program for a computer;

- the presentation of information – again copyright protection will apply;
- any variety of animal or plant or any essentially biological process for the production of animals or plants, not being a micro biological process or the product of such a process;
- methods of treatment of the human or animal body by surgery or therapy and diagnostic methods practised on the human or animal body – products, substances or compositions for use in any such methods are patentable; and
- inventions where the commercial exploitation of which would be contrary to public policy or morality – a letter-bomb is an often quoted example.

For all but the last two areas, the exclusion only relates to the extent that the patent 'relates to that thing as such'. Taking a mathematical method as an example, it has always been possible to obtain a patent for a non-obvious invention that uses a mathematical method to achieve an advantageous result. The use may, for example, be in the use of a device or in a process, or embodied in the final form of a device. In summary, a patent application for a mathematical method would be rejected but an application for a control system that used a mathematical method would most likely be accepted.

Computer implemented inventions

For many years there has been a misconception that software-based inventions are not patentable. However, there have been many tens of thousands of patents granted in Europe and in other countries covering computer software. Part of the problem is that there are categories of computer implemented inventions that are excluded from patentability.

If the end result of a computer implemented invention does not fall into one of the other excluded categories such as a mental act, presentation of information or method of doing business then the invention may be patentable in Europe – subject to novelty and inventive step.

While patent law in Europe is based on common concepts, its implementation has often differed. This is particularly the case for granting patents for computer implemented inventions. Many inventions fall into the definition of a computer implemented invention and are generally agreed to be patentable – for example, telecommunications systems, control systems, etc.

Take, for example, the following examples of patents granted for software inventions. These have been selected as being closer to the borderline between what is and is not allowable. There are many granted patents for inventions that include software components where problems are not even encountered. The commentary provided on why the patents were most likely granted are the author's opinions only:

Data Processing System (GB1274768). This patent was granted under the previous version of the UK Patents Act and in fact covered spreadsheets. It was dressed up to look like hardware – a dodge that patent examiners are now very aware of and does not work. It is unlikely that such a patent would have been granted under the current laws.

Complier (GB2391348). This patent covers an improved compiler in which non-invasive information on compilation is obtained and used to improve effectiveness of compilation without the intervention of a programmer. The patent was originally objected to for being directed to a computer program but was granted after a hearing. The decision stated that the ability to modify compilation in response to performance data, results in a faster, more accurate and adaptable compiler that constituted technical advances rather than cosmetic changes that took the invention beyond being a computer program as such.

Proxy server (EP0892947). This patent covers a proxy server for mobile devices in which downloaded web pages are transposed into appropriate size and resolution for the device. During a UK patent infringement action brought by the proprietor, Research In Motion, the defendant, Inpro Licensing SARL, argued that the patent was directed to a mere collection of computer programs and was excluded from patentability. The Judge disagreed, saying that 'the claims give this a technical effect: computers running faster and transmitting information more efficiently, albeit ultimately for the purpose of displaying part of that information'.

Graphics file format (EP129439). This patent was directed to a method and system of compressing data that was faster and produced better compression ratios on data – particularly image data – than prior methods and systems. The method was used for the GIF file format. It was not a specific software algorithm that was claimed but rather a new and non-obvious way of compressing data that could have been implemented in circuitry as well as in software.

Computerized diary scheduling system (EP326778). This patent covers a diary scheduling system that operates over a network. Meeting invitations are displayed simultaneously to a number of users allowing them to accept, reject or save the invitation. The operation of the system over a network and simultaneous display of data were most likely key to avoiding rejection of this case as a computer program or presentation of information as such.

Computer file system (EP375188). This patent covers a computer file system and method in which physical disk space is divided into large blocks. At least some of the large blocks are subdivided into smaller blocks. When a file is created, it is designated as small or large. If a file classified as large is extended, it is allocated an appropriate number of large blocks. If a small file is extended then it is allocated an appropriate number of small blocks. The intention was to manage disk space allocation to avoid small files wasting space if they were written to large blocks. An additional advantage was that, where possible, files were written contiguously to avoid excessive head movement while reading. It was most likely decided that this was not a computer program as such because a physical disk was being controlled.

Teaching systems (EP461127). This patent covered an interactive learning system in which selected model text is displayed and also converted to audio and output to the user. The user's own speech is recorded and played back after the model text to enable comparison. The claims in this case were directed to a system including storage for the model text and a text-to-speech system that amounted to more than a computer program as such.

MP3 data structure (EP287578). This patent covers the digital coding process for audio signals used for the MP3 format. The patent was most likely granted for the same reasons as that covering the GIF format, discussed above.

Amazon 1-click (EP927945). There was a great deal of controversy concerning the US version of this patent which covers an online system allowing customers to enter their credit card number and address information just once so that on follow-up visits to the website all it takes is a single mouse-click to make a purchase from their website. Amazon successfully enforced the US patent against Barnes and Noble. The European patent cited above was ultimately granted but is much more restricted than its US counterpart. Its claims in fact do not even directly cover 1-click ordering but instead are concerned with buying gift purchases. The purchaser identifies the intended recipient of the gift and the system communicates with the recipient to arrange delivery etc. Amazon is still pursuing an application[207] with many similarities to the corresponding US patent but this is still under examination.

Full details of these and other patents can be found at http://ep.espacenet.com.

Patent applications are more likely to be rejected for lacking novelty or inventive step than because they are directed to excluded subject matter. For example, EP0390041 – directed to a system in which a cursor could be moved diagonally using a single keystroke – was rejected for lacking inventive step.

In the past few years, the European Commission and Parliament attempted to pass a law that would clarify what aspects of computer implemented inventions are patentable. A great deal of press coverage was given to this. Unfortunately, much of it was inaccurate. For example, a number of stories stated that if the law was passed, scroll bars used in graphical user interfaces would be patentable. The overriding requirements of novelty and inventive step – which would have prevented grant of such a patent – were overlooked. The proposed law would not have made computer implemented inventions patentable for the first time, nor would it have opened up the possibility of business method patents, it was merely an attempt to make the national procedures applied by patent offices and courts consistent – indeed, the proposed law was based on those already being performed by the UK Patent Office.

There are opponents of 'software patents', particularly the supporters of open source software who argue that patents covering software are damaging to innovation and competition. This argument has little to do with software per se and there has been a notable lack of evidence showing specific damage to the software field. It can in fact be argued that patents are one of the few ways a small innovative company can protect its ideas from the bigger players in the market. It is relatively common for the smaller companies to be bought specifically for their IPR and there is as much evidence that patents are beneficial as there is to the contrary. Unfortunately, those against patents were much more efficient and vocal in their lobbying and so much confusion was created that the European Parliament rejected the proposed directive outright. The overall effect is that patents for computer implemented inventions are still patentable, it is just that your application or patent may be treated differently in different EU countries – even though they have the same law.

Recently, a series of test cases[208] have caused the UK Court of Appeal to specifically consider patentability of business methods and computer programs in what is referred to as the Aerotel/Macrossan decision. While this decision does not substantially change the approach applied by the UK Patent Office and courts – it is still essentially as described above – it criticizes the often-contradictory approaches applied by the European Patent Office in this area. The approach adopted by the UK Court of Appeal is different to that currently applied by the European Patent Office. While all of the approaches are said to lead to the same result – which is what you would hope for given the written law that is being interpreted is word for word identical – this is unlikely to always be the case. This is an area of particular concern because while an inventor may be able to secure grant of a patent via the European Patent Office that covers the UK, the patent may later be found to be invalid during infringement proceedings in the UK – which are dealt with by the UK Courts using UK-based procedures/approaches.

Steps in obtaining a patent

Although individuals may file a patent application, applicants are strongly advised to obtain professional advice since patent procedure is not simple and mistakes can result in not getting the best protection for an invention. Many applicants who do not employ professional advice find that their granted rights are not adequate for their needs or that it is too easy for a competitor to design around them.

Figure 4.2 illustrates the steps involves in obtaining a patent in the UK.

A patent application must include:

- a technical description – called the specification – of the invention that is clear and complete enough for the invention to be reproduced

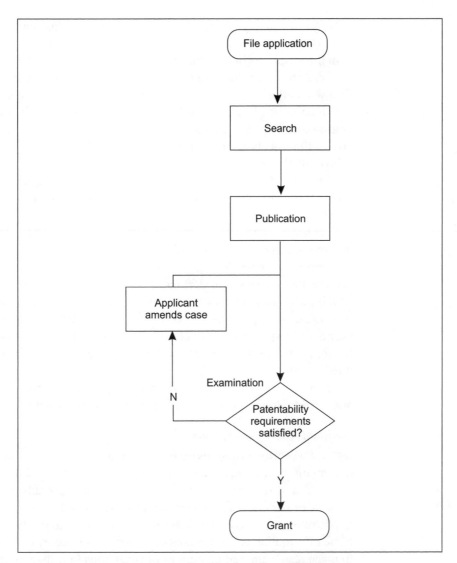

FIGURE 4.2   *Steps in obtaining a UK patent*

by a person skilled in the technology of the invention. The description does not limit the scope of protection and is merely illustrative; and

- one or more claims that define, in words, the matter for which protection is sought. The claims are what limit the scope of protection and determine whether someone infringes or not. The claims are also what are evaluated for novelty and inventive step. If claims are too broad, they will not be novel or inventive – if they are too narrow, a patent would be granted for something that is easily designed around and therefore has limited value.

The search is based on the claims filed and identifies any prior art published prior to the date of filing the patent application that the Patent Office considers falls within the scope of the claims.

At approximately 18 months from filing the application, it is published by the Patent Office (copies are available at http://gb.espacenet.com) along with the results of the search. This is the first time the contents of the patent application are available to the public. From this point onwards, details of the prosecution of a patent application are publicly available.

The applicant has six months from publication to request examination. During examination, a Patent Office official examines whether or not the application meets all the requirements of the law for example, is it new? Is it inventive? Is there sufficient disclosure? The applicant is advised of any objections and is given the opportunity to amend the application to address them. At the end of this process and, assuming all has gone well, a patent is granted.

After grant, an annual renewal fee will have to be paid to keep the patent in force – subject to a maximum term of 20 years.

At grant, the specification and claims are published again and it is this version that is relevant for infringement. If you look at published applications – their publication number ends with an A – the claims may look incredibly broad and unsupportable. However, for infringement purposes it is only the claims of the granted application – their publication number ends with a B – that is relevant. The claims will most likely have evolved and narrowed during examination.

The average length of time between filing a patent application in the UK and the decision by the Patent Office to grant or refuse it is three to four years.

National security provisions

National security provisions exist within patent systems of a number of countries including the UK, USA and France to prevent sensitive information being disseminated without that nation's permission. Generally, where national security provisions exist, an applicant is required to file his or her first patent application for an invention in his or her country of nationality or residency. If the information is deemed sensitive, a national security order may be put in place restricting publication or other actions in respect of the invention. In the UK, these provisions only apply in respect of military technology or information prejudicial to national security.

Paris Convention and priority rights

A single national patent can have value. However, most companies do not have a single country as their market. For commercially important inventions, patent protection is normally desired covering a number of countries – typically the USA, at least part of Europe, possibly Japan. Among other things, the Paris Convention was drawn up to make the absolute novelty requirements that these countries apply compatible with the possibility of filing for patent protection in multiple territories.

The Paris Convention provides priority rights to an applicant that enable him or her to file subsequent patent applications within 12 months of his or her first patent application for that invention and yet benefit from the filing date of the first application. In this way, all applications for that invention benefit from the first filing date for novelty and inventive step purposes. Disclosures made in the first 12 months can be discounted and it is even possible to have the first application searched within the 12 months to determine whether expenditure on other applications is worthwhile. The date of filing of the first application is called the priority date.

Patent systems

In addition to national patent offices, there are various collective patent systems that can be used for filing patent applications covering more than one country. These systems keep prosecution central and in some cases keep costs down. However, they do not ultimately result in a collective patent. For example, a patent application can be filed and prosecuted at the European Patent Office covering most European countries – and some others. However, upon grant, the European Patent breaks down into a bundle of national patents, just as if a patent application had been filed and prosecuted in each country. There is an International Patent System called the Patent Cooperation Treaty (PCT), through which provisional protection for over 100 countries can be secured. However, in order to progress an international application to grant, it must ultimately be prosecuted within each country of interest according to their national laws and procedures.

Third-party interaction

While the public may observe aspects of the prosecution of a patent application after publication at 18 months from the priority date, they are not normally able to take part in the prosecution proceedings. Before grant of a patent application in the UK, it is possible for the public to submit third-party observations on the novelty, inventive step or other aspects of a patent application. These will be taken into account by the UK Patent Office examiner when deciding whether or not to grant the application. After grant, it is possible to request revocation of a patent at the UK Patent Office or via the courts. Revocation is often requested during infringement proceedings and grounds for revocation are discussed in the section dealing with infringement.

Some patent offices, including the European Patent Office, have a post-grant opposition procedure in which interested parties can oppose the grant of a patent without having to resort to the costs involved in going to court.

Petty patents/utility models

Although patents are the only true way of securing a monopoly on how something works or is manufactured in the UK, some jurisdictions – principally Japan, China, Korea, Taiwan and Germany – offer a petty patent or utility model system. This is similar to the patent system except that there are typically lower costs, a lower duration for protection and limited or no examination – typically validity is assessed upon attempted enforcement.

In some cases, a lower threshold – or possibly no threshold – is applied to inventive step.

US patent system

Although the US patent system shares a number of concepts with the UK including novelty and inventive step, there are also significant differences. It is worth noting that there are slight differences in terminology too. In the USA, patents are called 'Utility Patents' and registered designs are called 'Design Patents'.

The key differences include:

- **Entitlement to a patent.** Entitlement is determined on a first-to-invent basis rather than first to file. This is important because in the USA it is possible to 'swear back' and establish an earlier filing date to overcome prior art or actually take over another person's application or patent through interference proceedings. Elsewhere, as long as the applicant is entitled to grant of a patent, the first to file for a patent is awarded grant. For example, if two scientists A and B independently invent something, outside of the USA the scientist who will be awarded a patent for the invention would be the first to file a patent application. In the USA, the scientist who can prove he or she invented the invention first would be awarded the patent, irrespective of whether they filed first.

- **One-year grace period.** A disclosure made within 12 months of filing in USA is not counted against the patent for purposes of novelty or inventive step.

  Note that novelty in other countries applies on a worldwide basis so a disclosure made up to 12 months before filing may not count against a US patent application but would do elsewhere.

- **Excluded subject matter.** Very little subject matter is excluded from patentability. US patent law requires an invention to have a useful, concrete and tangible result to be awarded a patent. Laws of nature, natural phenomena and abstract ideas are generally not patentable. So long as there is a practical real-world application then an invention is generally patentable is the USA – it does not even have to be that useful, a recent patent has been issued for a method of swinging a swing. Business methods are also patentable in the USA.

  The key decision in this area is *State Street Bank & Trust Co. v Signature Financial Group*.[209] This was a decision made in 1998 by the US Federal Circuit – approximately equivalent to the English High Court – in which a business method was decided to be patentable in the USA, irrespective of whether it was computer implemented. The patent in question was directed to a data processing system for implementing an investment structure that was developed for use in Signature's business as an administrator and accounting agent for mutual funds. Mutual funds have their assets pooled into an investment portfolio organized as a partnership, providing the administrator of the mutual fund with the combination of economies of scale in administering investments and the tax advantages of a partnership.

- **US national security provisions.** A patent must be first filed in the USA if the invention is first made – reduced to practice – in the USA. If a patent is to be first filed elsewhere then permission must be first sought from the US Patent Office for a foreign filing license.

4.1.4 Other types of intellectual property

Confidential information

There is no registration process for confidential information; rather, it must be protected by agreement to keep the information confidential. It can cover anything that has the necessary quality of confidence about it and is not in the public domain. In order for there to exist a duty of confidence, the information must be communicated in circumstances where the confidant ought reasonably to have known that the disclosure had been made in confidence. Furthermore, for a breach of confidence action to be successful, there must be a risk of damage from the information being used or disclosed in an unauthorized way.

Confidentiality is generally used to protect technical and commercial information that is not patentable. It can embrace the minor details of a manufacturing process that, although not necessarily inventive, are essential for a commercial product to be obtained. Examples are the tolerances involved in the manufacture of an article, and the detailed operating procedures of a machine. Of course, such information is valuable only so long as it is kept confidential. Thus, persons or companies should make sure that they take adequate steps to keep details secret, and make sure that everyone in the organization knows this. Also, when negotiating a transfer of technology, it is important not to disclose know-how until it is covered by a written agreement. Once published, it is not reasonable to expect anyone to pay for it.

The existence of know-how is a useful back-up in case a patent is not granted, since it still enables royalties to be charged – even if at a reduced rate. If a binding know-how agreement is broken by unauthorized use of the information or by unauthorized disclosure it will be possible to bring a legal action for breach of contract.

While a duty of confidence can arise through a verbal disclosure, this can be difficult to prove and it is common for confidential information to be distributed on media marked as such. Ideally, a non-disclosure agreement (NDA), also known as a confidentiality agreement, should be signed by the receiving party prior to disclosure. Breach of confidentiality is typically a breach of contract and dealt with as such by the courts.

Trade marks and passing off

Trade marks protect the way in which goods and services are identified. As evidenced by discussions in the financial press over recent years, trade marks are now widely recognized as very valuable company assets. One only needs to refer to the instant worldwide recognition achieved by such marks as Kodak and Coca-Cola.

Background

The marking of goods to identify their crafter can be traced back to ancient times. However, it was only in the 19th century that the idea of a trade mark, as is known today, came about.

Trade mark protection generally does not come about by registration of a company name at companies house or by registration of a domain name and mere registration of either of these is no guarantee that you can trade using that name or domain.

There are two types of trade mark: registered and unregistered.

A registered trade mark involves the owner of the mark registering it with a country's Trade Marks Registry as a mark applying to one or more classes of goods or services. Owners of registered trade marks have the exclusive right to the use of their marks in the territory in which the mark is registered.

It is not essential to register a mark and many marks are used unregistered. A disadvantage of unregistered use is that it is much more difficult to prevent competitors from appropriating the goodwill in the mark. To do this, in the UK, one must resort to the common law and to a legal action known as 'passing-off'. This protects the reputation associated with products and services on the market. It applies not only to unregistered marks but also to instances where a competitor attempts to confuse customers by adopting a similar package or 'get-up' to that used for an existing product or service.

The principle of passing off is that a third party cannot lawfully pass itself or its goods or services off as being yours, being associated with you or being in some way authorized by you. Passing off can take many forms, from using the same trade name to get up of goods or premises. It is necessary, however, that you possess so-called 'goodwill', in the UK – defined as 'the attractive force which brings in custom'; that there is a 'misrepresentation' – such as confusion on the part of the public as to trade origin; and that this is likely to cause you damage.

Registered trade marks are identified with the symbol ® while unregistered marks are followed by the letters TM.

A trade mark is not necessarily the same as the name of a business, for example, the mark 'St. Michael' is employed by Marks and Spencer. A trade mark is a word or device (logo) or a combination used to distinguish one's goods or services from those of one's competitors.

Registered trade marks

A trade mark or service mark can be registered by filing an application at the Trade Marks Registry, which is part of the UK Patent Office.

Monopoly provided

A registered trade mark provides exclusive rights to its proprietor to use the trade mark for the goods or services for which it is registered.

A major part of the value attributed to trade marks is due to their association with goodwill for a brand. Trade marks can help customers and traders to recognize a business and identify it with the quality of product or service for which the company is known. Brands are central to marketing programmes and it is a trade mark that protects the distinctive elements that make up the market identity element of most brands. Many celebrities seek to profit through merchandizing using the reputation of their name. By registering their name as a trade mark, they can control the way their reputation is used to endorse products in the marketplace.

Due to the different nature of trade marks from patents and registered designs, their registration can be extended indefinitely provided renewal fees are paid. A trade mark is first registered for 10 years and then renewed for a fee at 10-yearly intervals. Subject to renewal, trade mark protection is indefinite in duration. In the UK, a registered trade mark must be in constant, relevant use.

What can be a trade mark?

Almost anything can be a trade mark. Most good registered trade marks are made up words, shapes, logos or combinations – it is easier to state what cannot be a trade mark.

To be registrable, the mark should not be misleading nor should it be descriptive of the goods or services covered. Surnames and geographical names can be difficult to register. In addition, an official check is made to ensure that a proposed mark is not confusingly similar to an existing registration or application in respect of similar goods or services.

The mark must act as a badge of origin for a product or service. Sometimes, a mark may be eligible because it has been in use for some time and is recognizable as belonging to somebody already. Laudatory terms normally may not be registered, nor may descriptive terms in the relevant class – for example 'apple' in grocery – so that all traders retain basic freedoms.

Registrable marks include: names, logos, shapes, colours, smells, jingles etc. For example, the distinctive shape of the 'Coca-Cola' bottle and perfume bottles are registrable, the smell of strong bitter beer for dart flights has been registered.

It is necessary to register a trade mark in respect of relatively specific goods and services. For example, UK registered trade mark No. 1 is for the mark 'Bass & Co's PALE ALE' and is registered for pale ale. It is common for more goods and services to be covered, although broad ranging coverage of goods and services is only usually allowed for well-known trade marks.

On average, 80,000 trade marks are registered in the UK each year.

It is possible to oppose registration of a trade mark during or after registration.

It should be noted that unlike patents and registered designs, there is no worldwide novelty requirement for trade marks. Indeed, it is possible to register a trade mark many years after public use as long as nobody else has beaten you to the post. Similarly, different owners can hold the same registered trademark in different countries. The mark BUDWEISER is a classic example: in some countries it refers exclusively to the beer brewed by the Czech brewery; in some countries the trade mark is owned by the USA brewers of Bud.

Trade mark systems

As with patents, in addition to national trade mark registration systems, there are various collective systems through which trade marks can be registered. Most notably, the European Union operates a European trade mark system through which a European trade mark registration can be obtained. Unlike with patents, the European trade mark remains a single right that covers the whole of the EU and only one renewal fee is payable.

Domain names

In its strictest sense, a domain name is not an intellectual property right. A domain name is simply an internet address that is leased from a generic domain register operator – such as .com, .org or .net – or a country-level domain register operator – such as .uk.

However, in a similar manner to trade marks, domain names have acquired a further significance as business identifiers and, as such, have come into conflict with the system of business identifiers that existed before the arrival of the internet and that are protected by IPRs.

In the early days of the web, domain name registration operated on a first-come, first-served basis and once someone had registered a domain name, it was theirs to do whatever they wished until their lease expired due to non-renewal.

This quickly gave rise to cybersquatting. Cybersquatters exploit the first-come, first-served nature of the domain name registration system to register names of trade marks, famous people or businesses with which they have no connection. Since registration of domain names is relatively simple, cyber-squatters can register numerous examples of such names as domain names. As the holders of these registrations, cybersquatters often then put the domain names up for auction, or offer them for sale directly to the company or person involved at prices far beyond the cost of registration. Alternatively, they keep the registration and use the name of the person or business asso-ciated with that domain name to attract business for their own sites – this in itself could be passing off or trade mark infringement depending how it is done.

Most of these registry operators have developed, or are in the process of developing, specific dispute resolution policies designed to resolve disputes occurring during a start-up, or 'sunrise' phase of a domain. In the case of the .eu domain, two sunrise phases were provided. The first allowed owners of registered trade marks to reserve associated domains and the second allowed those with unregistered trade marks and the like to reserve associated domains. Only once the two sunrise periods ended were the general public allowed to register .eu domains.

Where cybersquatting is encountered, beyond negotiating with the cyber-squatter and walking away, there are two options: court action and using a dispute resolution procedure such as the UDRP (Uniform Domain Name Dispute Resolution Policy) provided by ICANN (Internet Corporation for Assigned Names and Numbers).

UDRP is limited to certain domain types and only in cases of abusive registrations (cybersquatting) where a trade mark is involved. The only available remedy is cancellation or transfer of the registration (no damages). However, the proceedings are generally only in writing and are quick (45–60 days) and relatively cheap. Nominet offers a similar procedure for .uk domains.

Many well-known companies including Marks & Spencer, Ladbrokes, Sains-bury, Virgin and British Telecom have taken cybersquatting disputes to court for trade mark infringement and have won.

Where there is no abusive registration, it is not necessarily the case that a registered trade mark holder will always have the upper hand – although registration always helps prove you are serious about the trade mark. In the case of *Prince v Prince*,[210] a British computer consultancy company had registered *www.prince.com* in good faith and were using it. The USA company Prince, who manufacture sports equipment had a US trade mark for, among other things, sports goods. They had no registered trade mark in the UK or anywhere for that matter for computer consultancy services. They threatened to sue the British company for infringement of the US trade mark. The British company counter-sued in the UK for unjustified threats of trade mark infringement and won. The US company had to settle for *www.princetennis.com*.

Designs (registered and unregistered)

Registered designs
Registered designs protect the appearance of a design. The protection is a monopoly, in that to show infringement by a competitor it is not necessary to prove copying. It is sufficient to show that the articles look the same.

Background
Laws protecting designs originated in the UK in the 18th century to protect those designing and printing fabrics. In the mid-19th century, a registration system was introduced and the system was extended to include articles of manufacture.

In 2001, the European Designs Directive came into force bringing harmon-ized design law throughout the European Union. The directive broadened

UK registered designs law such that it is the design itself that is protected rather than the article to which the design was applied.

Monopoly provided

Design registration gives the owner a monopoly on their product design. For a limited period, the owner may stop others from making, using or selling a product to which the design has been applied, or in which it has been incorporated, without their permission. This is additional to any design right or copyright protection that may exist automatically in the design.

Initially the right lasts for five years, renewable every five years to a maximum of 25 years. Like any other business commodity, it can be sold or licensed under terms agreed with the registered owner.

What designs can be registered?

A registered design is a monopoly right for the appearance of the whole or part of a product, resulting particularly from the features of lines, contours, colours, shape, texture and materials of a product or its ornamentation.

Protection can also be obtained for the 'get-up' of a product, for graphic symbols – such as computer icons – and typographical typefaces.

A registrable design may be:

- a new article – for example, the shape of a computer case;
- a new part of an article – for example, an elaborate switch for the computer case;
- a new two-dimensional pattern or ornament suitable for use on an article – for example, a decorative pattern for a plate, or fabric etc.; or
- a new computer icon.

There must have been a 'freedom of design' in the creation, so where a jug has a distinctive shape it is registrable because it could have had many other shapes and still have been a jug. However, where form is dictated by function, or dictated by the need to fit with other parts – for example, a brake pad, which needs to fit in the callipers – no registration is possible.

The design must be new on the day the application is filed, that is to say not likely to be previously known anywhere in the world by a designer working in the same field. Furthermore, the design must have 'individual character'. This means it must not give the notion of déjà vu in the mind of an 'informed user', namely one familiar with the product in question who is not a designer.

The design will still be judged as novel on the filing date even if the designer has disclosed their design – for example, sold it – at any time in the 12 months prior to filing. This one-year 'grace period' allows designers to test the market before deciding if registration is appropriate. However, any disclosures by others of designs that are the same or similar, even if they occur during those most recent 12 months, will count against the applicant when assessing novelty.

A design may constitute the whole or a part of a product, a part being taken to mean an individual feature that is an integral piece of a product as distinct from a 'component part' that can be removed or replaced. Thus, a registered design can cover the head of a toothbrush, for example. Furthermore, registered designs can now also protect a one-off product, rather than a product manufactured in quantity, which was not the case previously.

Protection is not necessarily limited to features on the outside of a product. For example, protection can be obtained for the appearance of the inside of a suitcase.

Furthermore, the features of the design must not be dictated solely by their technical function. However, interlocking components – such as plugs and sockets – can be protected.

The registered design covers any designs that do not produce on the informed user a different overall impression. This definition is fraught with difficulties and no doubt will result in much litigation over the next few years. The only real guidance at present is that the scope of a registered design will depend upon the freedom that the designer had in choosing the design and in what was known in the industry before the date of the registered design. Thus, highly functional designs where the designer must respect given parameters are likely to be infringed only by very similar designs.

How are designs registered?

An application for design registration only requires a few pictures showing different views of the design, and an indication as to what the design might be applied to – though this does not limit the legal protection just to that application. Registration is possible even for handicraft items and one-off items.

Registered design systems

The European Union operates a European registered design system through which a European design registration can be obtained. Unlike with patents, the European registered design remains a single right that covers the whole of the EU and only one renewal fee is payable.

Unregistered design right

Unregistered designs are a version of copyright that protects any original aspect of the shape or configuration of the whole or a part of an article. As with copyright, copying of the design or a substantial part of it must be proven for infringement.

Independent production of a similar design is not an infringement.

There are a number of important distinctions from copyright. There are currently two forms of design right in the UK. The first form comes from old UK copyright law and only protects shapes. There is no protection for surface patterns. Protection lasts for either 15 years from creation or 10 years from first marketing, whichever expires earlier. The second form is based on current registered design law and covers anything that satisfies the criteria for a registered design but only for three years from first marketing in the EU.

4.2 FIRST OWNERSHIP OF IPR

The owner of IPR is usually its author or creator. If the author or creator is employed and the creation of the IPR is in the course of their employment then the first owner will be the employer. No assignment is necessary to effect ownership by the employer in this situation. If an employee's duties do not include anything that would be expected to result in the creation of IPR – for example if the employee was a cleaner – any IPR created would be owned by the employee. In the case of directors, a greater duty to the company is expected and it is quite likely that the company will own IPR created by its directors.

A contractor normally retains the copyright in any commissioned work unless their contract is explicit to the contrary.

For the purposes of copyright, the author of a computer-generated work is 'the person by whom the arrangements necessary for the work to be generated are undertaken'.

Joint ownership (and inventorship or authorship) of IPR is possible. In assessing whether there is joint ownership, the courts typically look at the contributions made by participants.

4.3 LICENSING AND ASSIGNMENT

Licences and assignments are merely contracts and can contain whatever provisions the parties are willing and able to include.

In every case, general provisions in law about what contractual terms are acceptable need to be considered carefully as well as the nature of the IP that is the subject of the contract. In particular, competition law and company law may be relevant.

An assignment is typically an outright transfer of rights by the holder of the rights (the assignor) to another party (the assignee).

A licence involves a continuing relationship between the rights holder (the licensor) and the organization wishing to exploit the rights (the licensee). The relationship may involve the continuing flow of information and technical assistance from the licensor in return for financial payments or royalties from the licensee. Improvements to the technology might be made in the future by either party and these can also be covered in the initial licence agreement.

4.3.1 Assignments

There are some specific formal requirements for IP assignments. In the UK, patent assignments must be in writing and require the signature of the assignor, elsewhere it is still the case that assignments must be signed by both parties and some countries, such as Canada, require witnesses. In certain countries including the UK, there is a deadline – typically six months from the date of execution – for registration of assignments at the relevant Patent Office. If this deadline is missed then damages from subsequent infringement proceedings may be restricted until registration is completed. An assignment of copyright in the UK must be in writing and signed by the assignor.

4.3.2 Licences

A licence gives the right to do something that would otherwise be an infringement of rights. As far as licensing is concerned it is a permission to do something, which the law says is the exclusive right of the owner of the IPR, which is licensed.

Only the owner of the IPR can grant a licence – if there is more than one owner then all must agree. However, any inventor may make and sell the product without a licence from any co-inventor.

Normal licences are non-exclusive – the number of licensees who may be granted a licence is not limited. However, there are two special licence types commonly used in IP.

- Where the licensee and licensor are permitted to perform the acts covered by the licence, this is referred to as a sole licence.
- Where IPR is licensed to the exclusion of even the person who owns the IP, this is known as an exclusive licence. Such a licence could be worthwhile where IP owners do not want to exploit the IP themselves as it may be possible to seek a higher royalty payment than for a non-exclusive licence.

There are many reasons for granting a licence.

(1) It may be the easiest way to gain entry to a particular market. The licensee may be well established in a particular market with marketing and distribution resources, customer base and reputation needed to exploit the IP and product(s).

(2) The licensor may be granted a cross-licence in return and gain access to a right that will enhance its own business.

(3) It may be the simplest and most cost-effective way of resolving an infringement of the rights in question.

(4) A licence removes the risks inherent in manufacture and sale.

When it comes to negotiating a licence it cannot be over-emphasized how important it is for both parties to have a common understanding of everything that is involved. Do not assume that one party's understanding of a particular technical or legal term is the same as that of the other party. Simple misunderstanding on issues such as the basis upon which a percentage royalty rate is to be calculated can and do occur. While it is not possible to completely specify all the topics that a licence should cover there are certain basic issues, which should always be considered, as follows.

- Subject of the licence – specific reference to a patent or some other enforceable right will usually form the basis here.
- Rights being granted – what is the licensee being given permission to do?

- Payment – how is it to be calculated? Should it be a percentage of the selling price or a fixed sum per item? Upon what basis should any percentage be calculated? When should payment be made? Can the payment be independently audited?

- Warranties – if, for example, a licence is based on a patent then the licensee may require the licensor to indemnify them against infringement actions by agreeing to defend the action and pay any legal costs or damages.

- Improvements – if the licensee produces improvements to the invention or product, how does this affect the licence? Does the licensor have access to these improvements?

- Disputes – any licence should contain a provision on how to deal with any disputes between the parties that occur during the life of the licence. It can be very expensive if, for example, the licensor is based in one country and the licensee is based in another.

- Term of the licence – how long does the licence last? Can it be terminated before full term and if so under what circumstances? For example, company takeover.

- Continuation after lapse of the IPR – if the patent, trade mark or registered design lapses or expires, does the licence continue, if so is it on the same terms?

- Termination – one or both parties may wish to terminate the licence for a whole host of reasons such as non-payment of royalties, bankruptcy of either party, and a whole host of terms and conditions in the agreement that are not adhered to – for example, the licensee producing goods of inferior quality or the licensor not supplying agreed 'know-how'. Clearly it is desirable for the licence to cover these eventualities.

- Applicable law – if the other party is not based in the same country, chances will be that they will want the agreement to be governed by the law of the country in which they are domiciled.

Competition law is applicable to licence agreements and care should be taken to ensure provisions do not have the object or effect of preventing, restricting or distorting competition within the UK/EU.

IP rights can normally be exercised without fear of breach of competition law – for example you can use patent rights to control who is authorized to sell a patented article in a territory. However, there is a generally accepted principle called the doctrine of exhaustion that only allows IP rights to be applied once within Europe. A patented article bought from a licensee of the patent in one EU territory can normally be sold in another territory – even if patent rights exist there too – because the patent rights are said to have been exhausted – the proprietor has already received the benefit.

As far as software and database licences are concerned, additional provisions may be included such as:

- Can the software be transferred to another machine or is it tied to a single machine?
- What rights does the licensee have in respect of data migration?
- Do they have sufficient rights to obtain information on database, program or data structure and format?
- Is there provision for access to the source code by the licensee via escrow or the like – for example if the licensor was to go out of business?

Open source software/GNU General Public License (GPL)

Although there are various forms of open source software licences in existence, the GNU General Public License appears most used at present.[211]

Open source software licences are a standardized form of licence. However, they typically include provisions that require source code of the software to be available to anyone on request and that royalty free licences are normally required for any patents or patent applications associated with a product sold that uses open source code.

GPL licences are written to ensure: users have the freedom to distribute copies of the software – and charge for this service if they wish; that source code can be obtained; and that the software can be changed or pieces of it be used in new applications.

No warranty is generally provided in GPL licensed software and this can be an issue to some purchasers. However, it can be seen why warranties are avoided – it is unlikely that the author will be responsible for all components. If the software is modified by someone else and passed on, it would be foolish to warrant other's work.

Shrink-wrap licences

In a shrink-wrap licence, acceptance on the part of the user of the terms of the agreement is indicated by opening the shrink-wrap packaging or other packaging of the software, by use of the software or by some other specified procedure. Shrink-wrap licences may, among other things, restrict the use of the software, declare the governing jurisdiction, disclaim legal warranties and limit the availability of monetary damages. The English courts have declared such licences valid. In the case of *Beta v Adobe*[212] it was held that the terms of a licence created by a software producer had been validly incorporated into a contract between the customer and a software distributor. Although the licence terms were not brought to the customer's attention until the software packaging was opened, it was held that the contract between customer and distributor was not concluded until this stage. The licence offered the customer an unqualified right to reject the software if its conditions were considered unacceptable, a right that was held to be enforceable against the distributor. It will be appreciated that such licences allow the normal privity of contract principles to be bypassed, creating a contract between the software producer and purchaser, even if the software was not directly purchased from the software producer.

Shrink-wrap licences are starting to appear in the USA on hardware items. In one case, printer cartridges were offered at a discount if the purchaser agreed not to refill the cartridge through anyone other than a licensed refiller. In 2005, a lower US court has indicated that this practice is acceptable as long as the item in question was patented. It may well be tested at a higher court level.

Click-wrap and browse-wrap licences

Terms such as click-wrap and browse-wrap are being more and more regularly used to describe licences where a user indicates acceptance of a licence prior to downloading or installation of a software product. While these licences have not been tested in the English courts, it is likely that they will follow a similar logic to the above decision in shrink-wrap licences. If there is an unambiguous agreement by the licensee to the terms of the licence then the licence will most likely be found to be enforceable.

Freeware and shareware

Freeware, as the name suggests, does not cost any money. However, it is still copyrighted, and will include some form of licence agreement in which its modification and usage are limited or prohibited. In the case of shareware, licence terms typically stipulate that a licence must be purchased for commercial use or use beyond a set trial period. By using freeware or shareware, the user is accepting the terms of the licence agreement and breach would constitute breach of contract and possibly copyright infringement.

4.4 INFRINGEMENT

The uses that are restricted by IP depend on the IP right and have been discussed in their respective sections. It is important to remember that much material will be protected by more than one IP right.

For example, a music CD will generally involve copyright in both the music and the sound recording itself, performers' rights for the singers and musicians and a trade mark for the company under whose label the CD is sold. The band's name may even be a trade mark. There will also be copyright in any graphics on the insert of the CD case.

A cooling fan for a central processing unit (CPU) may involve patent rights in several different aspects of its design and operation. Each patent may be owned by a different person. Additionally, there may be registered design or design right protection in the shape of various components.

You may need a licence if you want to use anything protected by IP. This will largely depend on what uses are restricted by the IPR and whether there are any exceptions to these restricted uses. Otherwise, use without permission will infringe an IPR and you could be sued by the right holder.

It is important understand the restrictions on use of IP. This will depend on what type of IP it is.

For example, copyright gives the creator the right to control copying and first publication of works. Another creator who has independently thought of something similar, that is they have not copied from the first creator, would not infringe the first person's rights.

The registered rights – registered designs, patents and registered trade marks – give monopolies so that even someone who does not know of the IPR could perform an act falling within the scope of the IP and would not have permission to use the IP.

In some very limited cases, a use that does fall within the scope of what is restricted by the IP right may not require the permission of the IP owner. For example, doing something for private or experimental purposes relating to the subject matter of an invention is not normally an infringement of a patent. Similarly, an act that is done for private or experimental purposes that would normally be an infringement of a registered design is not normally an infringement.

In registered trade marks, it is not an infringement to:

- use a person's own name and address – if either happened to be a registered trade mark;
- use a registered trade mark that is an indication of kind, quality, quantity, intended purpose, value, geographical origin, time of production or rendering or other characteristics of goods or services; or
- use a registered trade mark where it is necessary to indicate the intended purpose of a product or service, for example for spare parts.

In the case of patents, registered trade marks and registered designs, you cannot generally be prevented from doing something you did before the date of application of the IPR. For example, if someone happened to patent something that you had done – and not made public – before their application was filed, they would be awarded the patent but would not be able to stop you continuing that act. Similarly, if you used a sign, mark etc. in the course of trade and someone subsequently registered a trade mark for it, your use would co-exist with their rights and could not be stopped. Prior user rights are typically very limited and you would not normally be allowed to expand your use – for example license someone else for the act covered by someone else's patent.

There are many exclusions – and exclusions to those exclusions – from infringement of copyright. The more common ones are highlighted here:

- Making a transient copy of a copyright work for the purposes of transmission of the work, in a network or for a lawful use of the work, is not an infringement of copyright. This exception covers situations such as caching content while browsing a website.

- Decompilation of software for interface production and making back-up copies of software is not normally an infringement of copyright.

- Limited use of copyright works is also permitted for research and private study, criticism or review, reporting current events, judicial proceedings and teaching in schools. However, copying large amounts of material or making multiple copies will require permission. Publication of excerpts, such as quotes, from a copyright work will require an acknowledgement.

There are special provisions applying to the use of programme listings for television, radio etc. A publisher of a newspaper or magazine cannot be stopped from using the listings of any channel, although a royalty fee is normally payable. Recording broadcasts for time-shifting purposes does not infringe copyright in the broadcast or any work included in it as long as the recording is made for personal and domestic purposes and is made in domestic premises.

It is important to remember that just owning a copy of a copyright work does not give you permission to use it in a way that would infringe copyright.

Exceptions do not generally give you rights to use IPR; they just state that certain activities do not infringe. So it is possible that an exception could be overridden by a contract you have agreed limiting your ability to do things that would otherwise fall within the scope of an exception.

Someone planning to use IP should carefully consider whether they need to seek a licence. This is often the safest route and avoids any doubt of infringement. Often, an organization representing the user's interests may be able to give more advice about such matters.

Another possible, but not common, use without permission can occur in the case of compulsory licences. Compulsory licences are generally granted in the situation where the rights holder fails to 'work' the invention. For example, if a company obtains rights to an invention and then fails to work the invention – i.e. sell the patented article, use the patented method, etc. – and refuses to license the patent rights to another company to work the invention, a compulsory licence may be applied for through the courts who will set reasonable licence terms if these cannot be agreed.

4.5 IPR AND THE INTERNET

Although IPR such as patents are national rights, use of the internet to position servers etc. offshore does not necessarily avoid infringement. This was discussed in *Menashe Business Mercantile Ltd v William Hill*[213] in which the judge stated:

> If the host computer is situated in Antigua and the terminal computer is in the United Kingdom, it is pertinent to ask who uses the claimed gaming

> system. The answer must be the punter. Where does he use it? There can be no doubt that he uses his terminal in the United Kingdom and it is not a misuse of language to say that he uses the host computer in the United Kingdom. It is the input to and output of the host computer that is important to the punter and in a real sense the punter uses the host computer in the United Kingdom even though it is situated in Antigua and operates in Antigua. In those circumstances it is not straining the word 'use' to conclude that the United Kingdom punter will use the claimed gaming system in the United Kingdom, even if the host computer is situated in, say, Antigua. Thus the supply of the CD in the United Kingdom to the United Kingdom punter will be intended to put the invention into effect in the United Kingdom...A punter who uses the William Hill system will be using the whole system as if it was in the United Kingdom. He will in substance use the host computer in the United Kingdom, it being irrelevant to the punter where it is situated.

Similar decisions have been reached in the USA concerning both patent and trade mark infringement where not all infringing acts are within the territory in question.

4.5.1 Copyright and the internet

Copyright law applies on the internet just as it does to paper.

It is an infringement of copyright to post material on a website without the consent of the copyright holder. This applies whether the site is on an intranet – accessible only to members of an organization – or the internet.

The internet is subject to copyright in many different ways:

- Web pages and any textual articles contained on a web page are separate literary works. Graphics are generally artistic works, while any sound files are sound recordings that contain separate musical works. In a single web page there are likely to be many different copyrights.

- To copy and paste anything from a web page into a document of your own or to print out a web page, you should have the permission of the copyright owner. Many websites contain a copyright notice detailing how the material they contain may be used. Permission may already have been granted within this notice.

- While the practice of including a hyperlink to someone else's web page is generally accepted and often welcomed, 'deep linking' and 'framing' are more controversial. In the case of deep linking, the website's homepage is bypassed. One of the reasons complaints arise from deep linking is that the terms and conditions and advertising on most sites are found on or linked to their home page and deep linking bypasses this. Best practice is to check a site's linking policy and seek clarification from the site where necessary. You should only link directly to pages and not images, sounds and video as this could give the impression that the material is yours and would be a potential copyright infringement. Framing differs from linking in that instead of providing a direct link to another page, it imports a page into the framing site. The framing site links to another site, but the crucial difference is that it displays the linked content within a frame including content from the framing site. This practice has attracted legal action in that it is seen as effectively hijacking another site's content as opposed to a straightforward link.

One particular area where copyright infringement is being applied at present is against peer-to-peer file sharers and the underlying networks. In January 2006, two men were ordered to pay the British Phonographic Industry (BPI) between £1,500 and £5,000 for copyright infringement by illegally making thousands of songs available online. One of the men said he did not know he was acting illegally. The other said there was no evidence against him. The cases, in which both men were ordered to stop sharing files illegally, were the first of their kind to be heard in the British courts. The first defendant said there was no direct evidence of infringement, but the judge dismissed this and ordered him to make an immediate payment of £5,000. His total costs are estimated at £13,500 and damages are expected to take the bill even higher. The other man said he was unaware that what he was doing was illegal and did not seek to gain financially. His defence was also thrown out, with the Judge declaring: 'Ignorance is not a defence.'

The BPI has launched over 140 cases, most being settled out of court for up to £6,500. Other media companies and organizations are pursuing similar cases with similar results.

4.6 ENFORCEMENT

Enforcement of IPR in the UK is typically slow, expensive and complex. The Chancery Division of the High Court will hear all IP actions but the complexity of most cases will require a legal team including a barrister and possibly a solicitor or patent attorney. The Patents County Court will hear patent and registered design-related actions and is theoretically quicker and cheaper and does not necessarily require as large a legal team.

4.6.1 Copyright enforcement

Because copyright is not registered, three hurdles must be overcome to bring an action against infringers. First, you must convince a court that your complaint concerns copying. If another person's work is the same or similar to yours by coincidence then you have no case against them. Second, you must show that you own the copyright in the original work you allege has been copied. Finally, you must show that the work in question falls within the scope of those creative works afforded protection under the Copyright, Designs and Patent Act 1988.

For an act to be an infringement, it does not necessarily need to concern the whole copyright work. Infringement is defined as doing an act that is restricted by copyright in relation to the work as a whole or any substantial part of it, either directly or indirectly. A 'substantial part' is not defined and varies depending on the circumstances. Depending on the work, even very small parts of a copyright work may count as a substantial part.

Infringement is also possible:

(1) by removal or alteration of electronic rights management information without permission;

(2) by circumvention of effective technological measures – any technology, device or component in the normal course of operation is designed to prevent or restrict acts in respect of copyright works that are not permitted by the copyright owner; and

(3) by manufacture, import, distribution, sale, rental, possession or advertisement for commercial purposes of products, components or services intended to achieve either of (1) or (2).

Under the EU's Electronic Commerce Directive – applicable to all EU countries – ISPs are said not to be liable for copyright infringement by:

- acting as a mere conduit;
- caching; or
- hosting.[214]

Unregistered designs are enforced in a similar manner to copyright.

4.6.2 Patent enforcement

Granted patents have assumed validity so, unlike copyright, it is not necessary to prove a patent's validity unless it is called into question by a defence. For infringement to occur, all of the features of a granted claim must have been performed by the accused infringer or included in the infringing product. If a claim includes a requirement that is not performed or included, this is not infringement.

4.6.3 Registered trade mark enforcement

As with patents, registered trade marks have assumed validity unless it is called into question. There are various ways to infringe a registered trade mark including:

- use of identical mark for identical goods and services;
- use of identical mark for similar goods and services;
- use of similar mark for identical goods and services where there is a likelihood of confusion by the public;
- use of similar mark for similar goods and services where there is a likelihood of confusion by the public; or
- use of identical or similar mark to one having a reputation in the UK where unfair advantage is taken or use is harmful or detrimental to the repute of the mark.

4.6.4 Registered design enforcement

Registered designs have assumed validity unless it is called into question. However, unlike patents and trade marks, there is little or no examination during the registration of a design and the validity and scope of protection will be assessed during court proceedings.

Any of the following acts will infringe a registered design:

- the making, offering, putting on the market, importing, exporting or using of a product in which the design is incorporated or to which it is applied; or
- stocking such a product for those purposes.

4.6.5 Remedies

Assuming the case is found in favour of the proprietor, various remedies are available including an injunction restraining the defendant from future infringement and damages or an account of profits and costs. However, no recompense will be obtained for 'innocent' infringement, so it is important to mark your product with the trade mark number, registered design number or patent number to ensure that others are aware of the existence of your rights.

4.6.6 Injunctions

An interlocutory or interim injunction is granted to stop the defendant performing certain acts before the case reaches full trial. Such injunctions are granted in effect to stop the proprietor suffering large and irrecoverable damage by an alleged infringer during litigation proceedings leading to the trial and final court order. However, such injunctions are granted only if strict requirements are met in terms of proving irreparable damage and the proprietor giving undertakings to compensate the alleged infringer if the proprietor fails at trial.

If the proprietor is successful in proving the validity of the IPR and in proving infringement, the court will impose a full injunction against the defendant to stop the defendant repeating the infringing activity.

4.6.7 Damages and account of profits

Damages represent the monetary value of the damage incurred by the claimant (proprietor) as a result of the infringement. An account of profits represents the profits made by the infringer by the infringing activities. A proprietor has the option to elect for either damages or an account of profits.

Damages are more commonly requested than an account of profits because they can be calculated by the plaintiff, rather than having to rely on and argue over alleged profits made by the defendant. However, the actual selection should depend of the financial circumstances.

In patents cases, damages or an account of profits can be obtained from the date of the A publication of the application but only to the extent that it was reasonable to expect grant on the basis of the A publication and only if the granted claims and the A publication claims cover the infringing act.

Damages or an account of profits are also subject to the six-year limit in the Limitation Act 1980.

4.6.8 Costs

These represent the legal costs incurred in bringing the action. In theory, the court will grant the winning party its costs, which would have to be paid by the losing party. However, costs are 'taxed' by the court, in other words the court will assess the costs claimed to see whether there were any wasted costs or costs incurred in matters (points) that the winning party did not succeed on. In general, the court will only award 50–75 per cent of the costs actually incurred. Therefore, the winning party will almost always be out of pocket in terms of the legal costs.

4.6.9 Third-party support

Particularly in the case of infringement cases involving pirated or counterfeit goods, various UK governmental and non-governmental organizations may be able to provide assistance in seizing infringing articles. These include the Federation Against Software Theft (FAST), HM Revenue and Customs and Trading Standards.

4.6.10 Challenges against an infringement attack

Unjustified threats

In respect of patents, trade marks and registered designs, a third party is able to seek recourse in respect of an unjustified threat. The remedies include damages, a declaration of non-infringement and an injunction preventing such threats. Therefore, it is very important not to take any action in this regard without first seeking advice.

Avoiding a finding of infringement

If you are accused of infringement, you should check the following.

(i) Has the patent/trade mark/registered design been granted?
(ii) Is it still in force?
(iii) Does the alleged activity actually fall within the scope of protection?
(iv) Are the infringed rights valid? Consider arranging for further searches with a view to counter-claiming for revocation of the patent, trade mark or design. (The validity of the right may be challenged at any time.)

Even if all the checks are adverse you should consider 'designing around' the patent or negotiating a licence with the patentee.

Request for revocation

Revocation of registered rights can be requested at any time, although it is common for a counter-claim to be brought in response to infringement proceedings. Revocation is possible on many points, although the main ground used is that the invention, trade mark or design did not satisfy the necessary legal requirements for grant or registration.

REFERENCES

Legislation

- Limitation Act 1980
- Copyright, Designs and Patents Act 1988

Cases

- *John Richardson Computers Ltd v Flanders* (1993)
- *Beta Computers (Europe) Limited v Adobe Systems (Europe) Limited* (1995)
- *Prince v Prince* (1997)
- *State Street Bank & Trust Co. v Signature Financial Group* (1998) US Case
- *Menashe Business Mercantile Ltd v William Hill* [2002]
- *Navitaire v easyJet Airline Co* [2004]
- *British Horseracing Board (BHB) v William Hill* [2005]
- *Aerotel Ltd v Telco Holdings Ltd (and others)* [2006]
- Macrossan's Application (2006)

5 Employment

JOHN ANTELL

There are no special employment laws that apply solely to IT staff and the law covered by the syllabus applies to all sectors of the economy. However, because the use of freelance workers is more widespread in the IT industry than in many other sectors, the syllabus gives as much weight to the law relating to freelance and other workers, who may not be employees in the strict sense, as it does to the law relating to employees.

5.1 CONTRACTUAL AND STATUTORY RIGHTS

When a worker is carrying out work for an employer in return for payment there will almost always be a contract between the two parties. The contract may be in the form of a formal written contract signed by both parties or the contract may have been formed by a verbal acceptance of a job offer.

The worker – and the employer – have the contractual rights defined by the terms of the contract but the worker will generally have additional rights conferred by statute. (Strictly a statute is an Act of Parliament but regulations – called statutory instruments – can be made by government ministers under powers delegated to them by parliament, and the word statute will be used to refer to both types of legislation.) These additional statutory rights generally operate in one of two ways.

- Statutes sometimes modify the terms of the contract between the parties so as to enable the worker to sue for breach of contract not only when the explicit terms of the contract have been broken by the employer but also if the employer breaks any of the additional contract terms imposed by statute.
- Sometimes statutes do not change the contractual rights of the worker but instead give the worker statutory rights that exist in parallel with the worker's contractual rights.

Although there is some overlap, generally 'parallel' statutory rights – such as the right not be unfairly dismissed – can only be enforced in a special court known as an employment tribunal whereas contractual rights – whether under the explicit terms of the contract or under the contract as modified by statute – can only be enforced in the County Court – or, for very high value cases, the High Court. In addition the rules governing the award of compensation and what defences may be available to an employer against whom a claim is made, differ between parallel statutory rights and contractual rights.

5.2 DUTIES OF THE EMPLOYER TO THE EMPLOYEE

5.2.1 Payment of remuneration

An employee is entitled to be paid remuneration in accordance with the terms of the contract. Typically contracts of employment will provide either for an annual salary to be paid in 12 monthly instalments or for a weekly wage at a given rate per hour. There may be provision for higher rates for overtime. The National Minimum Wage Act 1998 prescribes the minimum hourly rate that may be paid.

Most contracts will provide for paid holiday and under Regulation 13 of the Working Time Regulations 1998, employees are entitled to a minimum of four weeks paid leave per year.

It is usual for contracts of employment to provide for sick pay at the full remuneration rate, often limited to a maximum period of, say, three months per year at full pay and a further three months at half-pay. The statutory minimum, known as statutory sick pay, is far less than is typically provided by contract. The statutory minimum for the 2007/8 year is: nil for the first three days than then £72.55 per week for up to 28 weeks.

There are also statutory minima for maternity and paternity pay.

5.2.2 A safe working environment

Every employer has a legal duty to take reasonable care for the safety of his employees. The employer must provide safe fellow employees, safe equipment, a safe place to work and safe access to it, and must provide a safe system of work.

'Safe' in this context does not mean zero risk. Under this general duty an employer will only be liable to an injured employee if the employer has been negligent. An employer is not required to, for example, spend enormous amounts of money eliminating very small risks, but to take reasonable measures to reduce foreseeable risks.

In addition to this general duty not to be negligent, however, many regulations issued under the Health and Safety at Work Act 1974 impose strict duties on employers so that the employer is liable if injury results from an inadvertent breach of the regulations, even if the employer has taken all reasonable care.

> **EXAMPLE**
>
> Regulation 5 of the Provision and Use of Work Equipment Regulations 1998 requires every employer to ensure that work equipment is maintained 'in an efficient state, in efficient working order and in good repair'.
>
> In *Stark v Post Office* (2000) the employer was liable for an accident caused by a defect in a postal worker's bicycle even though a rigorous examination of the bicycle would not have revealed the defect.

The Employers' Liability (Compulsory Insurance) Act 1969 requires all employers to be insured against liability to employees.

5.2.3 Rest breaks and holidays

The Working Time Regulations 1998 give employees rights to certain rest breaks, and holidays, and limit the total number of hours that can be worked each week. In general these are not simply rights that an employee can exercise or not as he pleases but they are, in many cases, requirements that the employer has a legal duty to insist its employees comply with.

- Every employee who works more than six hours a day is entitled to an uninterrupted rest break of at least 20 minutes.
- Employees must have a break of at least 11 consecutive hours in each 24-hour period.
- Every employee is entitled to at least one day (period of 24 hours) off each week.
- An employee must not work more than 48 hours per week on average – averaged over a 17-week period – unless the employee has agreed in writing to do so.
- Every employee is entitled to – and must take – at least four week's holiday per year. It should be noted that while most contracts of employment provide for a least four weeks' holiday plus public holidays, the statutory minimum is four weeks in total and not four weeks plus public holidays.

Additional restrictions apply to night workers and to those aged under 18.

5.2.4 Fair disciplinary/dismissal and grievance procedures

A **grievance procedure** is a procedure designed by the employer to be used by employees who wish to seek resolution of any grievance they may have about their employment. A **disciplinary/dismissal procedure** is a procedure designed by the employer to be used by the employer when considering whether an employee should be disciplined or dismissed. Discipline and dismissal overlap in that dismissal is one of several disciplinary sanctions open to an employer, but not all dismissals are disciplinary because an employee may be dismissed because, for example, he is redundant or because he has reached retirement age, without there being any suggestion that he is being disciplined.

Disciplinary/dismissal procedure

All employers must have a disciplinary/dismissal procedure in place and, within two months of an employee commencing work, the employee must be given a written statement of particulars of employment, which includes details of the disciplinary rules applicable to the employee and of the disciplinary/dismissal procedure. The statement of particulars of employment may either itself set out the disciplinary rules and disciplinary/dismissal procedure or else may specify where they made be found – such as in an employee handbook made available to the employee. A separate statement of particulars of employment does not need to be given to employees who have a written contract of employment providing that contract specifies all the details required – the full details required in a statement of particulars of employment or written contract are specified in sections 1 to 7B of the Employment Rights Act 1996 and include the date that employment began, the rate and frequency of pay, hours of work and entitlement to holiday pay and sick pay.

Minimum statutory requirements for the disciplinary/dismissal procedure
The minimum statutory requirements are set out in Schedule 2 of the Employment Act 2002 and are as follows.

- The employer must give the employee a written statement of the employee's alleged conduct or the circumstances – for example that the employee's job is no longer needed – which lead the employer to contemplate dismissing or taking disciplinary action against the employee, and invite the employee to attend a meeting to discuss the matter.
- Before the meeting takes place the employer must give the employee details of the evidence – for example witness statements, logs or other documents – of the conduct or other basis for invoking the procedure – if the written statement gives does not itself give full details – and the employee must have a reasonable opportunity to consider his response before the meeting takes place.
- The employee has the right to be accompanied at the meeting by a fellow worker or trade union official of his choice.
- After the meeting the employer must inform the employee of the employer's decision and notify the employee of his right to appeal if he is not satisfied with the decision.
- If the employee exercises his right to appeal the employer must invite the employee to a further meeting at which the appeal will be considered.
- The employee has the right to be accompanied at the meeting by a fellow worker or trade union official of his choice.
- After the appeal meeting the employer must inform the employee of the employer's final decision.

The above summarizes the specific statutory requirements but it should be noted that the procedure as actually followed must in total be fair if the employer who dismisses is to avoid an unfair dismissal claim.

There is no specific statutory requirement to use the disciplinary procedure before issuing a warning – or suspending on full pay – and it is often appropriate to deal with minor matters informally. However, it should be noted that under section 10 of the Employment Relations Act 1999, employees have the right, if they so wish, to be accompanied at anything that could be described as a 'disciplinary hearing' even if the hearing is not held as part of the formal disciplinary procedure. In addition care needs to be taken by employers to ensure that there is not a sudden escalation from informality to the imposition of serious sanctions such as demotion or dismissal. Dismissal of an employee – for a matter that is not gross misconduct – after two previous informal warnings may be held to be unfair dismissal: if a matter has hitherto been subject only to **informal** warnings then formal warnings – using the disciplinary procedure – should be issued before dismissal is considered.

ACAS Code of Practice 1: Disciplinary and Grievance Procedures gives detailed guidance on drafting disciplinary and grievance procedures and on the way disciplinary meetings and the investigations leading up to them should be handled. The Code of Practice is not actually compulsory but in deciding whether a dismissal is, overall, 'unfair' an employment tribunal will take compliance – or lack of it – with the Code of Practice into account. In practice therefore an employer should always follow the Code of Practice unless there is some special circumstance justifying a departure from it, and in any event the minimum statutory requirements set out above should always be followed.

Important points from the Code of Practice include:

- Minor matters of misconduct or unsatisfactory performance should be resolved informally if possible.
- Disciplinary procedures should be used primarily to help and encourage employees rather than as a way of imposing punishment.
- Following the first meeting at which it is decided that an employee's performance is unsatisfactory, the employee should be given a note setting out the performance problem, the improvement that is required, the timescale for achieving the improvement, a review date and any support or training that the employer will provide to assist the employee. The consequences of failure to improve – usually a final written warning and ultimately dismissal – should be stated.
- Following the first meeting at which it is decided that an employee is guilty of misconduct, the employee should normally be given a written warning setting out the nature of the misconduct and the change in behaviour required. The consequences of failure to improve – usually a final written warning and ultimately dismissal – should be stated.
- Disciplinary rules should be specific, clear and in writing.
- The likely consequence of breaking various rules should be stated. In particular those rules – for example theft, fraud, violence etc. – the breaking of which will normally lead to dismissal for a first offence – gross misconduct – should be clearly identified.

Grievance procedure

As with the disciplinary/dismissal procedures, the grievance procedure must be specified in the statement of particulars of employment.

Minimum statutory requirements for the grievance procedure

The minimum statutory requirements are set out in Schedule 2 of the Employment Act 2002 and are as follows:

- The employee must set out his grievance in writing and give it to the employer.
- The employer must invite the employee to attend a meeting to discuss the grievance.
- Before the meeting takes place the employee must give the employer details of the grievance – if the written grievance statement does not itself give full details – and the meeting must not take place until the employer has had a reasonable opportunity to consider his response.
- The employee has the right to be accompanied at the meeting by a fellow worker or trade union official of his choice.
- After the meeting the employer must inform the employee of the employer's decision as to his response to the grievance and notify the employee of his right to appeal if he is not satisfied with the decision.
- If the employee exercises his right to appeal the employer must invite the employee to a further meeting at which the appeal will be considered.
- The employee has the right to be accompanied at the meeting by a fellow worker or trade union official of his choice.
- After the appeal meeting the employer must inform the employee of the employer's final decision.

An employee can, of course, raise grievances informally but where the matter complained about is one that can form the basis of a claim to an employment tribunal, the employee will not be able to bring a claim until he has at least started the formal grievance procedure.

Discrimination

Discrimination is the less favourable treatment of one employee compared to another, on grounds that the law prohibits, currently the grounds of sex, race, religion, age and disability. Discrimination against part-time and fixed-term employees is also restricted. The main legislation is as follows:

- Employment Equality (Age) Regulations 2006;
- Employment Equality (Religion or Belief) Regulations 2003;
- Employment Equality (Sexual Orientation) Regulations 2003;
- Fixed-Term Employees (Prevention of Less Favourable Treatment) Regulations 2002;
- Part-time Workers (Prevention of Less Favourable Treatment) Regulations 2000;
- Disability Discrimination Act 1995;
- Race Relations Act 1976;
- Sex Discrimination Act 1975; and
- Equal Pay Act 1970.

Direct and indirect discrimination

Discrimination can be classified as 'direct' or 'indirect'. An example of direct discrimination would be the situation where an employer does not offer a job, or promotion, or some benefit, to a job applicant or employee because of their race.

If the law prohibited only direct discrimination, it would be possible for an employer who wished to discriminate on the ground of, for example, race, to do so indirectly by applying a criterion that disproportionately excluded those of a particular race. For example, an employer who wished to employ as few people of African origin as possible could state that 'applicants must have blond hair' – a criterion that is not explicitly racial (because no single race has a monopoly on a particular hair colour) but that nevertheless puts certain racial groups, for example people of African origin, at a disadvantage.

In order to prevent the prohibition on racial discrimination being so easily circumvented, the law also prohibits 'indirect' discrimination, which – although defined in slightly different terms in different Acts – is essentially the applying of a provision, criterion or practice that is such that a particular group – racial group, age group, sex etc. – is put at a particular disadvantage compared to everyone else.

However, there are many requirements that employers may legitimately have that are indirectly discriminatory. A university employing a lecturer in Computer Science will doubtless require applicants to hold a first degree in Computer Science. This would be indirectly discriminatory because the proportion of different age groups, racial groups and of the two sexes who will hold such a degree will, for all kinds of reasons, vary.

The law therefore allows employers to discriminate **indirectly** if the discrimination arises from the imposition of a provision, criterion or practice that the employer can show is 'a proportionate means of achieving a legitimate aim'.

Permitted direct discrimination

The circumstances in which the law allows an employer to **directly** discriminate vary according to the type of discrimination. For example, direct sex and racial discrimination is allowed only in very limited circumstances – including, for example, waiters in a Chinese restaurant. In the case of religion, the extent to which direct discrimination is permitted depends on whether the employer has a religious ethos or not. Churches can give preference when recruiting to members of the relevant faith in appropriate cases but non-religious organizations can discriminate directly only in very limited circumstances – such as hospital chaplains. In the case of age discrimination and discrimination against part-time and fixed-term employees, the employer can discriminate directly providing the discriminatory treatment is 'a proportionate means of achieving a legitimate aim' or is 'justified on objective grounds', a wider and more general exception.

Victimization

It is unlawful for an employer to treat someone less favourably because the person has complained of discrimination or given evidence or information about discrimination against them or someone else.

A summary of the main provisions of the non-discrimination legislation that applies in different fields is given below.

Employment Equality (Age) Regulations 2006

The regulations prohibit direct and indirect discrimination but there is a defence if the employer can show that the discrimination is 'a proportionate means of achieving a legitimate aim'. Unlike in the case of some other types of discrimination this general defence is available for direct age discrimination as well as for indirect age discrimination.

In addition to that general defence, there are specific provisions that allow benefits to be linked to length of service and for the low paid to receive different hourly rates depending on age in accordance with the different age-related rates prescribed under the National Minimum Wage Act 1998. An employer is also entitled to impose a retirement age of 65 or over and there are exemptions for occupational pension schemes to permit age-related differences based on genuine actuarial criteria.

Employment Equality (Religion or Belief) Regulations 2003

The regulations prohibit direct and indirect discrimination. In the case of indirect discrimination there is a defence if the employer can show that the discrimination is 'a proportionate means of achieving a legitimate aim'. In the case of direct discrimination, however, the situation is more complex and, in particular, a distinction is drawn between organizations with a religious ethos and other organizations. Churches and other organizations with a religious ethos can give preference when recruiting to members of the relevant faith in appropriate cases where it is a 'genuine occupational requirement' for the job and it is proportionate to apply the requirement. This means that, for example, the Catholic Church is entitled to require its priests and laymen connected with its ministry to be Catholics but that in the unlikely event that it insisted that, for example, an engineer employed to maintain the central heating system in a cathedral had to be a Catholic, that might well be held to be disproportionate.

In the case of organizations that do not have a religious ethos, the circumstances in which they can use the 'genuine occupational requirement' defence are more limited. It is only if it can be said that a position has to be occupied by a member of a particular faith – and not simply that it is preferable – that direct discrimination is permitted. An obvious example would be a non-religious organization such as a hospital, prison or the armed services, where the organization wishes to appoint a chaplain of a particular faith.

The regulations apply to discrimination on the grounds of religion or belief, which is defined as 'any religion, religious belief, or similar philosophical belief'. Until cases that raise the issue are decided by the courts it is not possible to be precise as to what non-religious beliefs will be considered similar to religious belief and so be covered by the regulations.

Employment Equality (Sexual Orientation) Regulations 2003

The regulations prohibit direct and indirect discrimination. In the case of indirect discrimination there is a defence if the employer can show that the discrimination is 'a proportionate means of achieving a legitimate aim'. In the case of direct discrimination, however, the situation is more complex and, in particular, a distinction is drawn between employment 'for the purposes of an organized religion' and other employments in a similar – if not quite identical – way to the distinction made in the Employment Equality (Religion or Belief) Regulations 2003 as described above.

Fixed-Term Employees (Prevention of Less Favourable Treatment) Regulations 2002

The regulations prohibit direct (but not indirect) discrimination against fixed-term employees as compared to permanent employees but there is a defence if the discrimination is 'justified on objective grounds' or where the terms of employment of the fixed-term employee, taken as a whole, are no less favourable than those of permanent employees.

The regulations only apply to employees in the strict sense and in particular do not apply to agency workers.

There is no equivalent prohibition against discrimination against permanent employees.

Where an employee is employed for four years on successive fixed-term contracts, then the contract automatically becomes one of permanent employment if fixed-term employment is 'not justified on objective grounds'. Fixed-term employment would normally be 'justified on objective grounds' where a person was employed on, and only for the duration of, a particular project such as development of a particular computer system.

Part-time Workers (Prevention of Less Favourable Treatment) Regulations 2000

The regulations prohibit direct (but not indirect) discrimination against part-time workers as compared to full-time workers but there is a defence if the discrimination is 'justified on objective grounds'.

The pro-rata principle applies so that a worker who is paid the same hourly rate as a full-time worker is not counted as being discriminated against merely because, working fewer hours, their weekly wage is less than that of the full-time worker.

The regulations also specifically allow an employer to, for example, pay higher rates for overtime and to define overtime as, say, more than 40 hours in a week, even though that means that part-time workers are less likely than full-time workers to work sufficient hours in a week to qualify for the higher rate.

Disability Discrimination Act 1995

The Act prohibits direct discrimination against disabled employees. A disability is defined as 'a physical or mental impairment which has a substantial and long-term adverse effect on [the employee's] ability to carry out normal day-to-day activities'. 'Long term' in this context means that the disability has existed for at least 12 months, or is expected to last for at least 12 months – or is expected to last for the rest of the employee's life if that is expected to be less than 12 months. Certain conditions that would otherwise come within this definition are nevertheless defined in the Disability Discrimination (Meaning of Disability) Regulations 1996 as not being disabilities. So for example, hay fever, alcoholism and kleptomania are not regarded as disabilities for the purposes of the Act.

There is no specific prohibition of indirect discrimination as such but instead there is a positive duty on the employer to make 'reasonable adjustments' to accommodate the disabled person. What is a reasonable adjustment depends on the circumstances. For example, if some working practice causes great difficulties for a disabled employee and the working practice is one that could easily be changed at no cost to the employer and with minimal disadvantage to the employer's operation then it will clearly be reasonable to make the adjustment. At the other extreme, a small employer with limited financial resources would not be required to make major costly and disruptive changes if they would have only a marginal effect in assisting the disabled employee.

Race Relations Act 1976

The Act prohibits direct and indirect discrimination on the grounds of race, colour, nationality and ethnic or national origins.

In the case of indirect discrimination there is a defence if the employer can show that the discrimination is 'a proportionate means of achieving a legitimate aim'.

There are some limited defences that allow direct discrimination on the grounds of race, or ethnic or national origins – but not on the grounds of nationality – where its is a genuine occupational requirement. An example would be a waiter in a Chinese restaurant. Discrimination on the grounds of nationality, place of birth or length of time of residence in an area – but not on the grounds of race – is permitted when selecting a sports team to represent a country, place or area, so there is no obligation on the England football team, for example, to select players from Scotland.

Sex Discrimination Act 1975 and Equal Pay Act 1970

The Act prohibits direct and indirect discrimination on the grounds of sex but in the case of indirect discrimination there is a defence if the employer can show that the discrimination is 'a proportionate means of achieving a legitimate aim'.

There are some limited defences that allow direct discrimination on the grounds of sex where being of a particular sex is a 'genuine occupational qualification', for example for reasons of authenticity or decency – for example an actress playing a female character or someone working in a public toilet, and in the areas of sport and insurance.

An employer is allowed – and, indeed in certain respects required – to accommodate women who are pregnant or on maternity leave. The Act exempts such actions from its scope insofar as male employees cannot complain that such treatment discriminates against them.

The Act also covers discrimination on the grounds of marital status or gender reassignment.

Unfair dismissal

A dismissal of an employee will be 'unfair' – entitling the employee to bring a claim to an employment tribunal – if the dismissal is for a prohibited reason. A dismissal will be automatically unfair if the decision to dismiss is because the employee:

- has joined a trade union;
- is pregnant or has taken maternity or paternity leave;
- has raised a health and safety issue;
- has insisted on his employment rights such as rights to rest period and holiday or the right to be accompanied at a disciplinary or grievance meeting;
- has complained – to the employer or to others – that the employer has failed or is likely to fail to comply with any legal obligation – whether to the employee or anyone else – to which the employer is subject (sometimes known as 'whistleblowing');

as well as if the dismissal is an act of discrimination or victimization.

In addition, where an employee has been employed for more than 12 months, **any** dismissal will be unfair (under section 98 of the Employment Rights Act 1996) unless the employer has 'acted reasonably' in dismissing the employee. In determining whether an employer has acted reasonably, an employment tribunal will look both at the employer's reason for dismissing and at the procedure the employer has used. For example, it will in principle be reasonable for an employer to dismiss an employee who is incapable of doing the job to the proper standard, but in most cases it will be unreasonable for the employer to dismiss without first giving warnings and offering advice or training and giving the employee a chance to improve. Whether the procedure used by the employer is reasonable will be judged in the light of all the circumstances including the size and administrative resources of the employer's organization, but the dismissal will always be found to be unfair if the employer has not complied with the minimum statutory requirement of the disciplinary/dismissal procedure (see above under 'Minimum statutory requirements for the disciplinary/dismissal procedure').

Wrongful dismissal

The right not to be 'wrongfully dismissed' is a contractual right distinct from the statutory right not to be 'unfairly dismissed'. An employee has a contractual right to a certain period of notice – or payment in lieu – unless the employee has committed a breach of contract (e.g. gross misconduct) that is so serious that it amounts to a 'repudiation' of the contract in which case the employer is entitled – in contract law at least – to terminate the employment without notice.

It is possible for a dismissal without notice – or payment in lieu – to be 'unfair' without being wrongful. For example, if an employee, who is guilty of gross misconduct, is dismissed by the employer without the minimum statutory requirements of the dismissal procedure being followed, then the dismissal will be automatically unfair but will not be wrongful because the statutory requirements are not contractual. On the other hand if an employer, dismisses an employee – using the proper procedure – because the employer honestly, but, as it turns out, wrongly, believes, after having carried out a thorough investigation, that the employee was guilty of some gross misconduct such as theft, the dismissal will be wrongful but not unfair because the statutory concept of unfair dismissal takes account of the reasonableness of the employer's belief whereas contract law takes into account only the facts subsequently proved to the court and not the employer's belief, reasonable or otherwise.

An employee who is wrongfully dismissed can recover in damages his notice pay whereas an employee who is unfairly dismissed can recover his full continuing loss of earnings until he manages to find another job paying as well as the job he was dismissed from. It is usual therefore for disputes to centre on whether an employee has been unfairly dismissed rather than on whether he has been wrongfully dismissed. However, where the contract of employment contains a restraint of trade clause, the question of whether the employee has been wrongfully dismissed assumes greater importance because if he has been wrongfully dismissed he will be completely free from the restraint of trade clause.

Where the contract of employment contains a restraint of trade clause that the employer wishes to enforce, many employers will 'play safe' by ensuring that if the employee is dismissed, he is given pay in lieu of notice so that even if the employee successfully claims unfair dismissal he will still be subject to the restraint of trade clause – assuming the clause itself is valid.

Maintenance of trust and confidence

The law recognizes a duty on the part of the employer not, without reasonable and proper cause, to conduct itself in a manner calculated and likely to destroy or seriously damage the relationship of confidence and trust between employer and employee. An employer must, for example, avoid acting capriciously by singling one employee out for less favourable treatment, unless, of course there is a good reason.

Where an employer is in breach of this duty – or commits some other breach of contract that is so serious that it is a 'repudiatory' breach – the employee could resign immediately and claim 'constructive unfair dismissal'. Resigning in such circumstances is, however, a gamble for the employee. When a claim of constructive unfair dismissal is brought before an employment tribunal the tribunal might conclude that the employer's actions are not so bad as to 'seriously' damage the relationship of confidence and trust, and in that case the employee will have lost his job and be denied compensation. The decision as to whether to resign is thus a difficult one for the employee.

However, if the employee has suffered actual monetary loss as a result of the employer's breach of this duty – for example, if the employer, without good reasons, has given everyone else a pay rise – then the employee can recover the loss in a breach of contract claim. In this case the employee does not have to resign before making a claim. Likewise if the employer's breach constitutes prohibited discrimination or victimization then a claim can be made without the employee first having to resign.

Redundancy payments

Where an employee is fairly dismissed by reason of redundancy – because the requirements of the business for employees to carry out work of a particular kind has diminished or is expected to diminish – then the employee will be entitled to a statutory redundancy payment the amount of which is decided according to a formula[215] that takes account of both the number of years service and the salary of the employee. However, the salary used in the formula is subject to a fairly low 'cap' and many contracts of employment contain provision for redundancy payments in excess of the statutory minimum.

It is important that redundancies are handled fairly because even if there is a genuine redundancy situation an employee may succeed in an unfair dismissal claim – and may be awarded compensation greatly in excess of the statutory redundancy payment – if the procedure used to select them rather than someone else for redundancy was unfair, because, for example, there has been insufficient consultation over other jobs within the company that the employee might consider applying for, or if the minimum statutory requirements of the dismissal procedure have not been complied with.

5.3 DUTIES OF THE EMPLOYEE TO THE EMPLOYER

5.3.1 Duty to exercise skill and care

Where an employee when applying for a job has claimed to have certain skills, there will be an implied term in the contract of employment that the employee will exercise reasonable care and skill. Although it is relatively rare for employers to sue employees for failure to exercise reasonable care and skill – the employer usually being content simply to discipline or, in appropriate circumstances dismiss, the employee – an employer could bring a claim for damages against an employee if, through the employee's failure to exercise reasonable care and skill, the employer has suffered proven monetary loss.

An employee must co-operate with the employer as far as is necessary to enable to employer to comply with its duties under health and safety legislation.

5.3.2 Obedience to lawful and reasonable orders

Every employee impliedly agrees to carry out the lawful and reasonable orders of the employer.

5.3.3 Good faith

While the employee remains employed, he owes the employee a duty of fidelity or 'good faith'. He must not compete against – or work for another employer who competes against – his employer and he must keep his employer's confidential information, secret. (The obligation of secrecy does not of course extend to information about any wrongdoing.)

5.3.4 Duties after employment has ceased

The duty to preserve confidentiality will continue after employment has ended but the duty not to compete against the employer will cease when employment ends unless the contract of employment contains a 'restraint of trade' clause under which the employee agrees not to compete against the former employer.

In general the law favours free trade and it is considered that the public interest is served by ensuring that those who wish to offer goods and services to the public are free to do so. Of equal importance is the principle that a man should not be deprived of the opportunity to earn a living. If a restraint of trade clause is too wide, the courts will hold it to be completely void so that the former employee is not bound by it at all. The drafting of a restraint of trade clause in a contract of employment therefore needs to be carried out with great care to ensure that it is wide enough to afford the employer some protection for his business without being so wide that it risks being held to be completely void. The general principles that the courts follow when deciding whether a restraint of trade clause is enforceable are:

- An employer is not entitled to protect himself from mere competition by a former employee.
- The employer must show that it has some interest, such as the goodwill of a customer base, which the restraint of trade clause is designed to protect.
- Area restraints – where the former employee is precluded from working within a certain radius of the employer's base – are more difficult to justify than restraints on soliciting business from companies who were customers of the employer at the time of the employment.
- The longer the duration of the restriction the less likely it is to be reasonable.

An employee who is wrongfully dismissed or constructively dismissed is not bound by any restraint of trade clause.

5.4 OUTSOURCING

Outsourcing, that is the process of an employer replacing a service provided in-house with an equivalent service provided by an external supplier, will involve a number of legal issues but for the purposes of this chapter on employment law, the issue we will concentrate on is the position of any employees who were providing the in-house service.

The effect of the outsourcing will generally be to transfer the employment of those employees engaged in providing the in-house service to the employment of the external supplier and the external provider will become responsible both for future obligations under the contract such as payment of future salary and for any past obligations owed by the previous employer so that, for example, if an employee had suffered an injury at work for which the previous employer was liable or was a victim of discrimination before the transfer, legal liability to compensate the employee will transfer to the external provider.

These consequences of a transfer are set out in the Transfer of Undertakings (Protection of Employment) Regulations 2006 – often known as 'TUPE' – and they apply not only where an in-house service is outsourced but also where an outsourced service is brought in-house, or where the external provider of an outsourced service changes from one contractor to another.

Where there is a TUPE transfer the transferor cannot simply dismiss the employees to prevent them transferring over. Dismissal is only a possibility if there is an 'economic, technical or organizational reason entailing changes in the workforce'. And even where there is an 'economic, technical or organizational reason' the transferee can dismiss only if it can establish that it is acting reasonably in dismissing so that the dismissal is not an 'unfair dismissal' under section 98 of the Employment Rights Act 1996.

Before the TUPE transfer takes place the transferee and transferor must consult with employees who:

- may be transferred;
- are not being transferred but may be affected by the transfer; or
- are employed by the transferee and may be affected by the transfer.

The consultation must take place with the trade union, if one is recognized, or else with elected employee representatives.

5.4.1 What is an employee?

The rights and duties so far described apply to employees. But what is an employee? What is the dividing line between an employee and a self-employed worker?

In the 19th century the law regarded any worker who could be told by his employer how to do his job – and not merely what job to do – as an employee. Conversely anyone providing services who could not be told how to do their job – for example, a professional person such as a surgeon or lawyer – was regarded as a self-employed independent contractor. The law has since evolved a more complex test that involves two mandatory elements – without which a worker cannot be an employee – and a number of general principles or factors none of which is necessarily determinative but that, taken together, are used to determine whether a worker who meets the first two mandatory requirements is, on balance, an employee or is self-employed.

First requirement

There must be a contract – not necessarily written – between the worker and the employer under which the worker agrees to personally carry out some service and the employer agrees to pay remuneration.

Second requirement

It must be a term of the contract – either expressly or by implication – that the worker, in carrying out the service, will be subject to control by the employer. 'Control' can consist of control over what is done, where, when and how, but not all types of control need be exercised to the fullest extent as long as there is overall 'sufficient control'.

If either of the above two requirements is not met then the worker is not an employee. If both requirements are met then whether the worker is an employee or not depends on all the circumstances including in particular the following important factors.

Further factors to be considered

- whether the worker provides his own equipment and the nature of the equipment involved in the work;
- the degree of financial risk the worker takes – for example, as a result of delays in the performance of the services agreed;
- the extent of the worker's responsibility for investment and management;
- how far the worker has an opportunity to profit from sound management in the performance of his task;
- the understanding or intentions of the parties – i.e. whether the parties intend that the worker should be an employee;
- whether the worker has set up a business-like organization of his own;
- the degree of continuity in the relationship between the worker and the employer; how many engagements he performs and whether they are performed mainly for one employer or for a number of different people;

- whether the worker's services are accessory to the employer's business or whether the worker has become 'part and parcel' of the employer's organization;
- whether the worker hires any staff to help him – clearly the worker, in order to meet the first mandatory requirement, must undertake to do **most** of the work personally, but it may be that he hires staff to **help**: the greater the degree of help, the less likely the worker is to be an employee; and
- the degree of control exercised over the worker – clearly some 'sufficient' degree of control is necessary to meet the second mandatory requirement but the extent of control beyond this becomes one of the factors to be taken into account: the more control the more likely the worker is to be an employee.

It will be readily apparent that determining whether a worker is an employee is not straightforward. In some cases all the factors will point towards the worker being an employee; in others the factors may all point in the other direction. But many cases will be on the borderline with many factors pointing in one direction and many other factors in the opposite direction.

5.4.2 Consultants and contractors

If a worker is not an employee according to the legal test explained above then he may, nonetheless, have some more limited 'employment rights'. The law provides uneven coverage: not only do workers who are not employees have fewer rights than employees, but between different categories of non-employee worker, the extent of protection differs.

EXAMPLES

- Only employees who have been employed for at least a year have a general right not to be dismissed without a good reason – i.e. the **general** right to continuation of employment beyond the notice period specified in the contract; of course all employees, no matter how recently employed, are protected from dismissal for a specifically prohibited reason such as racial discrimination.
- Any worker who has a contract to carry out work personally has the right not to be discriminated against no matter how short the engagement is. For example, if a company books a specific well-known self-employed speaker to give a short talk, the speaker is protected from sex, race, disability, religious and age discrimination.
- The right to paid holiday applies to a group of workers sometimes termed 'semi-dependent' contractors. This group of workers includes all employees and some, but (not all) workers who have a contract to carry out work personally. The courts have held[216] that in order to determine whether a worker comes within this group, the employment test –

i.e. the two mandatory requirements plus consideration of the further factors as described above – is applied but with a 'lower pass mark'.

The 'employment' rights of consultants and contractors

What group of workers a consultant or contractor falls into determines which subset of employment rights they have, as shown in Table 5.1.

TABLE 5.1 *Employment rights of various classes of workers*

Type of protection or right	Employees	Semi-independent con-tractors who agree to carry out work person-ally	Independent contract-ors who agree to carry out work personally
General protection from unfair dis-missal	After 12 months	No	No
Right to be accompanied at discip-linary and grievance meetings	Yes	Yes	No
Sick pay	Yes	No	No
Maternity/paternity leave and pay	Yes	No	No
Rest breaks	Yes	Yes	No
Holiday pay	Yes	Yes	No
Sex discrimination	Yes	Yes	Yes
Racial discrimination	Yes	Yes	Yes
Disability discrimination	Yes	Yes	Yes
Religious discrimination	Yes	Yes	Yes
Age discrimination	Yes	Yes	Yes
Discrimination against part-timers	Yes	Yes	No
Discrimination against fixed-term employees	Yes	No	No
Minimum wage	Yes	Yes	No
TUPE	Yes	Yes	?
Whistleblower protection	Yes	Yes	No

Health and safety

A company that engages contractors or consultants is under a duty to take reasonable care for their safety but the precise extent of the duty depends on the degree to which the employer has control over whatever it is that might cause the contractor injury. For example, if the contractor is carrying out work at the employer's premises or at a site under the control of the employer, the employer will be liable to the contractor if he suffers injury due to the dangerous condition of the premises. On the other hand where the contractor provides his own equipment the employer would not generally be liable for injury caused to the contractor by defects in the contractor's own equipment.

Statutory regulations issued under the Health and Safety at Work Act 1974 vary in the extent to which they impose duties on employers in respect of self-employed workers and because many regulations are made in response to EU directives the courts can use the original EU directive as an aid when interpreting the UK regulations, which may mean that even duties that appear, under the UK regulations, only to apply to employees, may be held by the courts to apply more widely – for example to semi-independent contractors.

Grievance and disciplinary procedures

There is no statutory requirement for an employer to use a grievance or disciplinary procedure for workers who are not employees. However, the *ACAS Code of Practice 1: Disciplinary and Grievance Procedures* recommends that procedures should nevertheless be used for all workers and not just for employees. While workers who are not employees cannot claim 'unfair dismissal' as such they are protected against, for example, discrimination and under the working time regulations. An employer who dismisses suddenly without using at least some formal procedure runs the risk he may inadvertently contravene such legislation if there are outstanding issues that he is unaware of.

It should be noted that while there is no specific statutory right to a grievance and disciplinary procedure, if a disciplinary or grievance meeting does take place then semi-independent contractors do have a statutory right to be accompanied by a fellow worker or trade union official.

Agency workers

In IT the use of 'agency workers' is widespread. The employer contacts a 'contract agency' and gives the agency the specification of the kind of worker it requires. When the agency has found a suitable worker, instead of charging the employer a placement fee, the agency enters into a contract with the employer to supply the worker's services at a certain rate per hour, and at the same time enters into a contract with the worker to pay him a lower rate per hour to carry out the work for the employer.

Because the agency worker has no contract with the employer he would, in the absence of special legislation, be protected from discrimination or victimization by the agency but not from discrimination or victimization by the ultimate employer with whom the agency worker will have most contact. Most legislation, however, contains special provisions that protect agency workers against discrimination or victimization by the ultimate employer irrespective of whether there is one agency, or many agencies and a Personal Service Company – see below for definition – interposed in the contractual chain between worker and ultimate employer.

Contract agencies

Parliament considers that both workers and employers require protection from unscrupulous contract agencies. The resulting legislation is found in the Employment Agencies Act 1973 and in the regulations issued under it: Conduct of Employment Agencies and Employment Businesses Regulations 2003. The main requirements of the regulations as they apply to contract agencies (called 'employment businesses' in the Act and regulations) are as follows.

- Before providing any services to the employer the agency must set out the terms that will apply in a single document that states that the agency is operating as an 'employment business', the fees payable, and the procedure to be used if the worker proves unsatisfactory.

- Before providing any services to the worker, the agency must set out the terms that will apply in a single document that states that the agency is operating as an 'employment business', the type of work that the agency will seek to find for the worker, whether the worker will be an employee of the agency under a contract of service or engaged as a self-employed person under a contract for services and in either case the terms and conditions of employment, an undertaking that the agency will pay the worker for work done whether or not the employer has paid the agency, the period of notice that must be given by either party to terminate an assignment with an employer, the minimum rate of remuneration that the agency expects to achieve, the frequency of payment, and any entitlement to paid or unpaid holiday.

- Before introducing a worker the agency must obtain sufficient inform-ation from the employer including the employer's identity and the nature of its business, the date the work is to commence and its likely duration, the type of work, location of work, hours of work, health and safety information, the experience, training and qualifications neces-sary, any expenses payable by or to the worker, and must confirm with the worker that he has the necessary experience, training and qualifications and is willing to work in the position described.

- During the assignment the agency must not withhold payment from the worker for work done merely because of the worker's failure to produce a timesheet signed by the employer.

It often happens that once a worker has completed the initial period of the assignment, the employer wishes to engage him directly rather than through the agency. The agency may wish to have, in its contract with the employer, a clause that provides that in these circumstances a 'placement fee' must be paid by the employer. The regulations provide for this situation in the following way.

- The agency must not directly seek to prevent the worker taking up any position with the employer – any restriction or condition must be in the agency/employer contract and not in the agency/worker contract.

- If the agency wishes to charge the employer a placement fee in these circumstances, the agency/employer contract must provide that the employer can, instead of paying such a fee, opt for a further period of 'hire' through the agency – at the current fee rate – after which it can engage the worker directly without payment of any placement fee. If the agency/employer contract does not contain the 'further period of hire' option then the clause providing for payment of the placement fee is unenforceable and the employer is free to engage the worker directly straight away without payment of any placement fee.

- If eight weeks have elapsed since the worker last worked for the employer through the agency, then the employer is free to engage the worker directly without payment of any placement fee – providing at least 14 weeks have elapsed since the worker **first** worked for the employer via the agency.

With one exception, the regulations are mandatory and cannot be excluded by agreement between the agency and the worker or employer. The exception is that if the worker contracts with the agency not directly but via an incorporated company, such as a Personal Service Company (see below) then if both worker and Personal Service Company agree and give notice to the agency before the worker is introduced by the agency to the employer, the regulations will then not apply. In this case all of the regulations are disapplied – both those that would protect the worker and those that would protect the employer.

PAYE and contractors

Employees come within the Pay-As-You-Earn system under which employers are obliged to calculate and deduct from the employee's gross wages the tax and Class 1 National Insurance contributions due. The amounts deducted must be paid over to HM Revenue and Customs (HMRC) monthly. Employers must not make PAYE deductions from payments to independent and semi-independent contractors. However, if the contractor is engaged by an agency ('employment business') the agency may have to make PAYE deductions from payments it makes to the contractor. Whether or not the agency must make PAYE deductions depends, under Chapter 7 of Part 2 of the Income Tax (Earnings and Pensions) Act 2003, on whether the contractor would have passed the old employment test used in the 19th century – i.e. whether the employer or agency can tell the contractor how to do his job and not merely what job to do. Because of the difficulty for the agency in determining whether or not PAYE is to be deducted, many agencies encourage contractors to incorporate their own limited companies – often called Personal Service Companies (PSC) – with which the agency enters into a contract. PAYE does not apply to company-to-company payments so the agency can pay fees gross and leave the PSC to account to HMRC for PAYE deductions on payments the PSC makes – or is deemed for tax purposes to have made under Chapter 8 of Part 2 of the Income Tax (Earnings and Pensions) Act 2003 (the 'IR35' provisions) – to the worker.

Formal contracts with consultants

When using the services of a contractor or consultant it is important for the employer to give some thought to the contract. A formal written contract is the best way of ensuring that the expectations of both parties coincide.

The terms on which consultants are engaged varies from a contract under which the consultant is essentially another pair of hands carrying out work as directed – in the same way as the employer's employees but without the expectation of long-term employment – for an hourly rate, to contracts under which the consultant carries out a well-defined piece of work for a fixed price agreed in advance.

The simplest solution of an hourly rate may not be in the employer's best interests because it provides little opportunity for budgetary control unless the employer has the project management expertise to effectively manage the consultant's work so as to control costs.

A fixed price is generally a better solution but it does require that the work to be carried out is sufficiently well understood to be specified in a schedule to the contract in sufficient detail to reduce the risk of disputes about whether the work has been completed to specification or not. In addition the consultant is unlikely to agree to a fixed price contract unless he is provided with sufficient information to enable him to estimate the work involved. If the necessary information is not readily available then it might be possible to agree an initial contract at a fixed price for the production of an initial feasibility report that will then provide sufficient information for a fixed price to be agreed for the main work.

It might be thought that consultants would resist fixed price contracts but there is a growing tendency by consultants to consider them, because a fixed price contract is one way for the consultant to demonstrate that he is truly self-employed – with the tax advantages that follow from self-employed status. Where, however, the consultant is not engaged directly but through an agency, the agency is unlikely to agree to payment on anything other than an hourly rate basis.

Variations combining fixed prices and hourly rates are possible. One possibility is for the consultant to be paid at an hourly rate but with a 'target' total number of hours. If the work is competed in less than the target number of hours, the money 'saved' is divided between the parties. A target completion date can also be built into the formula. The object is to provide incentives to both parties: an incentive to the consultant to complete the work efficiently, and an incentive to the employer to co-operate with the consultant in making available information and other agreed resources in a timely manner.

5.5 LIABILITY OF THE EMPLOYER TO THIRD PARTIES FOR THE WORKER'S ACTIONS

5.5.1 Vicarious liability

'Vicarious liability' refers to the liability of an employer for the negligent acts of its workers where those negligent acts cause harm or loss to third parties.

Where a third party is injured or they suffer some other kind of loss because of the carelessness (negligence) of a worker, the worker will be liable for that injury or loss.

> **EXAMPLE**
>
> A worker engaged by a computer supplier incorrectly wires a bank's ATM machine so that metal parts of the machine become 'live' causing serious injury to the bank's customer. The worker is liable to the bank's customer.
>
> However, the worker's 'employer' will also be liable to the bank's customer. The liability of the employer does not depend on the employer being at fault – the employer may have taken great care when recruiting the worker and in subsequently training and supervising him, but the employer will nonetheless be liable for the worker's negligence. This is why the employer's liability is known as 'vicarious' liability.

Through the principle of vicarious liability the law assists third parties who are injured by workers acting in the course of their employment. Instead of having to sue the worker, who may have limited means, the injured third party can sue the employer who will generally have deeper pockets and should be insured.

A worker's 'employer' for the purposes of vicarious liability is not necessarily the same as the worker's contractual employer for employment rights purposes. For example, where a company uses an agency (employment business) to engage contractors who work within the company's organization and under the company's control, with the agency having no day-to-day control, the company will be the 'employer' for vicarious liability purposes.

In some cases vicarious liability may be shared between two companies.

> **EXAMPLE**
>
> A contractor is employed by a consultancy company that provides him with training and some degree of general supervision but hires him out for short periods to work as part of a client's team. In this case vicarious liability would be shared between the client and the consultancy company.

Accidents at work

Vicarious liability will also apply in the situation where one worker (A) employed by a employer (E) negligently injures another worker (B) employed by the same employer. E will be vicariously liable to B even though E may have done everything it could – in terms of, for example, training and supervision of A – to avoid the accident.

5.5.2 Agency

In the case of an employer who is an individual with no, or very few, staff, customers may deal directly with the employer, but otherwise it will be usual for customers to communicate not with the employer himself but with his employees who act on the employer's behalf. Similarly, except in the smallest organizations, employees will not generally deal with their employer directly but rather with directors or managers who are also employed by the employer.

When, in such situations, employees act on behalf of their employer in dealing with third parties – whether those 'third parties' are other employees, customers or suppliers – they are said to be acting as the employer's 'agents' and the area of law concerned with the actions of agents and in what circumstances the 'principal' (in this case the employer) is bound by the actions of the agent, is called the 'law of agency'. ('Agents' in this legal sense should not be confused with 'contract agents', 'estate agents' etc. whose main function is to find contractors or house buyers and not generally to enter into contracts on behalf of anybody.)

Appointment as an agent

It is possible for a person to be appointed agent of a principal by a formal written agency contract but in the case of employees or self-employed workers it is more usual for the agency to be implied by the circumstances. For example, an employee recruited for a telesales position with a computer supplier will have implied authority from the employer to enter into contracts of sale on the employer's behalf in the ordinary course of his work but not, unless specifically authorized, authority to enter into contracts with wholesalers for the purchase of computers.

Apparent authority

A third party will not normally have detailed knowledge of the exact terms of the actual authority that the employer has given to the employee, and an employer will be bound by contracts entered into by its employee with the third party if the employee has, from the viewpoint of the third party, 'apparent' authority.

For example, if the employer tells a wholesaler that its buyer has authority to enter into contracts worth up to £1,000,000 and then subsequently reduces the buyer's authority to £500,000, but does not inform the wholesaler of the reduction of authority, then the employer will still be bound by any contract entered into by the buyer up to £1,000,000 because the buyer still has 'apparent authority' to enter into such contracts on behalf of the employer. If the employer has suffered loss by being bound by the employee's actions to a contract for which the employee did not have actual authority, the employee will be liable to compensate the employer.

In practice apparent authority usually arises not from an explicit statement by the employer to a third party but by implication from the position the employer has placed the employee in. If the employer sends an employee whose job title is 'buyer' to a meeting with wholesalers, the buyer will have apparent authority to enter into contracts for the kinds of goods or services that it is normal for the employer to buy.

If the employer has not, expressly or by implication, given the employee apparent authority but the employee purports to enter into a contract with a third party on the employer's behalf, then the employer will not be bound by the contract, though the employer can subsequently choose to be bound by the contract by telling the third party that the employer 'ratifies' the contract. If the employer decides not to ratify the contract, and so is not bound by it, then the employee himself is liable to compensate the third party for any loss it has suffered – for example if the market price for the third-party's goods has dropped so that, on discovering that it did not have a binding contract with the employer, it is unable to sell the goods to another buyer at the same price.

5.6 DEALING WITH EXAMINATION QUESTIONS: THE FOUR STEPS

Because some employment statutes modify contractual rights (as explained in 5.1) while others create parallel statutory rights, it will generally be necessary – when answering questions in the examination – to consider both and hence to go through four mental steps before deciding on the right answer to the question.

Step 1

Decide what contractual terms have been agreed – either in writing, by word of mouth or by implication from the parties' actions.

Step 2

Consider whether the contract terms that are relevant to the question have been modified by statute.

Step 3

Consider whether the contract terms, as modified by statute, have been broken.

Step 4

Consider whether there are, in addition, parallel statutory rights that have been breached.

You should then be in a position to decide which of the four multiple choice answers to the question is correct.

THE FOUR STEPS: AN EXAMPLE

Phillip has worked for HAL Computers Ltd for 7½ years as a program developer. When he started he signed a written contract with HAL, which contained this term:

Clause 18: Either party to this Agreement may terminate this Agreement by giving one calendar month's notice in writing to the other party.

HAL computers has decided that, because of the replacement of an in-house developed system with a software package from an external supplier, it no longer needs as many program developers as it currently has and, without any warning or discussion, Phillip's manager gives him a letter that states:

'**HAL Computers Ltd hereby gives you one calendar month's notice to terminate your employment. We wish you all the best for the future.**'

What are Phillip's rights in this situation?

In order to answer this question we need to go through the four steps outlined above.

STEP 1   The contractual term agreed by the parties is that HAL can terminate Phillip's employment by giving him one calendar month's notice in writing.

STEP 2   Does statute modify this agreed contractual term? Section 86 of the Employment Rights Act 1996 (ERA) provides that for an employee who has been employed for between two and 12 years is entitled to not less than one week's notice for each year of employment and that any provision in a contract for shorter notice is subject to this minimum. So statute does modify the contractual term and the contractual term, as modified by statute, is that HAL can terminate Phillip's employment by giving him seven weeks' notice in writing.

STEP 3   Has HAL broken the contractual term (as modified)? Yes, HAL has only given just over four weeks' notice when they should have given a minimum of seven weeks' notice.

STEP 4   Are there any parallel statutory rights that may have been breached? Yes, HAL has not consulted Phillip so on that ground alone the dismissal is likely to be unfair under section 98 of the ERA. In addition because the statutory dismissal procedure has not been complied with, the dismissal will be automatically an unfair dismissal under section 98A of the ERA.

So we conclude that Phillip is entitled to about 2 ½ weeks of extra contractual notice pay plus an award for unfair dismissal.

REFERENCES

Other resources

- *ACAS Code of Practice 1: Disciplinary and Grievance Procedures* (available from the ACAS website: www.acas.org.uk)
- Daniel Barnett and Henry Scrope (2006) *Employment Law Handbook*. Law Society, London. ISBN 1 85328 929 9 gives a good coverage of employment law as it relates to employees.
- John Antell (2002) *Employment Status*. Butterworths, London. ISBN 0 754518124 concentrates on the law as it applies to various kinds of contractors and consultants who are not employees.

Acts of Parliament and Regulations

The further reading above should provide sufficient information without the reader having to refer to the actual text of Acts and Regulations. However, if it is desired to refer to Acts of Parliament and Regulations, they can be found in *Butterworths Employment Law Handbook*. It is also possible to find some legislation on the web using a search engine such as www.google.co.uk but it should be noted that Acts are frequently amended – when using a copy found on the web it is essential to ensure that it is up to date with all amendments, and is not simply a copy of the Act as originally enacted many years ago.

Legislation

Relevant Statutes include:
- Employers' Liability (Compulsory Insurance) Act 1969
- Equal Pay Act 1970
- Employment Agencies Act 1973
- Health and Safety at Work Act 1974
- Sex Discrimination Act 1975
- Race Relations Act 1976
- The Workplace (Health and Safety and Welfare) Regulations 1992
- The Personal Protective Equipment at Work Regulations 1992
- The Manual Handling Operations Regulations 1992
- The Health and Safety (Display Screen Equipment) Regulations 1992
- Disability Discrimination Act 1995
- Employment Rights Act 1996
- Disability Discrimination (Meaning of Disability) Regulations 1996
- Provision and Use of Work Equipment Regulations 1998
- Working Time Regulations 1998

- National Minimum Wage Act 1998
- Maternity and Parental Leave Etc Regulations 1999
- National Minimum Wage Regulations 1999
- Employment Relations Act 1999
- The Management of Health and Safety at Work Regulations 1999
- Part-time Workers (Prevention of Less Favourable Treatment) Regulations 2000
- Fixed-term Employees (Prevention of Less Favourable Treatment) Regulations 2002
- Employment Act 2002
- Income Tax (Earnings and Pensions) Act 2003
- Employment Equality (Age) Regulations 2006
- Employment Equality (Religion or Belief) Regulations 2003
- Employment Equality (Sexual Orientation) Regulations 2003
- Conduct of Employment Agencies and Employment Businesses Regulations 2003
- Employment Act 2002 (Dispute Resolution) Regulations 2004
- Transfer of Undertakings (Protection of Employment) Regulations 2006

Cases

Similarly for this syllabus it is not necessary to study in detail the actual text of cases decided by the courts. However, readers who are interested will be able to find the text of most cases at www.bailii.org

6 Accessibility and Information Security

VIVIAN PICTON

6.1 WEB ACCESSIBILITY

6.1.1 What is accessibility?

> *The power of the internet is in its universality. Access for everyone regardless of disability is an essential aspect* [**Sir Tim Berners-Lee**]

This quote is often used when discussing accessibility in relation to the internet. Primarily accessibility is about making websites and online services available to everyone regardless of any disability. It also relates to the way in which websites are designed, the use of assistive technology and the overall usability of websites. The more accessible and usable a website is, the better the experience for everyone.

6.1.2 Legal landscape

Disability Discrimination Act 1995 and Code of Practice

The key piece of legislation in the United Kingdom is the Disability Discrimination Act 1995 (DDA) and the Codes of Practice that flow from it. In relation to web accessibility the relevant Code of Practice is the Rights of Access, Goods, Facilities, Services and Premises, which was published in 2002 (Code of Practice).[217] Part III of the DDA applies to Goods, Facilities and Services and came into force on 1 October 1999.

Part I of the DDA defines disability as:

> **physical or mental impairment which has a substantial long term adverse effect on his ability to carry out normal day-to-day activities.**[218]

There are three key elements to this.

- First, there has to be an impairment. For the purposes of the DDA, an 'impairment' includes sensory impairment such as blindness and deafness but also learning disabilities and mental illness.
- Second, in order to be substantial, the impairment must not be minor or trivial and must be long term. This means that it must be capable of lasting for at least 12 months.
- Third, the impairment will be relevant only if it has an adverse effect on the ability to perform normal day-to-day activities. Schedule 1

paragraph 4 of the DDA provides that an impairment affects the ability of a person to carry out normal day-to-day activities only if it affects the person's:

- mobility;
- manual dexterity;
- physical coordination;
- continence;
- ability to lift, carry or otherwise;
- speech, hearing or eyesight;
- memory and ability to concentrate, learn or understand; or
- perception of the risk of physical danger.

The definition of a disabled person applies equally to adults and children.

The Code of Practice deals with the duties imposed by Part III of the DDA 1995 on those providing goods, facilities or services to the public and those selling, letting or managing premises. The Act makes it unlawful for service providers, landlords and other persons to discriminate against disabled people in certain circumstances.

Section 19(3) of the DDA defines what a 'service provider' is; and in particular section 19(3)(c) gives 'access to and use of information services' as one of the examples of services to which this section and sections 20 and 21 apply.[219] This, together with the Code of Practice, makes it clear that the provisions of Part III of the DDA apply to websites.

In section 19(2) of the DDA, the provision of services includes the provision of goods or facilities and, subject to certain exclusions, the Act affects everyone concerned with the provision in the United Kingdom of services to the public, or to a section of the public, whether in the private, public or voluntary sectors. It does not matter if services are provided free – such as access to a search engine – or in return for payment – for example, accessing an online magazine.

The duties imposed on service providers were introduced in three stages:

- since 2 December 1996 it has been unlawful for service providers to treat disabled people less favourably for a reason related to their disability;
- since 1 October 1999 service providers have had to make 'reasonable adjustments' for disabled people, such as providing extra help or making changes to the way they provide their services; and
- since 1 October 2004 service providers may have to make other 'reasonable adjustments' in relation to the physical features of their premises to overcome physical barriers to access.

A service provider discriminates against a disabled person:

- 'in refusing to provide, or deliberately not providing, to the disabled person any service which he provides, or is prepared to provide, to members of the public'[220]
- 'in the standard of service which he provides to the disabled person or the manner in which he provides it to him'[221]
- 'in the terms on which it provides a service to the disabled person'.[222]

Paragraph 4.15 of the revised Code of Practice suggests that 'this is a duty to disabled people at large, and applies regardless of whether the service provider knows that a particular member of the public is disabled or whether it currently has disabled customers'.

The idea of 'reasonable adjustment' is one of the cornerstones of the DDA. In section 21 of the DDA, where a service provider offers services to the public, it has a legal duty to take such steps as it is reasonable for the service provider to have to take in all the circumstances of the case in the situations described below. Therefore, where a service provider has an existing website and it discovers that it is not accessible, it has an obligation to make reasonable adjustments to the site 'in circumstances in which the effect of that failure is to make it impossible or unreasonably difficult for the disabled person to make use of any such service'.[223]

The duty to make reasonable adjustments comprises a series of duties falling into three main areas:

- changing a practice, policy or procedure that makes it impossible or unreasonably difficult for disabled people to make use of its services;[224]
- providing an auxiliary aid or service if it would enable – or make it easier for – disabled people to make use of its services;[225] and
- providing a reasonable alternative method of making its services available to disabled people where a physical feature makes it impossible or unreasonably difficult for disabled people to make use of the services.[226]

Companies can be sued for damages if they fail to make the necessary adjustments after complaints of poor accessibility.

Discrimination occurs when a service provider:

- treats the disabled person less favourably, for a reason relating to the disabled person's disability, than it treats (or would treat) others to whom that reason does not (or would not) apply;
- or he fails to comply with a duty imposed under section 21 – a duty to make reasonable adjustments;

and in each case it cannot show that its actions or inaction are justified.

In certain circumstances, service providers may defend discriminatory treatment of disabled persons or failures to make adjustments under the DDA. To establish justification for its actions, the service provider must first show that it considers one of these following conditions to be satisfied and it is reasonable for the service provider to hold such belief:

(1) the particular treatment of the person is necessary not to endanger the health and safety of that person or anyone else;

(2) the disabled person is incapable of entering into a binding agreement or of giving informed consent;

(3) where the service provider refuses or deliberately fails to provide a service to a disabled person because otherwise the service provider would be unable to provide a service to the public;

(4) where the service provider provides a service to a lower standard or on different terms for a disabled person, such action is necessary, otherwise the service provider would be unable to provide the service to the disabled person or to the public; or

(5) where the service provider provides a service on different terms to a disabled person, the difference reflects the greater cost in providing a service tailored to that individual's need.[227]

The test under the Act has two elements. First, what did the service provider believe? This is a subjective test. Second, was that belief reasonably held? This is an objective test.

However, as is pointed out in the Code of Practice:

> **A service provider should not be looking for reasons or excuses to discriminate against disabled people who wish to use its services. It is in the service provider's own best interest to ensure that its services are fully accessible to all customers.**

Given the similarities between the UK and Commonwealth disability rights legislation and the obligations set out under section 24 of the Commonwealth Disability Discrimination Act mirror those of section 19 of the UK Act, it is worth considering the outcome of *Maguire v Sydney Organising Committee for the Olympic Games*,[228] an Australian case.

Maguire was a blind internet user. He was also the supplier of assistive technology to enable blind users to access information on the internet. In 1999 he lodged a complaint against the Sydney Organising Committee for the Olympic Games on the basis that their website was not accessible to blind users. This was due to the way in which the various navigation links were set out in the site. Maguire believed he was being discriminated against. The Commission found that Maguire had been discriminated against and that the Sydney Organising Committee for the Olympic Games had caused 'considerable feelings of hurt, humiliation and rejection' and fined them A$20,000. The Commission said that the minimum standard that should be adopted by bodies providing services via the internet was the Priority 1 or Priority A checkpoints, set out by the World Wide Web Consortium Accessibility Initiative.[229]

On 8 March 2006 the British Standards Institution published a 'Publicly Available Specification' (PAS) dealing with accessibility of websites.

Rather than establishing technical standards, the PAS creates a process that developers should adopt to ensure that their websites are accessible. Every organization with a website should have an 'accessibility policy'. This policy should set accessibility targets, include references to the relevant World Wide Web Consortium guidelines and be available online. The annexes to the PAS provide useful information in relation to the issues that need to be considered when developing an accessible site.[230]

Disability Rights Commission Act 1999 (DRCA)

The main purpose of the DRCA was to establish the Disability Rights Commission (DRC) as an Independent Statutory Body. It gives the general functions[231] of the DRC as being:

(a) to work towards the elimination of discrimination against disabled persons;

(b) to promote the equalization of opportunities for disabled persons;

(c) to take such steps as it considers appropriate with a view to encouraging good practice in the treatment of disabled persons; and

(d) to keep under review the working of the DDA and the DRCA.

Along with these general functions the DRC is also required to:

- assist disabled people by offering information, advice and support in taking cases forward;
- provide information and advice to employers and service providers;
- undertake formal investigations;
- prepare statutory codes of practice providing practical guidance on how to comply with the law; and
- arrange independent conciliation between service providers and disabled people in the area of access to goods and services.

6.1.3 W3C

The World Wide Web Consortium (W3C) is an international consortium that seeks to develop web standards.[232] It was founded in 1994 and comprises 300 organizations, which include technology suppliers, such as EDS, Nokia and Microsoft, research bodies and governmental departments.

Web accessibility initiative

W3C's states that its mission is:

> To lead the World Wide Web to its full potential by developing protocols and guidelines that ensure long-term growth for the Web.

In this respect the W3C has developed detailed technical guidelines on how to ensure that websites are accessible.

Web content guidelines

W3C has issued guidelines (Web Content Accessibility Guidelines) as to what constitutes an 'accessible website'. Accessibility is defined by such matters as text size, font and colour, background colour, the use of graphics and frames, software and compatibility with assistive technology.

These guidelines recommend 14 general principles of accessible design not just enabling better access for the disabled but enabling better access for all users; and there are compelling commercial reasons for ensuring a website is fully accessible by all.

> **Guideline 1** – Provide equivalent alternatives to auditory and visual content. Provide content that, when presented to the user, conveys essentially the same function or purpose as auditory or visual content.
>
> **Guideline 2** – Don't rely on colour alone.
>
> **Guideline 3** – Use markup and style sheets and do so properly.
>
> **Guideline 4** – Clarify natural language usage.
>
> **Guideline 5** – Create tables that transform gracefully.
>
> **Guideline 6** – Ensure that pages featuring new technologies transform gracefully.
>
> **Guideline 7** – Ensure user control of time-sensitive content changes.
>
> **Guideline 8** – Ensure direct accessibility of embedded user interfaces.
>
> **Guideline 9** – Design for device-independence.
>
> **Guideline 10** – Use interim solutions.
>
> **Guideline 11** – Use W3C technologies and guidelines.
>
> **Guideline 12** – Provide context and orientation information.
>
> **Guideline 13** – Provide clear navigation mechanisms.
>
> **Guideline 14** – Ensure that documents are clear and simple.[233]

These checkpoints are ranked into three categories, defined by the Web Accessibility Initiative as Priorities 1, 2 or 3.

> **Priority 1 (Level A):** 'Site must satisfy this checkpoint, otherwise, one or more groups will find it impossible to access.'
>
> **Priority 2 (Level AA):** 'Site should satisfy this checkpoint, otherwise, one or more groups will find it difficult to access information in the document.'
>
> **Priority 3 (Level AAA):** 'Site may address this checkpoint, otherwise, one or more groups will find it somewhat difficult to access information in the document.'

6.2 REGULATION

6.2.1 Computer Misuse Act 1990

Crimes committed with the assistance of a computer or to a computer system have always presented problems for the prosecutors of such crime.

In a notable case predating the Computer Misuse Act 1990, Gold and Shifreen, were convicted at Southwark Crown Court in April 1986 of offences of forgery under the Forgery and Counterfeiting Act of 1981. The defendants in this case had gained access to Prestel Gold email accounts, one of which was that belonging to HRH Duke of Edinburgh.

The two men were journalists who claimed they only hacked into this system in order to highlight its weaknesses. It was alleged they had produced a 'false instrument' with the intention of inducing another to believe it was genuine. In this case it was said to be the CIN (customer identification number) and password. Section 8 of the Forgery and Counterfeiting Act stated the false instrument may be 'recorded or stored on disc, tape, sound track or other device'. The trial judge in his ruling said:

> the defendant here made a series of electrical impulses which arrive at, effect and operate on what is called a user segment. These impulses are recorded or stored albeit for a limited period only...By section 9(2) an instrument is sufficient and here there was, as I see it, an alteration to a user segment.

The two men appealed. The Law Lords interpreted the particular section to mean the process must be lasting in nature and one that could be retrieved later. Clearly the CIN and password were only temporarily held in the computer system. With the Law Lords saying:

> the Forgery Act was not intended for computer misuse offences. The problem was that the machine was the 'deceived' and the 'false instrument' at the same time.

Lord Lane, the Lord Chief Justice, said that the act of accessing the Prestel Gold system by what amounted to a dishonest trick was not a criminal offence. This decision was confirmed by the House of Lords. Lord Brandon in the House of Lords said:

> The Procrustean attempt to force these facts into the language of an Act not designed to fit them produced grave difficulties for both judge and jury which we would not wish to see repeated. The appellants' conduct amounted in essence, as already stated, to dishonestly gaining access to the relevant Prestel data bank by a trick. That is not a criminal offence. If it is thought desirable to make it so, that is a matter for the legislature rather than the courts.

Normally in a forgery case it was necessary to prove that some person was deceived. In this case the machine was both instrument and deceived entity.

Other offences could have been committed under the Theft Acts of 1968 and 1978, and the Telecommunications Act 1984.

The act of 'hacking' into a computer system was an act for which, under legislation available at the time, it was found to be difficult to bring charges against the perpetrators.

The late 1980s saw both politicians and lawyers appreciating the risks and developing a strategy to deal with it, although it was thanks to the determined efforts by two different MPs to support a Private Members Bill, which eventually became the Computer Misuse Act 1990 (CMA). The Law Commission in 1989 had highlighted the issue too but it was still left to individuals to deal with rather than the government despite the obvious commercial consequences.

The CMA was created in light of the Law Commission Working Paper no. 186; Criminal Law: Computer Misuse, Cmd 819, October 1989, in order to create specific offences to secure computers against unauthorized access or modifications and states:

> The main argument in favour of a hacking offence does not turn on the protection of information, but rather springs from the need to protect the integrity and security of computer systems from attacks from unauthorized persons seeking to enter those systems. . . It is for those reasons that we propose, as a deterrent to hacking, two offences; the first, a broad offence that seeks to deter the general practice of hacking by imposing penalties of a moderate nature on all types of unauthorized access, and the second a narrower but more serious offence, that imposes much heavier penalties on those persons who hack with the intent to commit. . . serious crime.

When the CMA was passed it introduced three new offences into English Law.

The first offence related to unauthorized access to computer material. This is sometimes referred to as the 'general hacking offence'. Under this section, a person commits an offence if he obtains unauthorized access to any program or data held in any computer that he knew he was not permitted to access.

Section 2 of the CMA created what has become known as the 'aggravated hacking offence'. In essence, a person commits an offence if he hacks into a system with the intention of commissioning or facilitating another offence.

Finally, section 3 introduced an offence in relation to unauthorized modification of computer programs, which was intended to deal with viruses, worms, trojans and the like.

The provisions of the CMA have been amended by the Police and Justice Act 2006.

Section 1

Under section 1(1) (Unauthorized access to computer material) of the Computer Misuse Act 1990:

> **A person is guilty of an offence if:**
>
> (c) he causes a computer to perform any function with intent to secure access to any program or data held in any computer;
>
> (d) the access he intends to secure is unauthorized; and
>
> (e) he knows at the time when he causes the computer to perform the function that this is the case.

This section has been amended by the Police and Justice Act 2006 so that it now catches anyone who enables such access to be secured.[234]

> **The intent a person has to have to commit an offence under this section need not be directed at:**
>
> (a) any particular program or data;
>
> (b) a program or data of any particular kind; or
>
> (c) a program or data in any particular computer.[235]

A person guilty of an offence under section 1 will be liable on summary conviction to imprisonment for a term not exceeding six months or to a fine not exceeding level 5 on the standard scale or to both. At present this is not an indictable offence. However, the provisions of the Police and Justice Act 2006 will increase the penalties that may be imposed. The term of the sentence on summary conviction will be increased to 12 months and the offence will now be triable either way with a maximum sentence on indictment of two years.

Section 2

Under section 2 of the Act (Unauthorized access with intent to commit or facilitate commission of further offences) it is an offence to commit an offence under section 1 with the intent to commit or facilitate a further offence, whether or not both offences occur on the same occasion.

> (1) A person is guilty of an offence under this section if he commits an offence under section 1 above ('the unauthorized access offence') with intent:
>
> (a) to commit an offence to which this section applies; or
>
> (b) to facilitate the commission of such an offence (whether by himself or by any other person);
>
> and the offence he intends to commit or facilitate is referred to below in this section as the further offence.

(2) This section applies to offences:

    (a) for which the sentence is fixed by law; or

    (b) for which a person of twenty-one years of age or over (not previously convicted) may be sentenced to imprisonment for a term of five years (or, in England and Wales, might be so sentenced but for the restrictions imposed by section 33 of the [1980 c. 43.] Magistrates' Courts Act 1980).

(3) It is immaterial for the purposes of this section whether the further offence is to be committed on the same occasion as the unauthorized access offence or on any future occasion.

(4) A person may be guilty of an offence under this section even though the facts are such that the commission of the further offence is impossible.

(5) A person guilty of an offence under this section shall be liable:

    (a) on summary conviction, to imprisonment for a term not exceeding six months or to a fine not exceeding the statutory maximum or to both; and

    (b) on conviction on indictment, to imprisonment for a term not exceeding five years or to a fine or to both.

These offences relate to theft, blackmail, obtaining property or services by deception and many other offences having a penalty of five or more years imprisonment.

Both the section 1 and section 2 offences relate to unauthorized access to any program or data held on a computer. This gives rise to two questions:

    (a) What constitutes access?

    (b) What is meant by unauthorized?

The CMA does not provide any definition of 'computer' or 'program'. In each case the words need to be given their natural meaning. The meanings have developed since the CMA was passed and continue to develop with changes in technology. Section 17 of the Computer Misuse Act 1990 provides some interpretation.

In relation to the first question, the CMA provides that a person secures access to any program or data held in a computer if by causing a computer to perform any function he:

(a) alters or erases the program or data;

(b) copies or moves it to any storage medium other than that in which it is held or to a different location in the storage medium in which it is held;

(c) uses it; or

(d) has it output from the computer in which it is held – whether by having it displayed or in any other manner.[236]

The CMA provides that access to a program or data are unauthorized if the person obtaining access is 'not himself entitled to control access of the kind in question to the program or data and he does not have consent to access by him of the kind in question to the program or data from any person who is so entitled.'[237]

Where the alleged unauthorized access occurs by an employee the Law Commission considers that:

> An employer should only have the support of the hacking offence if he has clearly defined the limits of authorization applicable to each employee, and if he is able to prove that the employee had knowingly and recklessly exceeded that level of authority.[238]

In the case of *Denco Ltd v Johnson*,[239] it was held that an employee who used an unauthorized password to gain access to information stored in a computer and which he knew he was not entitled to see was guilty of gross misconduct and could be summarily dismissed from his employment. The Employment Appeal Tribunal and the Industrial Tribunal, which heard the case first, both criticized the employer's security arrangements. The Audit Commission noted a disregard for basic control safeguards and ineffective monitoring.

DPP v Bignell[240]

In this case two police officers, with the assistance of an operator, accessed the police computer system, for which they were authorized users. They accessed motor car details for private purposes, not connected to their duties as police officers. They were charged under Section 1 of the Computer Misuse Act 1990 and convicted at Bow Street Magistrates' Court. Their appeal to the Crown Court was allowed and subsequently confirmed by the Queen's Bench Divisional Court.

The question being raised in this case is whether a person who has authorized access to records or information can use that authority for unauthorized use, going by the judgment in this case it would appear so.

The decision in *DPP v Bignell* was reversed in 1999, however, by the House of Lords when they considered the case of *R v Bow Street Magistrates' Court and Allison (A.P.) ex parte Government of the United States of America*[241] and what was meant by 'authorization' within the context of the Computer Misuse Act. An employee of American Express in Florida who, as part of her duties, was authorized to access certain customer accounts, passed on details of other account holders to Mr Allison and others. American Express lost an estimated $1 million as a result of this. Mr Allison was arrested in London and was found to be in possession of counterfeit credit cards. An extradition request was finally granted when Mr Allison was committed on a charge of unauthorized modification of computer material. The House of Lords certified the question of law being:

> Whether, on a true construction on s.1 (and thereafter s.2) of the Computer Misuse Act 1990, a person who has authority to access data of the kind in question none the less has unauthorized access if:
>
> (a) the access to the particular data in question was intentional;
>
> (b) the access in question was unauthorized by the person entitled to authorise access to that particular data;
>
> (c) knowing that the access to that particular data was unauthorized.

The House of Lords did not disagree with the outcome of the original trial judge but did disagree with the reasoning for the decision.

Lord Hobhouse stated:

> The use of the phrase 'data of the kind in question' seems to derive from a simple misreading of section 17(5) (of the Computer Misuse Act 1990) and a confusion between kinds of access and kinds of data. Nor is section 1 of the Act concerned with authority to access kinds of data. It is concerned with authority to access the actual data involved. Because section 1(1) creates an offence which can be committed as a result of having an intent to secure unauthorized access without in fact actually succeeding in accessing any data, section 1(2) does not require that the relevant intent relate to any specific data. But that does not mean that access to the data in question does not have to be authorized.

Lord Hobhouse went on to state that section 17(5) had been misread by Kennedy LJ in his Court of Appeal judgment and went on to say that Kennedy LJ had confined the operation of section 1 to 'hacking', rather than the wider concept of using a computer to secure unauthorized access. This section of the Act is particularly suitable for activities carried out across networks.

Section 2 and section 3 offences are what are termed 'arrestable offences' and an individual may be arrested without warrant by a police officer if the police officer has reasonable suspicion that they have committed that offence. These offences are more serious than the section 1 offence.

Section 3

Under section 3 of the Act – Unauthorized modification of computer material:

> (1) A person is guilty of an offence if:
>
> (a) he does any act which causes an unauthorized modification of the contents of any computer; and
>
> (b) at the time when he does the act he has the requisite intent and the requisite knowledge.
>
> (2) For the purposes of subsection (1)(b) above the requisite intent is an intent to cause a modification of the contents of any computer and by so doing:

(a) to impair the operation of any computer;

(b) to prevent or hinder access to any program or data held in any computer; or

(c) to impair the operation of any such program or the reliability of any such data.

(3) The intent need not be directed at:

(a) any particular computer;

(b) any particular program or data or a program or data of any particular kind; or

(c) any particular modification or a modification of any particular kind.

(4) For the purposes of subsection (1)(b) above the requisite knowledge is knowledge that any modification he intends to cause is unauthorized.

(5) It is immaterial for the purposes of this section whether an unauthorized modification or any intended effect of it of a kind mentioned in subsection (2) above is, or is intended to be, permanent or merely temporary.

(6) For the purposes of the [1971 c. 48.] Criminal Damage Act 1971 a modification of the contents of a computer shall not be regarded as damaging any computer or computer storage medium unless its effect on that computer or computer storage medium impairs its physical condition.

(7) A person guilty of an offence under this section shall be liable:

(a) on summary conviction, to imprisonment for a term not exceeding six months or to a fine not exceeding the statutory maximum or to both; and

(b) on conviction on indictment, to imprisonment for a term not exceeding five years or to a fine or to both.

The scope of section 3 of the Computer Misuse Act 1990 would appear to suitable for catching a wide variety of 'crimes' committed with, by or to a computer, and should be capable of covering the intentional introduction into a computer system of viruses, worms, Trojan horses or any other program of a destructive nature. The language used in this section would also seem to indicate that if someone knowingly creates a program of a destructive nature and that program is innocently introduced into a computer system by a third party the creator would be liable.

It is worth considering the outcomes of two cases that were reported in 2001, with both offences being considered under section 3 of the Act. They are *R v Maxwell-King*[242]and *R v Lindesay.*[243]

In *R v Maxwell-King* the accused pleaded guilty to three counts of incitement to commit offences under section 3, the Court of First Instance found the defendant guilty of all charges and sentenced him to four months imprisonment and he appealed this decision. The Court of Appeal thought that what Maxwell-King had done was dishonest and was a form of theft; they also choose not take seriously his claim that he thought that what he was doing was not illegal. This was his first offence and he admitted guilt at the first opportunity.

The Court of Appeal distinguished an earlier case, *R v Carrey*,[244] where a custodial sentence was imposed on Carrey who had pleaded guilty to producing some 850,000 counterfeit smart cards with the intention to conspire to defraud; he made many thousands of pounds from this illegal activity. Maxwell-King, on the other hand, had manufactured an electronic gadget that was capable of bypassing the security on a cable television system and allowed its subscribers to receive all services and not just the ones they had paid for. The system was not very successful and Maxwell-King achieved a turnover of only £600 yielding minimum profit.

The Court of Appeal overruled the original decision in *Maxwell-King* to a community service order of 150 hours.

In the case of *R v Lindesay*, Lindesay had been employed as a computer consultant on a short-term contract by a computer company but, before the end of the contract, he was dismissed. Lindesay feeling rather aggrieved at this action gained unauthorized access to the company's computer websites – this required the use of confidential passwords. These websites were related to clients of the computer company. He made some changes to the websites and caused the company and its clients much inconvenience. Lindesay was sentenced, by the Court of First Instance, to nine months imprisonment following his plea of guilty to three counts of causing unauthorized modification to the contents of a computer contrary to the Computer Misuse Act 1990 section 3(1) and section 3(7). At the appeal Lindesay argued that the mitigating circumstances had not been fully taken into account and that further regard should have been given to the effect that a custodial sentence would have on both himself and his daughter.

The appeal judge held that the sentence was not excessive and that Lindesay had taken advantage of his knowledge and skill to exact revenge on the company that had employed him. The appeal was dismissed.

A further case worth considering under section 3 offences is that of *R v Simon Lee Vallor*.[245] In the Court of Appeal, Vallor appealed against the sentence of two years imprisonment set by the original trial judge. He was charged with offences of releasing computer viruses onto the internet contrary to the Computer Misuse Act 1990 section 3, a charge to which Vallor pleaded guilty. The viruses were detected in 42 countries. Two of the viruses were 'worms' in email messages, which caused the infected computers, estimated to be 200 to 300 computers, to stop and delete any unsaved material.

It was held, at the Court of Appeal, that the offences were planned and deliberate, calculated and intended to cause disruption. Vallor gave mitigation of youth, good character, co-operation with the police and the difficulty he had had following the death of his mother. The appeal was dismissed.

Changes to the Computer Misuse Act 1990

Over the past five years there have been various attempts to change the CMA. The first attempt was the Computer Misuse (Amendment) Bill, which was first introduced into the House of Lords by the Earl of Northesk in May 2002. The Bill was to amend the Computer Misuse Act 1990 in order to protect computerized systems against denial of service attacks. The Bill contained just one main clause and an associated minor clause; the main clause was to insert after section 3 of the Computer Misuse Act 1990 a new section '3A Denial of Service Attacks'. Although the Bill passed its first reading it failed to gain support in the House of Commons.

The concerns relating to the coverage of the CMA were highlighted when Aaron Caffrey, aged 19 from Shaftesbury in Dorset, was accused of launching an attack on 20 September 2001 on the port of Houston, Texas, which disabled the port's web service. This service held vital information for shipping and support firms responsible for navigating ships in and out of the harbour.

Although Aaron Caffrey admitted to hacking into computers for friends to test their security he denied being responsible for the attack on the port in Houston. He alleged that hackers had broken into his computer and used it to launch the attack. It was acknowledged that the attack had come from his computer. A forensic examination of Caffrey's computer failed to uncover a hidden program with an instruction to carry out the attack.

He was cleared by the jury in October 2003 at Southwark Crown Court of unauthorized modification of computer material.

The next attempt to change the CMA came in April 2004 when Derek Wyatt MP, also chairman of the then All Party Parliamentary Internet Group (APIG), introduced his Computer Misuse Act 1990 (Amendment) Bill, received as a 10-minute rule bill that was seeking to amend the Computer Misuse Act 1990.

It was reported in the House of Commons Hansard Debates for 5 April 2004 in a speech given by Derek Wyatt at column 1294: 'The Bill would add specific denial of service – DOS – and it would increase the tariff for Computer Misuse Act section 1 offences involving hacking from six months to two years.'

The Bill looked to introduce, after section 2 of the Computer Misuse Act, two new sections '2A Denial of service' and '2B Denial of service with intent to commit or facilitate commission of further offences'.

In January 2006 the Government introduced its Police and Justice Bill to Parliament; in part 5 of the Bill specific mention is given to Computer Misuse. On 8 November 2006 the Police and Justice Act 2006 received Royal Assent. In sections 35 to 38 of the Act particular reference is made to CMA. In addition to the changes to section 1 of the CMA,[246] there is the new offence of 'Unauthorized acts with intent to impair, or with recklessness as to impairing, operation of computer, etc.' This replaces the existing section 3 of the CMA and introduces a new section, '3A Making, supplying or obtaining articles for use in offence under section 1 or 3'.

The new section 3 provides that:

(1) a person is guilty of an offence if:

    (a) he does any unauthorized act in relation to a computer;

    (b) at the time when he does the act he knows that it is unauthorized; and

    (c) either subsection (2) or subsection (3) below applies.

(2) This subsection applies if the person intends by doing the act:

    (a) to impair the operation of any computer;

    (b) to prevent or hinder access to any program or data held in any computer;

    (c) to impair the operation of any such program or the reliability of any such data; or

    (d) to enable any of the things mentioned in paragraphs (a) to (c) above to be done.

(3) This subsection applies if the person is reckless as to whether the act will do any of the things mentioned in paragraphs (a) to (d) of subsection (2) above.

(4) The intention referred to in subsection (2) above, or the recklessness referred to in subsection (3) above, need not relate to:

    (a) any particular computer;

    (b) any particular program or data; or

    (c) a program or data of any particular kind.

(5) In this section:

    (a) a reference to doing an act includes a reference to causing an act to be done;

    (b) 'act' includes a series of acts;

    (c) a reference to impairing, preventing or hindering something includes a reference to doing so temporarily.

(6) A person guilty of an offence under this section shall be liable:

    (a) on summary conviction in England and Wales, to imprisonment for a term not exceeding 12 months or to a fine not exceeding the statutory maximum or to both;

    (b) on summary conviction in Scotland, to imprisonment for a term not exceeding six months or to a fine not exceeding the statutory maximum or to both;

    (c) on conviction on indictment, to imprisonment for a term not exceeding ten years or to a fine or to both.

The main change to the existing section 3 is the removal of the requirement to make any 'modification'. All that is required is that the act in question is unauthorized and that the perpetrator knew it was unauthorized. However, the act must have been committed with the intention of impairing the operation of a computer or hindering access to any program or data held in it or to impair the operation of any such program or the reliability of any such data. This distinguishes this offence from the two hacking offences. The main reason for the change was to ensure that the section 3 offence caught all forms of denial of service attacks. There was a concern that depending on the technology used to carry out the denial of service attack, no modification would be made to the computer in question and so no offence committed. By amending the section, this potential loophole has been closed.

The new section 3A offence of Making, supplying or obtaining articles for use in offence under section 1 or 3 is as follows:

(1) A person is guilty of an offence if he makes, adapts, supplies or offers to supply any article intending it to be used to commit, or to assist in the commission of, an offence under section 1 or 3.

(2) A person is guilty of an offence if he supplies or offers to supply any article believing that it is likely to be used to commit, or to assist in the commission of, an offence under section 1 or 3.

(3) A person is guilty of an offence if he obtains any article with a view to its being supplied for use to commit, or to assist in the commission of, an offence under section 1 or 3.

(4) In this section 'article' includes any program or data held in electronic form.

(5) A person guilty of an offence under this section shall be liable:

   (a) on summary conviction in England and Wales, to imprisonment for a term not exceeding 12 months or to a fine not exceeding the statutory maximum or to both;

   (b) on summary conviction in Scotland, to imprisonment for a term not exceeding six months or to a fine not exceeding the statutory maximum or to both;

   (c) on conviction on indictment, to imprisonment for a term not exceeding two years or to a fine or to both.

The new offence has been widely criticized as being too widely drawn and not taking account of the growing information security services such as penetration testing. Time will tell how the courts interpret theses provisions once they have come into force.[247]

6.3 INFORMATION SECURITY

All of us rely on information every day in just about every aspect of our lives. As information is so important, we tend to rank it by its reliability. There are some people whose opinion we trust implicitly on certain matters and we accept as a matter of course that information is only valuable if it is accurate. The most valuable sources of information are those that are seen to be reliable and easy to access such as the BBC News website or an ATM's display of our bank balance.

It seems strange then that when it comes to information in the workplace, we seem to place a far lower importance on ensuring the integrity and availability of the information on which we base our business decisions. This after all is what information security is all about. If a business wishes to survive, let alone prosper, it must grasp the nettle of information security and put in place appropriate measures and processes.

There is an increasing trend for businesses to share information with other businesses. Information is shared with customers and suppliers to make the contracting process more efficient and cost-effective. Also, information is shared in relation to projects on which a number of different businesses (including competitors) may be working. Information within an organization is no longer neatly ring-fenced and protected against the outside world.

6.3.1 Concepts and definitions

Information security

It is important to consider what exactly is meant by information security. The introduction to BS 7799 provides that 'information is an asset which, like other important business assets, has value to an organization and consequently needs to be suitably protected'. It goes on to say that information security is:

> characterised here as the preservation of:
>
> (a) Confidentiality: ensuring that the information is accessible only to those authorized to have access;
>
> (b) Integrity: safeguarding the accuracy and completeness of information and processing methods;
>
> (c) Availability: ensuring that authorized users have access to information and associated assets when required.

There has been an emphasis shift in relation to information security. This is reflected in the way in which the phrase 'information assurance' is often used in place of 'information security'. Businesses are beginning to see that good information security is intrinsic to the development of their business. Good information security can increase productivity, by ensuring that information systems are readily available and that the information can be relied upon.

The staple definition of information security found in the introduction to BS 7799 still holds good. However, the increased importance of information security within a business is reflected in the shift in emphasis away from 'security' to 'assurance'. The word 'security' suggests restrictions and is seen as negative, whereas the word 'assurance' suggests opportunities and is seen as positive. The shift in emphasis to 'assurance' means that the user is assured that the information:

- is only available to those entitled to view it, thus ensuring candour;
- is accurate allowing the user to rely upon it; and
- is available when he needs it, thus ensuring productivity.

Assets types (information, software, physical)

Assets can be divided into any number of different categories. For the purposes of information security, assets can be divided into physical or tangible assets and virtual or intangible assets. The latter category can be subdivided between information and software. The starting point for any information security assessment is to identify the assets owned or used by the organization.

The easiest category to identify is the physical assets. It is relatively easy to locate and record the physical assets owned or used by a business. The key physical assets from an information security perspective are computer equipment (servers, PCs, laptops, monitors, tokens, printers etc.), communications equipment (routers, PABXs, telephones, fax machines etc.).

It is far more difficult to identify the information assets. In theory, an organization should know exactly what software it has on its servers and computers and have a record of all of the associated software licences. However, this is often not the case and it is necessary to undertake a software audit in order to ascertain exactly what software is in use. The position is often worse in relation to the information assets, which will include electronic and paper-based information. Often the information will be located in numerous filing systems or databases and identifying the information assets can be time-consuming. However, unless the assets are first identified it is not possible to assess the risk to the business if such assets were lost or to determine how best to protect those assets.

Threats and vulnerability

In January 2003 the Henley Management College published a report entitled 'Information Security: Setting the Boardroom Agenda'.[248] The report gave three reasons why information security is an issue that needs to be addressed by senior management and ultimately by the board of directors.

The first reason that information security is a boardroom issue stems from the increasing desire of stakeholders to ensure that organizations are run in a competitive and yet risk-adverse manner. The report suggested that investors, particularly institutional investors, were paying increasingly close attention to the governance practices of the companies in which they invested. It also highlighted the scandals at Enron and WorldCom as having shaken public and investor confidence in the corporate sector.

The second reason it considered that information security was becoming a boardroom issue was due to the requirement to comply with codes of conduct. There has been a significant increase in regulation, which requires businesses to protect their data and take steps to ensure the integrity of their data.

The third reason why information security is becoming a boardroom issue is the trend for top-down management in relation to risk. These processes acknowledge the broad nature of risk and the need to embed risk management in all management processes. This largely follows the suggestion put forward by the Turnbull report.[249]

The report asks the question whether information security should be seen as a response solely to risk or an opportunity to drive a commercial advantage. In doing this, it considers that there are a number of drivers in relation to the need for information security.

These major drivers are identified as being:

- human;
- technology;
- environmental; and
- business process.

It is all too easy to focus on external risk. A lot of the technology used in protecting information is there to protect against external attacks to a system. The aim is to keep out viruses, worms and hackers. However, most surveys over the past 10 years in relation to security issues have identified that the majority of problems arise internally. The key is the adoption of a culture that is security minded. This involves the education of employees as to their responsibilities and duties.

Most employers allow their employees to receive and send personal emails and to have some personal use of the internet, not least access to online banking or food shopping sites to enable people to manage their lives in an efficient way. However, it is important to make it clear that the systems belong to the company and are provided for the business of the company. This is echoed in BS 7799.

A policy should be produced that clearly identifies the parameters of what personal and business use can be made of the system. It should also set out clear measures in relation to the enforcement of the policy. It is essential that if a policy is introduced it is made known to all employees and that they understand that they use the company's systems subject to that policy. Equally, if the policy is abused or breached, then the company must enforce its rights. If it does not do so, then its actual policy will be to allow people to use the system in breach of the policy that has been adopted.

In 2004, Henley Management and QinetiQ published a further report entitled 'Information Assurance Strategic Alignment and Competitive Advantage'. The report says that:

> an information assurance strategy determines how the reliability, accuracy, security and availability of a company's information assets should be managed to provide maximum benefit to the organization, in alignment with the corporate objectives and strategy.

The emphasis is clearly one of a strategic approach to the whole issue of information assurance.

This is reflected in a number of businesses where the responsibility for information assurance no longer sits in the realm of the IT department but has moved into the commercial departments of the business. What is clear from the report is that it is essential in the view of Henley Management that businesses take a holistic approach. This is very much in line with the principles put forward by the Turnbull Report[250] and those set out in BS 7799.

Information security is not just about firewalls and security patches. The electronic threat from without is very real and managing the threat from hackers and viruses is an essential element of any information security policy and information security management system. However, there are other threats that need to be considered. Employees need to be made aware of the security risks faced by an organization and their role in combating those risks. Equally an organization needs to protect itself against theft of information by its employees. The other vulnerability is in relation to physical security. There is little point in having extensive logical security if access to the server room is not controlled.

Information security policy concepts

It is essential that information security is seen within an organization as a management issue and the responsibility of each of the employees of that organization. The aim of an information security policy is to demonstrate the buy-in of management to the information security processes and policies of an organization and to provide information to employees as to what is expected of them.

Unlike an information security management system specification and the individual security policies adopted by an organization, the information security policy can be relatively short. It needs to encapsulate the importance of information security to the organization and make it clear that information security is the responsibility of each of the employees and not just the IT department or the risk management group. In this respect, it is essential that the document is published and communicated to all members of staff and also that it is clear that it has been approved and supported by senior management.

An information security policy does not set out the ways in which an organization intends to protect its information. Rather, it:

- explains what information security is and why it is important to the organization;
- explains the key information security issues that affect the organization and gives an explanation of the key policies, principles and procedures adopted by an organization to ensure that its information is kept secure;
- explains who is responsible for information security within the organization and in particular the names of those responsible for implementing the policy and to whom any potential security breach should be reported; and
- provides a list of the key information security policies and procedures and where information about these policies and procedures can be found.

As with any policy, an information security policy needs to be reviewed and evaluated on a regular basis. Ideally, an organization should appoint one person to be responsible for ensuring that the policy is monitored for its effectiveness and also is amended in light of any changes in the organization's business processes or the technology used.

Identity, authentication, authorization

Information security is all about ensuring the integrity of data and that data is available to those entitled to access it. A fundamental part of this is being able to identify users accurately when they log into the system.

The identity of a user is usually verified when the user is first employed. However, this is not always the case, especially where access is being given to third parties. There are numerous government guidelines on how to identify an individual, but these are beyond the scope of this text. Without wishing to diminish the importance of verifying the identity of an individual, the remainder of this section will consider the issues that arise in relation to 'authentication'.

When a user accesses a computer system, the user's identity can be authenticated by means of:

(i) something that the user knows, for example PIN or password;
(ii) something that the user possesses, for example smart card, token or fob;
(iii) something that the user is, for example a biometric; or
a combination of all or any of the above.

One of the most used forms of identity authentication is the use of passwords combined with user names. The more complex a password is the better. However, the problem is that long passwords using different character sets, which do not create words, are difficult to remember. The proliferation of password controls in the office, banking and online services means that there is a tendency for individuals to use the same password time and time again. This defeats the security objective as once the password has been cracked, all of the services become available. Most people know not to write down their passwords. This means that most people use passwords that are easily remembered, for example wife's birthday or dog's name. The problem is that such passwords are easily broken.

To overcome some of the risks associated with the use of PINs and passwords, some organizations issue their users with random password generators. These generate random passwords or PINs at regular intervals. The person accessing the service must not only know the user name but must have the random code generator in his or her possession at the same time. This removes the risk of the use of obvious passwords or PINs and reduces the risk in the event that a password or PIN is compromised. From an authentication perspective, the use of passwords or PINs only demonstrates that the user knows the password or PIN or has the random number generator in his or her possession. It does not confirm that person's identity.

An alternative to the use of passwords or PINs is the use of tokens or devices. These are electronic devices that must be plugged in to a computer before allowing the user of that computer to access certain software or information. Typically these devices use the ubiquitous USB (universal serial bus) port and are often used to regulate access to secure extranets and the like.

The use of tokens or fobs has two main advantages. First, they are extremely easy to use and second, being small they are easy to carry around. The main disadvantages are not surprisingly that anyone in possession of the token will have easy access to the restricted material and tokens and fobs are easy to lose. Once again from an authentication perspective, the use of tokens and fobs only demonstrates that the user has the electronic device in his or her possession. It does not confirm that person's identity.

Biometrics is the science of measuring behavioural and physiological characteristics of an individual. Biometrics technology can be used to provide a unique electronic identity for a person. In order for biometrics to provide an identity solution, it must rely on data that is universal in a sense that everyone must be able to create such data, while at the same time being unique to each person. It also needs to be permanent in that it must not change frequently or else the system will become bogged down in recapturing the individual's data. The typical biometrics that are used include fingerprints, facial thermograms, iris and retinal scans, hand geometry, voice recognition, signature recognition and keystroke analysis. However, at present the use of biometric technology is often too expensive and as yet is not sufficiently reliable to be a viable solution. It also raises a huge number of privacy issues.[251]

Information security management system concepts

Whereas an information security policy sets out at high level the approach taken by an organization to protect its information and other assets, the information security management system is the way in which that policy is implemented and managed. A typical information security management system will consist of processes, procedures, practices, systems, software and policies all of which are designed to work together to protect the information owned and used by an organization. In this respect, the information security management system will need to address such issues as the resources available for ensuring the integrity of information and identifying the responsibilities of each member of staff in relation to information security. This it will do by imposing a system of controls, which broadly speaking can be categorized as:

- physical controls: for example, restricting access to the server room and ensuring physical security of buildings;
- procedural controls: for example, business processes that must be adopted by an organization. This may include educating employees in respect of the importance of adopting such processes and procedures; and
- logical controls: for example, firewalls, filters etc.

By definition each information security management system will be unique to an organization. However, there are a number of processes which an organization should go through to ensure that it has implemented an effective information security management system. Part of this process will involve the ongoing review of the information security management system to ensure that it is effective and that it has kept pace with changes in the business and technology. In this respect, it is often sensible to obtain the services of a third party to test the information security management system and to provide a report on any of its failings.

There are a number of standards that have been developed in relation to information security management systems. The most well known are ISO 27001:2005 (which replaces BS 7799 Part 2) and ISM3.[252]

6.4 INTRODUCTION TO BS 7799/ISO 17799

BS 7799 started off life as a code of practice published by the Department of Trade and Industry in the United Kingdom. It went through a major revision in 1999 and was published as an ISO international standard in December 2000. It is a detailed security standard. There are 12 main sections covering the major issues that an organization needs to consider in relation to information security. These key issues are dealt with in the standard under the following headings:

(1) **Risk assessment and treatment**

The first step is to identify an organization's assets and then to assess the risk that exists in relation to those assets. Part of this process is an evaluation of the relative importance of different assets to an organization. Part 3 of BS 7799 establishes a standard for the assessment and management of risk.

(2) **Security policy**

As set out above, the importance of an information security policy is to promote within an organization the need for information security and to identify the steps that an organization is taking in order to protect its information.

(3) **Organisation of information security**

This section is divided into two parts, internal organization and external parties. The internal organization focuses on a need for management commitment and the way in which information security is organized within the organization itself. The section dealing with external parties looks at the information security issues raised when dealing with third parties including customers and suppliers.

(4) **Asset management**

This deals with the need to identify and create an inventory of assets and also the issues in relation to information classification. This is the starting point for any risk and security assessment.

(5) **Human resources security**

Employees are often the weakest link in relation to information security. The standard addresses this issue in the context of the steps to be taken prior to employing an individual, the steps to be taken during the employment and those to be taken on termination. These include vetting a potential employee, education of employees as to the importance of information security and the role that they play, and removal of access rights on cessation of employment.

(6) **Physical and environmental security**

It is all too easy to confuse information security with logical security. Physical security is just as important as logical security. Equally, protection against external loss of power, fire and environmental threats is essential.

(7) **Communications and operations management**

This section looks at the management of the communications system and deals with such things as capacity management, information back-up, network security management and exchanges of information. It also considers the development of electronic services and the monitoring of the use of the system.

(8) **Access control**

This section looks at the need to manage and police access to different aspects of the system including the network, operating system and applications. It also looks at managing access to information within an organization and the problems that arise in relation to mobile computing and remote working.

(9) **Information systems acquisition, development and maintenance**
This looks at the specification of information systems, the use of security within the systems and the way in which the development and support processes are managed and controlled.

(10) **Information security incident management**
The standard looks at the way in which breaches of security should be reported, how they are to be dealt with and what lessons should be drawn from them and implemented in an improved information security management system.

(11) **Business continuity management**
It is important that an organization plans for all eventualities. Power losses, floods and fires are all possibilities. The Buncefield catastrophe demonstrates that there is a risk that an entire office may be destroyed. This section looks at the planning of a business continuity plan and the way in which it is implemented and checked.

(12) **Compliance**
Often seen as the main reason for implementing an information security management system, compliance is left to the end. This section sets out the legal obligations typically faced by an organization. A failure to comply with applicable laws and regulation could subject an organization to civil and criminal sanctions. It is interesting to note that the majority of the sections within the standard deal with management or technical issues and only the last looks at the legal framework.

BS 7799 considers compliance in the context of an organization avoiding breaches of civil and criminal law, statutory, regulatory or contractual obligations and of any security requirements. The compliance section goes on to consider compliance in the context of assuring that the systems comply with organization of security policies and standards and maximizing the effectiveness of internal system audits.

6.4.1 Plan-Do-Check-Act

As with a number of the international standards, ISO 27001:2005 and BS 7799 adopt a 'plan-do-check-act model'. There is nothing new or particularly unique about this model. However, it is particularly suitable for information security management. The four stages of a model can be described as follows.

Plan

This stage requires an organization to assess its security requirements by identifying its assets, risks to those assets and the relative importance of those assets to the organization. It involves identifying the steps that need to be taken to protect those assets that will be a combination of the implementation of procedures, practices, policies and physical and logical security.

Do

This stage involves implementing the controls, systems and procedures identified and planned in the planning stage.

Check

This involves monitoring and reviewing the effectiveness of the information security management system. This may entail having third parties undertake a security audit or penetration testing. Also it will involve a review of any changes to the business of an organization and to the processes and procedures used by an organization. The check phase should identify any improvements or changes that need to be made to the information security management system.

Act

This stage involves putting into effect the corrective or preventive actions that are identified in the check phase.

The process is a continuous one as shown in Figure 6.1.

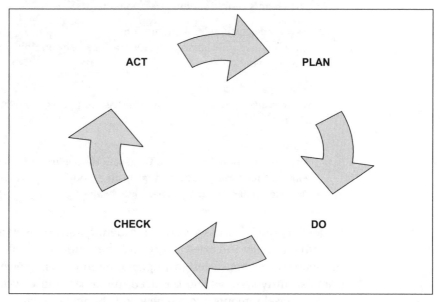

FIGURE 6.1 *Plan-Do-Check-Act*

6.4.2 International interest

Information security is a worldwide issue. BS 7799 is also an international standard (ISO 17799) and many other information security standards have been developed around the world.[253] In July 2002 the Organisation for Economic Co-operation and Development published 'Guidelines for the Security of Information Systems and Networks: Towards a Culture of Security'.[254] These guidelines promoted nine principles as follows:

(1) Awareness
Participants should be aware of the need for security of information systems and networks and what they can do to enhance security.

(2) Responsibility
All participants are responsible for the security of information systems and networks.

(3) Response
Participants should act in a timely and co-operative manner to prevent, detect and respond to security incidents.

(4) Ethics
Participants should respect the legitimate interests of others.

(5) Democracy
The security of information systems and networks should be compatible with essential values of a democratic society.

(6) Risk assessment
Participants should conduct risk assessments.

(7) Security design and implementation
Participants should incorporate security as an essential element of information systems and networks.

(8) Security management
Participants should adopt a comprehensive approach to security management.

(9) Reassessment
Participants should review and reassess the security of information systems and networks, and make appropriate modifications to security policies, practices, measures and procedures.

Under the principles, risk assessments identifying the effects and vulnerability both internally and externally need to be conducted. It also recommends the need for the proper design, implementation and management of appropriate security systems and the need to reassess those systems in light of ongoing developments and the new and changing threats and vulnerabilities that are continuously discovered. This echoes the approach taken by BS 7799.

REFERENCES

Legislation

- Theft Act 1968
- Theft Act 1978

- Forgery and Counterfeiting Act 1981
- Telecommunications Act 1984
- Computer Misuse Act 1990
- Computer Misuse Act 1990 (Amendment) Bill (2004)
- Computer Misuse (Amendment) Bill [HL] (2002)
- Disability Discrimination Act 1995
- Disability Rights Commission Act 1999 and Explanatory Notes
- Police and Justice Act 2006
- Regulation of Investigatory Powers Act 2000 and Explanatory Notes

Cases

- *McVeigh, O'Neill and Evans v United Kingdom* E.H.R.R. 71 (1981).
- *Gold and Shifreen* 1986
- *Denco Ltd v Johnson* [1991] IRLR 63
- *DPP v Bignell* [1998] 1 Cr App Rep 1
- *R v Carrey* [1999]
- *R v Bow Street Magistrates' Court and Allison (A.P.) ex parte Government of the United States of America* [1999]
- *Maguire v Sydney Organising Committee for the Olympic Games* [2000] (Australian Case)
- *R v Lindesay* [2001] EWCA Crim 1720,
- *R v Maxwell-King* [2001] 2 Cr App Rep (S) 136
- *Caffrey v Port of Houston Authority*, 2003, Southwark Crown Court
- *R v Simon Lee Vallor* (CA (Crim Div)) Court of Appeal (Criminal Division) 21 July 2003
- *Rotura v Romania* 8 B.H.R.C. 449

Reports

- APIG Report: Inquiry on revision of Computer Misuse Act (available via archives on http://www.apcomms.org.uk/apig/archive.html)
- BS 7799-2:2002: Information Security Management Systems
- Code of Practice (National Disability Council/DFEE *Code of Practice: Rights of Access: Goods, Facilities, Services and Premises (1999)* and regulations
- Countering Financial Crime Risks in Information Security; Financial Crime Sector Report, Financial Services Authority, November 2004
- *dti* – Achieving Best Practice in Your Business; Information Security: Protecting Your Business Assets
- *dti* Achieving Best Practice in Your Business; Information Security: Guide to the Electronic Communications Act 2000
- *dti* Achieving Best Practice in Your Business; Information Security: BS 7799 and the Data Protection Act

- *dti* Security Breaches Report 2004
- Hi-Tech Crime – The impact on UK business 2005; NHTCU
- Internal Control Guidance for Directors on the Combined Code, published by the Internal Control Working Party of the Institute of Chartered Accountants in England and Wales
- ISO 17799:2000: Information Technology – Code of Practice for Information Security
- The Department of Trade and Industry report; Information Security Breaches Survey (ISBS 2004). The revised Code of Practice deals with the duties placed by Part III of the Disability Act 1995
- Web Accessibility Initiative
- Web Content Accessibility Guidelines

Articles

- Sloan, Martin. Digital Discrimination; humanITy website, September 2001 (accessed March 2005)

Websites

- Web Accessibility Initiative (can be viewed at http://www.w3c.org/WAI/)
- Web Content Accessibility Guidelines (can be viewed at http://www.w3c.org/TR/2004/WD-WCAG20-20040730/)
- APIG report (available from the APIG archive accessible via www.apcomms.org.uk).
- DTI Security Breaches Report 2004 (can be viewed at www.dti.gov.uk/bestpractice)

Books

- Bainbridge, David (2004) *Introduction to Computer Law*. Fifth Edition. Pearson. England.
- Calder, Alan and Watkins, Steve (2005) *IT Governance – A Manager's Guide to Data Security and BS 7799/ISO 17799*. Kogan Page, London.
- Lloyd, Ian J. (2004) *Information Technology Law*. Fourth Edition. Oxford University Press, New York.
- Rowlands, Diane and Macdonald, Elizabeth (2005) *Information Technology Law*. Third Edition. Cavendish, London.
- Todd, Paul (2005) *E-Commerce Law*. Cavendish Publishing, London.

Notes

1 See paragraph 1.2.5(iii) on the Unfair Contract Terms Act 1977.

2 See paragraph 1.1.7(i).

3 Unfair Contract Terms Act 1977 (see commentary at paragraph 1.2.5(iii) below).

4 See sections 50A and 296A of Copyright Designs and Patents Act 1988.

5 For example, a term that goods are of satisfactory quality may be implied into contracts under the provisions of the Supply of Goods and Services Act 1982.

6 There are exceptions to this, most notably contracts for the assignment of land or copyright.

7 See *Carlill v Carbolic Smoke Ball Co.* [1891–94] All ER Rep 127.

8 This was decided in the case of *Pharmaceutical Society of Great Britain v Boots Cash Chemists* [1953] 1 All ER 482.

9 For example, offering to sell alcohol to minors.

10 See *Fisher v Bell* [1961] 1 QB 394 in which the courts held that the display of a flick knife in a shop window was not an offer to sell the knife but only an invitation to treat. Accordingly no offence was committed by the shopkeeper.

11 See *Carlill v Carbolic Smoke Ball Co.* [1891–94] All ER Rep 127.

12 See *Partridge v Crittenden* [1968] 2 All ER 421.

13 This will not always be the case. If an order constitutes an offer, it is essential that any automated response makes it clear that it is only a holding reply and that acceptance will not take place until the goods or notification of acceptance have been sent to the customer.

14 See *Carlill v Carbolic Smoke Ball Co.* [1891–94] All ER Rep 127.

15 In *Thornton v Shoe Lane Parking Limited* [1971] 1 All ER 686 the court held that the contract for use of the car park was at made at the point at which a machine in a car park issued a ticket.

16 *Currie v Misa* (1875) L.R. 10 Exch.153.

17 The rule in Pinnel's case (1602) 5 Co rep 117a, Moore KB 677.

18 A reasonable price for goods may be implied into a contract for the sale of goods in the absence of a price by the operation of the Sale of Goods Act 1979.

19 Anyone under the age of 18.

20 Also known as the 'General Rule'.

21 Established by the case of *Adams v Lindsell* (1818) 1B & Ald 681, 106 ER 250.

22 See paragraph 1.2.5 (iv) below re notices.

23 For a more detailed review of this topic see the Law Commission Advice on Electronic Commerce: Formal Requirements in Commercial Transactions (December 2001).

24 *Derry v Peek* (1889) 14 App. Cas. 337.

25 The classic statement of the principle of contractual damages is in *Hadley v Baxendale* [1854] 9 Exch 341: 'Where two parties have made a contract which one of them has broken, the damages which the other party ought to receive in respect of such a breach of contract should be such as may fairly and reasonably be considered either arising naturally, i.e. according to the usual course of things, from such breach of contract itself, or such as may reasonably be supposed to have been in the contemplation of both parties, at the time they made the contract, as the probable result of the breach of it.'

26 See paragraph 1.2.5 (iii).

27 See paragraph 1.2.5 (ii).

28 See paragraph on equitable remedies below.

29 Rescission and repudiation have been discussed at paragraph 1.1.3 above.

30 For a discussion of termination provisions see paragraph 1.2.5 (v) below.

31 S. 1(3) Contracts (Rights of Third Parties) Act 1999.

32 See comments re Argos in section 1.1.1 above.

33 See the Law Commission Advice on Electronic Commerce: Formal Requirements in Commercial Transactions (December 2001).

34 The enforceability of a shrink-wrap agreement was considered and approved in *Beta Computers (Europe) Limited v Adobe Systems (Europe) Limited* (1995) IP & T Digest 28.

35 1998 WL 388389, 1 (ND Cal.).

36 2001 WL 755396, 150 F. Supp. 2d 585

37 SI 2000:2334.

38 EU Directive 97/7/EC adopted on 20 May 1997.

39 There is a separate regime for the marketing of financial services set out in the Financial Services (Distance Marketing) Regulations 2004 (SI 2004:2095).

40 Regulation 7(1).

41 Regulation 7(2).

42 As amended following the changes made by the Consumer Protection (Distance Selling) (Amendment) Regulations 2005 (SI 2005:689).

43 The Consumer Protection (Distance Selling) (Amendment) Regulations 2005 (SI 2005:689).

44 See paragraph 1.1.7 (i) under the heading 'Right of Cancellation' below for a discussion of cancellation rights.

45 See Regulation 8(3) as originally drafted.

46 In view of the easyCar decision discussed at paragraph 1.1.7 in relation to the right of cancellation, it is ironic that the DTI consultation used car hire contracts as an example of distance sales agreements where issues might arise in relation to the right of cancellation.

47 See Regulations 11 and 12.

48 As amended by The Consumer Protection (Distance Selling) (Amendment) Regulations 2005 (SI 2005:689).

49 *easyCar (UK) Limited v Office of Fair Trading* (Case C-336/03) [2005] All ER (D) 175 (Mar).

50 Regulation 6 provides that 'Regulations 7 to 20 shall not apply to . . . contracts for the provision of . . . transport. . . services where the supplier undertakes, when the contract is concluded, to provide these services on a specific date or within a specific period'. The wording of Regulation 6 reflects that in Article 3 of the Directive.

51 Directive 97/7/EC of the European Parliament and of the Council of 20 May 1997 on the protection of consumers in respect of distance contracts.

52 Regulation 6 transposes Article 3 into English law.

53 Cars and Other Vehicles Sold by Distance Means Guidance on Compliance May 2005 (OFT689) available from www.oft.gov.uk

54 See Regulation 13(1)(c).

55 See Regulation 13(1)(c).

56 2000/31/EC adopted on 8 June 2000.

57 SI 2002:2013.

58 30 July 2002. Regulation 3(2).

59 Regulations 17–22. See paragraph 00 below.

60 Council Regulation (EC) No 44/2001 on jurisdiction and the recognition and enforcement of judgments in civil and commercial disputes.

61 Regulation 6.

62 Regulation 6.

63 Regulation 9.

64 A consumer is defined as a natural person who is acting for purposes that are outside his trade business or profession.

65 See discussion of the Argos case in section 1.1.1.

66 Regulation 11.

67 See Regulations 13–15.

68 EU Directive 2000/31/EC.

69 Regulation 18.

70 See comments above in relation to Regulation 18.

71 Regulation 19 (a)(i) provides that the service provider must not be 'aware of facts or circumstances from which it would have been apparent to the service provider that the activity or information was unlawful'.

72 The standard of reasonableness is that of 'a reasonable and prudent board of directors, acting properly in the interest of their company' *Terrell v Mabie Todd & Company Limited* [1952] 69 RPC 234.

73 This should be contrasted with the position in relation to the reasonableness test under UCTA and the remoteness of damages rule. See paragraphs 1.2.5(iii) and 1.1.4 respectively.

74 See paragraph 1.2.5(iii) below in relation to the Unfair Contract Terms Act 1977.

75 Small and medium-sized enterprises.

76 UCTA 1977 section 11. The key point to note is that it is the time at which the contract is made, and not the time at which the mischief arises, which is relevant.

77 See paragraph 1.1.1 on Postal Rule above.

78 See paragraph 1.1.5 above for a discussion of third-party rights and privity.

79 See paragraph 1.1.1 on equitable remedies above.

80 An example would be to provide that a software licence is subject to the laws of the State of New York so as to get around the prohibition in S. 50A of the Copyright, Designs and Patents Act 1988 on restricting a licensee's right to reverse engineer a software program.

81 For example, provisions dealing with limitation of liability, termination, governing law, etc.

82 See sections 50A–50C and 296A of Copyright Designs and Patents Act 1988.

83 For example, the testing may take place using the developers test platform or on the licensee's infrastructure.

84 For example, the parties may decide to ignore minor bugs/errors.

85 This is important to prevent the parties being locked in to a never-ending cycle of development and testing. Typically, the obligation to remedy any defects will cease after three unsuccessful attempts to pass the acceptance tests. The licensee may then have an option to either accept the software as it is or to terminate the contract.

86 See paragraph 1.1.4 for a discussion of liquidated damages and penalties.

87 See paragraph 1.1.5.

88 See paragraph 1.4.1 (ii).

89 For example, an obligation to correct any faults in the software.

90 See paragraph 1.4.1 for a review of the terms contained within a software licence.

91 Section 8(2) Late Payment Commercial Debts (Interest) Act 1998.

92 See paragraph 10.1.2.

93 See paragraph 1.1.3.

94 See paragraph 1.4.1 (v).

95 See sections 50A–50C and 296A of Copyright Designs and Patents Act 1988.

96 Helpdesk, site visit, remote access etc. Is the obligation to fix the fault or to find a work around?

97 By way of example, software 3.4 is a later release than software 3.3. Software 4.1 is a later version than software 3.4.

98 See paragraph 1.1.6 in relation to the liability of intermediaries.

99 Principle 7 Schedule 1 of the Data Protection Act 1998. The Act requires all agreements with data processors to be in writing.

100 An example of an independent escrow service is that provided by NCC Group Plc, which is a spin-off from the National Computing Centre (www.nccgroup.co.uk).

101 (1848) 1 Mac & G 25.

102 (1995) FSR 765.

103 (2005) Civ 595.

104 (2006) EWHC 522 Ch.

105 para 147.

106 See also ECHR cases *Wainwright v United Kingdom* (2006) and *von Hannover v Germany* (2004), and UK cases *McKennitt & Ors v Ash & Anor* (2006) and *CC v AB* (2006).

107 (1905) 122 Ga. 190; 50 SE 68.

108 1995 OJ L281/31.

109 (1992) 16 EHHR 97.

110 ECHR 23/11/92:29.

111 (1984) 7 EHRR 14.

112 ECHR 4/5/2000.

113 (2000) 30 EHRR 843.

114 ECHR 16/2/2000:69.

115 (1983) 5 EHRR 71.

116 para 255.

117 para 224.

118 (1985) 7 EHRR 14.

119 (1997) 24 EHHR 523.

120 (1998) EHRLR 121.

121 (1992) 14 EHRR 657.

122 para 35.

123 *X v Austria* (1979) 18 DR 154, also a breach of article 5 deprivation of liberty.

124 *Peters v Netherlands* (1994) 77 A DR 75.

125 2 EHRR 214.

126 ECHR 6/9/1978:49–50.

127 (1993) AC 534.

128 App. No 21132/93, Decision of 6 April 1994.

129 (1991) 71 DR 141.

130 (1987) 9 EHRR 433.

131 para 48.

132 (1989) 12 EHRR 36.

133 (1987) 9 EHRR 433 (para 74).

134 (1998) 26 EHRR 357.

135 para 57.

136 para 58

137 (1999) 27 EHRR 1.

138 para 101.

139 (1997) ECHR 49.

140 (1994) 776 A DR 140.

141 (1997) 25 EHRR 371.

142 para 95.

143 [2001] EWHC Admin 915.

144 (2004) UKHL 22.

145 [2003] All ER (D) 124 (Dec).

146 s28.

147 s29 (a).

148 s29(b).

149 s29(c).

150 s30.

151 ss31–33.

152 s36.

153 ss34–35.

154 s38.

155 s16(3).

156 s7(2)(a).

157 s7(2)(b).

158 Case C-101/01 (2003).

159 s84.

160 s8.

161 EU Draft Data Retention Directive, p3.

162 EU Draft Data Retention Directive, p3.

163 Civil Evidence Act 1995 section 1(2).

164 Civil Evidence Act 1995 section 2 & Rule 33.2 CPR.

165 *Hart v Lancashire and Yorkshire Railway Co.* [1869] 21 LT 261.

166 *Hollingham v Head* [1858] 27 LJ CP 241.

167 Section 10 (1).

168 [1975] Ch 185.

169 [1991] 2 All ER 901.

170 Civil Evidence Act 1995 section 9.

171 Rule 31.6 CPR.

172 *Alliance & Leicester Building Society v Ghahremani* [1992] 32 RVR 198.

173 Source: www.out-law.com

174 See the Australian case of *British American Tobacco v Cowell & McCabe* [2002] V.S.C.A. 197 and *Douglas and others v Hello! and others* (No.2) [2003] 1 All ER 1087.

175 Directive 1999/93/EC.

176 Article 5(2).

177 Interpretation Act 1978 Schedule 1.

178 Section 78 Police and Criminal Evidence Act 1984.

179 Rule 1.1 (2)(c) CPR.

180 [2003] EWCA Civ 151.

181 Section 69 Police and Criminal Evidence Act 1984, this was repealed by section 60 of the Youth Justice and Criminal Evidence Act 1999 and since 14 April 2000 computer record admissibility has been governed by common law.

182 Civil Evidence Act 1995 section 4.

183 Source: out-law.com

184 See for example section 103 in relation to audit work papers and other information related to audit reports.

185 Section 222(5) Companies Act 1985.

186 Finance Act 1998 (Schedule 18, paragraph 21).

187 Employers Liability (Compulsory Insurance) Regulations 1998.

188 Statutory Sick Pay (General) Regulations 1982.

189 *FSA Handbook*: Insurance Conduct of Business 5.7.1–3.

190 (November 2002) Lord Chancellor's Code of Practice on the Management of Records under section 46 of the Freedom of Information Act 2000.

191 ISO 15489.

192 Schedule 1, Principle 5.

193 Section 77 Freedom of Information Act 2000.

194 http://www.nationalarchives.gov.uk/policy/foi/

195 http://www.cipd.co.uk/subjects/hrpract/psnlrecrd/retrecords.htm?IsSrchRes=1

196 Harner, A. (2004) *The ICSA Guide to Document Retention*. ICSA Publishing, London.

197 (1996) 2 All ER 345.

198 Unreported 17 February 1998.

199 Directive 1999/93/EC.

200 Section 8 ECA.

201 At para. 3.28.

202 At para. 3.29.

203 European Commission Report on the operation of Directive 1999/93/EC 15.3.2006.

204 (1993) FSR 497.

205 (2004) EWHC 1725.

206 C-203/02 [2005] RPC 260.

207 EP1134680.

208 *Aerotel Ltd v Telco Holdings Ltd (and others)* and Macrossan's Application http://www.ipo.gov.uk/2006ewcaciv1371.pdf

209 http://www.law.cornell.edu/patent/comments/96_1327.htm

210 (1998) FSR 21.

211 Details can be found at http://www.gnu.org/copyleft/gpl.html

212 (1996) FSR 367.

213 (2002) EWCA Civ 1702.

214 See 'Liability of intermediaries' in section 1.1.6 above.

215 s.162 of the Employment Rights Act 1996.

216 *Byrne Brothers v Baird* [2002] IRLR 96.

217 This code replaces the original code of practice published in 1999.

218 s1(1).

219 s20 defines what constitutes discrimination and s21 imposes an obligation to make reasonable adjustments.

220 s19(1)(a).

221 s19(1)(c).

222 s19(1)(d).

223 s19(1)(b).

224 s21(1).

225 s21(1).

226 s21(4).

227 s20(4).

228 http://www.hreoc.gov.au/disability_rights/decisions/comdec/2000/DD000120.htm

229 See web Accessibility Guidelines at http://www.w3c.net

230 A copy of the PAS is available for free from http://www.bsi-global.com/

231 In s2(1).

232 http://www.w3c.net

233 Copyright © 2004–2006 W3C® (MIT, ERCIM, Keio), All Rights Reserved. W3C liability, trademark, document use and software licensing rules apply.

234 At the time of writing (March 2007) this amendment had not come into force and no date had been set for it to do so.

235 s1(2).

236 s17 (2).

237 s17(5).

238 Law Commission, 1989 Cmnd 829, para 3.37.

239 [1991] IRLR 63.

240 [1998] 1 Cr App Rep 1, 161 JP 541.

241 [2000] 2 AC 216, 225.

242 [2001] 2 Cr App Rep (S) 136.

243 [2002] Court of Appeal (Criminal Division); [2001] EWCA Crim 1720, (Transcript: Smith Bernal), 17 July 2001.

244 [1999] 1Cr App Rep (S) 322.

245 [2004] 1 CA (Crim Div); [2003] EWCA Crim 2288.

246 See above.

247 At the time of writing (March 2007) the amendments to the CMA had not come into force and no date had been set for them to do so.

248 A copy of the report may be obtained either through QinetiQ or Henley Management School.

249 *Internal Control: Guidance for Directors on the Combined Code* published in September 1999 by The Institute of Chartered Accountants in England & Wales and updated in 2005.

250 *Internal Control: Guidance for Directors on the Combined Code* published in September 1999 by The Institute of Chartered Accountants in England & Wales and updated in 2005.

251 See the EU Article 29 Working Party's Article 29 Data Protection Working Party: Working Document on Biometrics published in August 2003: http://ec.europa.eu/justice_home/fsj/privacy/workinggroup/index_en.htm

252 Information concerning standards can be found at http://www.iso.org and http://www.ism3.com

253 Two of the better known are ISM3 (http://www.ism3.com/) and COBIT (http://www.isaca.org/).

254 Available on the OECD website http://www.oecd.org

Index